# CONVICTING THE MOORS MURDERERS

The Arrest, Trial and Imprisonment of
Ian Brady and Myra Hindley

# CONVICTING THE MOORS MURDERERS

## The Arrest, Trial and Imprisonment of Ian Brady and Myra Hindley

### Chris Cook

PEN & SWORD TRUE CRIME

First published in Great Britain in 2023 by
PEN AND SWORD TRUE CRIME
An imprint of
Pen & Sword Books Ltd
Yorkshire – Philadelphia

Typeset in Times New Roman 10/12 by SJmagic DESIGN SERVICES, India.
Printed and bound in the UK by CPI Group (UK) Ltd, Croydon, CR0 4YY.

Pen & Sword Books Limited incorporates the imprints of Atlas, Archaeology,
Aviation, Discovery, Family History, Fiction, History, Maritime, Military,
Military Classics, Politics, Select, Transport, True Crime, Air World, Frontline
Publishing, Leo Cooper, Remember When, Seaforth Publishing, The Praetorian
Press, Wharncliffe Local History, Wharncliffe Transport, Wharncliffe True Crime
and White Owl.

*For a complete list of Pen & Sword titles please contact*
PEN & SWORD BOOKS LIMITED
47 Church Street, Barnsley, South Yorkshire, S70 2AS, England
E-mail: enquiries@pen-and-sword.co.uk
Website: www.pen-and-sword.co.uk

Or

PEN AND SWORD BOOKS
1950 Lawrence Rd, Havertown, PA 19083, USA
E-mail: Uspen-and-sword@casematepublishers.com
Website: www.penandswordbooks.com

# Contents

# Introduction

Following on from *The Moors Murderers*, this book tells the story of what happened at the trial of Ian Brady and Myra Hindley and of how David and Maureen Smith, Myra's sister and brother-in-law, dealt with the stigma of being labelled murderers during the trial.

Having been found guilty, this book also deals with how Ian Brady and Myra Hindley survived while in prison with large targets on their backs, and how and why Myra eventually broke off their relationship.

For the first time ever, using previously closed Home Office files, the full story of Myra Hindley's attempted jailbreak in 1973 is told, and the extraordinary lengths she went to in order to gain her freedom are exposed.

More importantly, following Myra Hindley's continuous attempts to deny her full role in the murders and gain her freedom, Ian Brady told a journalist in the 1980s that they had both murdered two further children – Pauline Reade and Keith Bennett. This opened up a reinvestigation of the case, led by Detective Chief Superintendent Peter Topping, and Myra Hindley eventually confessed to him that Ian Brady had indeed killed the two children, as well as John Kilbride, Lesley Ann Downey and Edward Evans – but that on all occasions she was either not present or in another room.

This led the police to search Saddleworth Moor again in the areas roughly pinpointed by the murderous couple, and eventually the body of Pauline Reade was recovered.

This is also the story of the strength of the families of those killed at the hands of Brady and Hindley in fighting to keep both of the murderers behind bars.

When we left the story in Part 1, Ian Brady had been charged with the murders of John Kilbride, Lesley Ann Downey and Edward Evans. Myra Hindley was also charged with harbouring Ian Brady knowing that he had killed John Kilbride, and with the murders of Lesley Ann Downey and Edward Evans.

At the committal, where the prosecution laid out their case against Brady and Hindley, it became quite clear that their chief witness was Myra's brother-in-law, David Smith, who had been present when Edward Evans was murdered. It also became clear that because he was on good terms with both Hindley and Brady at the time, that he was just as bad as them in the eyes of the public and this led to David and his wife Maureen (Hindley's sister) becoming hated by the public, and they were often attacked. Certainly, some members of the families of those children killed became convinced that David Smith knew, and had done, more than he would admit to.

# Acknowledgements

This book wouldn't have been possible without the close support and encouragement of my friends and family; in particular: Adrian Rodgers for giving me the encouragement to start writing, Rob Wittwer for all of his understanding over the years, my parents, sister, and her fiancé for their unconditional love and support and a particular 'Thank You' to Bob and Jane O'Hara and Nick Dexter for their help at the National Archives.

A huge 'Thank You' also goes to Karyn Burnham, Abigail Marlow, Rosie Crofts, Jonathan Wright and Adam Walsh.

# 1

# Family Fighting

The following account of what happened on the evening of 7 January 1966, is taken from police reports held in Home Office files.

At around 23.30, Ann Downey (mother of murdered Lesley Ann Downey), her partner (later to be her husband) Alan West and Ann's half-brother William (Billy) Shaw set out for Underwood Court but didn't know which flat belonged to the Smiths. They were unaware that David and Maureen Smith were out for the evening and the only person in the flat was David Smith's father, John.

As they approached, they asked an elderly gentleman which flat belonged to the Smiths, and he happily pointed out which flat was theirs. Ann West rang the bell at the entrance to the flats and spoke to John Smith over the intercom. He told them that he had been instructed by the police not to meet with other witnesses and refused to admit them. Alan West replied: 'So that's the way it is?' They waited by the entrance until other residents entered through the door and they followed them in, and a short time later knocked loudly on the door of Smith's flat .

John Smith answered the door after the third knock and told them that David and Maureen were not at home, but they demanded entry anyway. John Smith later said:

> By their speech and behaviour I surmised that they had been drinking. The brother [Shaw] was very aggressive and invited me to fight and said: 'I will fucking well top you, you and your son.' He made a motion with his right hand across his throat. Mrs Downey was also abusive and came out with a similar statement.

John Smith refused to let them in, but Alan West and Billy Shaw pushed past him and entered the flat to look for David Smith. As they were about to leave, David and pregnant Maureen returned home and met Ann standing on the landing. She warned David and Maureen not to enter the flat because Alan and Billy were in there and were drunk. Ann later recalled:

> As soon as we were inside I realised what I wanted. I had to have a photograph of Maureen's hellish sister. I wanted an original photograph, so that if ever Myra got out I would be able to track her down and give her the punishment she deserved.

David and Maureen entered the flat and Shaw immediately lunged at David, so Maureen went outside to call the police but was attacked by Ann as she left the flat, who apparently shouted: 'You are not going for the bloody police.' She grabbed Maureen by the hair and dragged her about the landing, kicked her in the back and punched her in the face. She also pulled clumps of hair out from her head. As David pulled Ann off of his wife he was attacked by Billy again, and in the fight Shaw got a black eye.

At this point, 19-year-old Christopher Swindells, who lived in flat 15, went out to protest at the noise as both he and his mother were ill. He saw Maureen lying on the floor and said that Ann and the two men with her were attacking her. He asked them to stop and to keep the noise down, but was told to 'fuck off' so he decided to go for the police.

John Smith's police statement said:

> I then got Maureen and David separated from the Downey people and took them back into the flat and locked the door. We then heard the door being forced and a smashing of glass. There were shouts and screams accompanying this and threatening abuse. We remained in the flat until the noise died down.

When Christopher Swindells moved towards the lift, Alan West asked him where he was going. Swindells told them he was going for the police; 'Like fuck you are' Alan replied. Ann Downey told the men to 'bleeding well let him'. Christopher was followed into the lift by Ann, Alan West and Billy Shaw. His statement read:

> While I was in the lift Mrs Downey started to grab hold of my hair; and started to scratch and bite me. On the way down to the ground floor these two men again asked me where I was going. I said 'I am going to get the police.' When the lift got to the ground floor I went towards Mr Page's door which is flat No.1. He is the caretaker of the flats. Before I could get to Mr Page's door, the two men started to punch me. Mrs Downey was still grabbing hold of my hair and she started to bite my left ear and neck. I then put my hand up and pushed Mrs Downey away from me. I then started to punch these two men who were still hitting me. By this time Mr Page the caretaker had come out of his flat. One of these men then turning round to me and said, 'By tomorrow your life will not be worth bleeding living. I am going to get the whole gang on to you.' Mrs Downey then picked up a milk bottle and hit me on the head with it. One of the men, the tallest of the two [Alan West] then started to move towards the main entrance of the flats. I then saw that this man had a photograph in his hand. He ran out of the front door of the flats. He returned back after a few seconds, and then both these men started punching me again. Two tall, heavy built men came into the flats and helped me.

John Smith's police statement continued:

> When it was quiet, I went to the flat door which had been burst open. Downstairs on the ground floor I heard a lot of screaming and shouting and smashing of glass. This eventually died down and I saw Chris Swindells with the left side of his face streaming with blood. … The lift then came up, stopped at our floor and Christopher Swindells … got out. His neck and the side of his face was covered in blood and his shirt was torn into ribbons.

It was alleged by the Smiths that during the fight a framed photograph of them and a duplicate notebook had been stolen from their flat. Swindells said in his statement that he saw Alan West with a photograph in his hand but all three denied they had taken anything from the flat. The caretaker, Alfred Page, said that after he had told the three to leave, he found the framed photograph and book on the doorstep. The frame was broken and the photograph smeared with blood, it appeared that it may have been used as a weapon by one of the parties.

At 00.05 on Saturday 8 January, an emergency call was made to Mottram Police Station where PC Smith went straight to Underwood Court. Sergeant Whittaker of the Motor Patrol also went, as did other officers, but by the time they arrived the three offenders had left the scene.

At 08.00, the police called round to talk to Ann and Alan West. A policewoman had a plastic bag that had clumps of Maureen's black hair in it.

William Shaw was interviewed by Chief Inspector Lowe, Alan West by Sergeant Brockbank and Ann by Police Woman Campion. Shaw and Alan West were very guarded in their statements and said it was David Smith who attacked them first and they were only defending Ann West, who was being attacked by Smith. They said that the incident in the lift with Chris Swindells came about because he attacked Ann West in the lift and they dragged him off her. Alan West said they had gone to the Smiths' flat in the first place because they wanted to know if it were true that Hindley and Brady wanted to get married.

When Ann arrived at the police station and was told why she was there she replied: 'Yes, I did go there, it's all my fault, it was the drink that made me do it. All this over Lesley has just got me down. I'll tell you everything that happened last night.'

She told how everything had got on top of her regarding the case and the upcoming trial and that the last straw was reading in the newspapers that Brady and Hindley wanted to get married. 'Really I just wanted to hurt somebody because Lesley had been so hurt. Then some weeks ago David Smith wrote to me and told me that if I ever wanted to go and see him I could do any time of day or night.'

She told how she had gone out for a drink with her husband Alan and her brother-in-law Billy to a local pub called the Chapman Arms. They had a couple of drinks there before Alan drove them to the New Inn. They had one drink there and then drove back to the Chapman Arms where they stayed until closing time. She said that her brother continued to drink but Alan switched to tomato juice. Before they left the pub she told

Alan that she wanted to go and see Smith about Hindley and Brady getting married, to see if he knew.

The rest of her statement generally agreed with what the Smiths had said, up to the point when Christopher Swindells got involved.

> I don't remember what he said but I know I said to him, 'Do you realise this was my daughter?' He said something like, 'She might have deserved it, but I didn't deserve this lot.' Then he pointed to a scar on his face and some on his hands. I said, 'She was only a baby.' I know I grabbed at his shoulder and I hit out at him and he started hitting me. He said he was going for the caretaker. By this time we all got in the lift and went downstairs. Alan went off through the door thinking we were following. I remember starting tussling again with this lad and he had me on the floor, and he kicked me on the head and face. I remember Billy pulling him off and saying, 'You don't fight a woman.' The lad ran to the caretaker's door and they both came out. The woman said to me, 'Don't take any notice of him he's mental.' Then Alan came in for me and we all went off home. We never took any photograph or anything from there. [This is a very similar story to that given by her partner Alan West in his statement].
> My coat got torn and I got scratches all over my face and on my head. Our Billy had a black eye. I think he got that from David Smith. I don't really know why all this started. I just think it was the drink and Mr Smith's attitude towards us. I'm only sorry that all this happened and I promise never to go there again.'

Chief Inspector Lowe had pushed for charges of 'Unlawfully wounding Christopher Swindells' against all three, and a charge of 'Assault causing Actual Bodily Harm' on Maureen Smith against Ann; all three of them were told that there would be no charges this time, but if it happened again there would be no choice other than to press charges.

There were no more incidents, but Ann recalled years later: 'to this day I am not convinced that Dave Smith had told anything like the full story of his relationship with Brady and Hindley'.

Not long after the attack on Maureen, she and David went on a trip to France, paid for by *The News of The World*.

David Smith again got into trouble with the police on 16 March. At about 21.00 a group of five boys were standing in the main entrance of the

Ann Downey (West), right, with friend.

flats at Hattersley Court where a couple of them were jumping up trying to catch hold of the edge of the veranda. While they were doing this some water was thrown down and drenched two of them.

They went around to the front of the flats on Hattersley Road West and heard the sound of a gunshot. A second shot then rung out and hit one of the boys in the back, he looked down and saw a lead pellet from an air rifle lying on the ground. He was uninjured. The shots were coming from the fifth floor of Hattersley Court. At this point the five boys were joined by another group, and a further shot was then fired at a group of girls standing on the opposite side of the road. One of the girls recalled:

> We were talking and I saw two boys and a girl on the veranda of the fifth floor flat. I saw one of the boys put what I definitely recognised as a rifle over the veranda opposite us … None of us said anything to Smith, he shot at us without any reason. I ran out of the way and Smith fired at me but missed.

One of the boys in the group said that at about 21.15 he and some friends left a youth football meeting and met up with other friends opposite Hattersley Court; one of the boys in the first group told him a man on the fifth floor had been firing a rifle. The witness said he looked up and saw two men leaning on the veranda. A verbal exchange took place, which ended with one of the boys goading the two men to come down and face them.

About five minutes later the men came down from the flat; David Smith was carrying a dog chain and his friend John Booth was carrying a studded belt. Smith asked: 'Who's the one with the big mouth?' One of the group of boys then asked Smith 'Who's the clever fellow with the air rifle?' Smith kicked him in the groin, then asked another of the boys what he had in his coat, as he had his hands in his pocket. When the boy didn't reply, Smith head-butted him then hit him with the chain across the neck. The boy later stated: 'I did not provoke him in any way by any spoken word or action. The attack made on me was entirely unprovoked and I wish some action to be taken by prosecution on my behalf against Smith.'

By this point, someone had called the police and Smith and Booth went back up to the flat after being shouted at by a Mr Victor Price, who had seen the attack.

Sergeant Brockbank went to Hattersley Road West, where he examined one of the youths and saw that his neck was bruised on the left side and his right eye was swollen. He went up to flat 28 and interviewed Smith and Booth, challenging them that 'some person has been shooting from the balcony of this flat and that two men had gone down and used a chain on a youth outside'.

Both Smith and Booth denied any shooting, saying that they did not possess a gun of any sort. Smith admitted that he had 'hit the lad with the chain and butted him'. He apologised, but said they had shouted something that had upset him. Booth denied striking anyone.

The following day Sergeant Brockbank spoke to John Booth again and said it had been alleged that he was carrying a studded belt at the time of the incident the previous day. Booth denied it and said he was wearing one, but not carrying it.

The next day DS Alexander 'Jock' Carr went to see John Booth at 22.10 at Hattersley Court. He asked Booth who owned the rifle, but Booth denied that either he or Smith owned a rifle and also denied that there had been any shooting. DS Carr pressed him further, stating that because the incident had occurred from Booth's balcony, he believed that Booth owned the rifle. At this Booth cracked, admitting he owned the rifle but had lied because his parents didn't know he had it. Then, probably because he was afraid of Smith, added: 'It was me that was shooting, not Smith. At least, that's what I'm saying.' Booth then went to his bedroom to fetch the Slavia .22 air rifle and pellets and gave them to the detective.

DS Carr then said it had been alleged that while Smith was assaulting the youth with the chain, he had stood nearby with a heavily studded belt. Booth said he had since burned the belt because his father had seen it and that the chain was a dog chain that belonged to his girlfriend. Not wanting to get her into trouble with her parents, he said that he would go and get the chain and take it to the police station.

Once in possession of the chain, the following day Carr went to see David Smith. Carr said he now believed that it was he who was firing the rifle, but Smith denied it and stated that he had only fired it in the house with some darts. He said that whoever had said he was firing it would have trouble identifying him as they were five floors up and both he and Booth were out on the landing. When confronted with the dog chain, Smith admitted it was the one he had used to hit the other youth with.

David Smith was then further cautioned before adding: 'They said I was no good without an axe. There was only two of us and a lot of them.'

From that day on, the Smiths had a policeman on their front door for protection. Smith later recalled that their neighbours would let the general public into the flats if they buzzed on their receiver and most mornings, when they left their flat, they found graffiti sprayed on their door and windows, and puddles of urine up their walls and front door.

Meanwhile, both Ian Brady and Myra Hindley were being held in Risley Remand Centre. They were, on occasions, allowed to see each other, along with their solicitor, to talk through their defence. They were also allowed to send each other letters, some of which were in code. They were in contact with their families, although Myra and her mother had cut off all contact with Myra's sister, Maureen, for siding with her husband, David Smith, over the family and giving evidence against Myra. Brady was also open with his views on race and religion with others being held at the remand centre.

On 28 March 1966, Brady was subject to a mental health examination which was carried out by Dr Lindsay Neustatter, a Senior Physician in Psychological Medicine. He commented: 'It is possible that it was an evasiveness that accounted for his rather oddly worded answers.' He also commented that a diagnostic label was difficult – 'a ruthless individual, cold and unemotional, without conscience or remorse … [Brady] showed a pathological admiration of power and unscrupulousness'.

He concluded that the factors 'could add up to regarding him as a psychopath, and to this extent, having an abnormality of mind due to inherent causes'. He went on to comment 'There have been no suicide attempts, depressive episodes, psychotic episodes of the kind which one sometimes finds in the history of unstable people which could have a bearing on impaired responsibility.'

On 4 April, a report was written by Senior Medical Officer R. Williams at Risley Remand Centre stating that Brady was:

in good general health and is of good average intelligence. He has at all times behaved in a moral manner. He has occupied himself with much reading and he has written to his co-defendant. It is part of my duty to read all incoming and outgoing letters in respect of persons on murder charges. In this way I have read almost all of the letters written by Brady and I think it may fairly be said that the quality of his correspondence is well above the average level.

I consider this man to be fit to plead and to be responsible in law in respect of the acts charged.

Dr Northage J. De V. Mather, a Consultant Psychiatrist for Manchester Regional Group of Hospitals and a Lecturer in Psychiatry at the University of Manchester wrote a letter to The Department of Public Prosecutions regarding Brady's upcoming trial:

The examinations took place on 15 January, 26 February and 9 April of this year. They were conducted to ascertain the mental state of the accused at the time of the offences for which he is charged, and subsequently while on remand.

I have carefully read the depositions with regard to the charges, have had talks with the medical staff in charge of the accused, and have seen and heard reports from the Hospital Officers who have been in charge of him. I have also read a number of letters which he has written to his co-defendant, Myra Hindley.

I will not recapitulate the history of this man's life, nor the list of his previous convictions. The statement he made to me of the crime was substantially the same as that made to the police on 7 October, 1965.

On examination he was entirely cooperative in giving his general information about himself and his family. There was no evidence of thought disorder in his conversation, no mental retardation and nothing to indicate that he was or had been deluded or hallucinated. There was no evidence of morbid depression and his general manner and demeanour were in keeping with his predicament. He was assessed as having above average intelligence. There was no evidence to suggest he had ever suffered from fits or blackouts.

He was in good physical health.

He was unwilling for an EEG examination.

Reports from the hospital staff were to the effect that during the whole of the time on remand he had never shown any sign of being anything but mentally and physically normal.

From my consideration of the deposition and the accused letters, and the evidence received from the Remand Centre staff I am unable to find any evidence of mental disorder, sub normality or psychotic disorder in the accused, nor can I find any medical evidence which would affect his responsibility for his acts.

I have no medical recommendation to make.

He is fit to plead to the indictment and stand his trial.

Hindley wrote a statement for the Home Office recording her version of events of the night the photographs and tape of Lesley Ann Downey were made. This is essentially the story that she would stick to in her defence at the trial. In regard to Lesley Ann Downey, she heavily implicated David Smith:

> On the evening of 26 December 1964, I had no idea that anything untoward was about to happen. It was my grandmother's eldest son's birthday, and as had been the custom for many years, I took her round to his house sometime during the day to spend the afternoon and evening there, planning to pick her up around 9 p.m.
>
> Ian and I were watching TV, when someone knocked on the door. Ian went to answer it. Ten minutes or so passed…
>
> Then I was called by Ian into the hall where he and David Smith and a child, a girl, were waiting. Ian told me, without preamble, that he was going to take some photographs of her and wanted me to be there as 'insurance' in case they ever fell into police hands, so I could be a witness that nothing other than the taking of photographs had taken place.
>
> I began to remonstrate immediately, shocked at the idea of a child being photographed, and indignant that they proposed to do it at my house.

She then said that she had an argument with Brady, where he told her that he and Smith had planned to take photographs of an 18-year-old girl, but Smith had turned up with the young girl instead. Brady said that he was reluctant to photograph her but didn't want to lose face in front of Smith. Later, while in prison, she expanded on this:

> I said I wasn't having anything to do with it and didn't want him too either. But after arguing again for several minutes, he just looked at me and said 'please yourself'. I know now and probably knew then that it was at this point that I could, and should, have stuck to my refusal, for it was my house and there was no obvious force involved. I should have said no, but I didn't, for I felt that in those words, 'Please yourself,' my whole future with Ian Brady lay in the balance.
>
> We had disagreements before, though not nearly as serious as this one, and I almost always ended up having to acquiesce – even about matters like where we went on holiday…
>
> Before I met him, I had a very strong character, but Ian Brady's character and personality were such that my whole individuality became completely submerged in him, almost to the point of complete submission.
>
> I think it was partly because of his forceful nature and selfish character that I became so fascinated by him, never able to fathom out what it was that had such an effect on me, that caused me to become so submissive and pliable when all the time I deeply resented the situation and was often filled with self-disgust.
>
> Yet I remained fascinated and unable to extricate myself from my tangled emotions. But I knew the decision over the matter of the photographs was

one which would affect my whole life and change it completely, whichever way I decided. Even though our relationship had survived over three years by then, I had never felt secure or completely sure of him…

So I felt that if I pleased myself and refused, where the photographs were concerned, there was a strong possibility that he would leave me.

For him to lose face was, I knew, an almost unforgivable thing and if I were the cause, it would be even worse. So even though I knew I would surrender all my self-respect and a great deal of my misplaced respect for him too, and shrinking from contemplating the consequences, I agreed to what was proposed.

I tried to justify it by telling myself that it wouldn't take long, that the child would not be harmed, and all sorts of other excuses.

I don't even have the excuse that she looked older than she was. She looked exactly what she was: a child of ten.

In her original statement while on remand, she then said that she followed behind Brady and Lesley Ann as they went up the stairs, before stopping to have a short argument with Smith, saying that she would never forgive him for what he had done, and wouldn't have anything to do with him if he wasn't on good terms with Ian and Maureen. She said that at this point she heard a scream from upstairs and ran into the bedroom where 'Ian was remonstrating with the child.' She continued:

I cannot recall what my first words were, but because I was so frightened that the neighbours would hear and perhaps come and investigate, I must have told her to be quiet or to shut up, and I did this several times during the next ten minutes or so.

For from the moment that Ian had told her to take her coat off, the child had panicked and became very frightened…

I wasn't very far off hysteria. I knew I was brusque to the point of cruelty, for I was so frightened about the noise, and instead of trying to calm her quietly, which I should have done, I probably frightened her even more…

At the time, I was unaware of the true value of fear in that room, fear from the child, from myself and probably from Ian too, for I don't think he had expected what was happening.

She then left the room to fetch Smith, who was out on the front path, and told him to go to the bedroom because the child had panicked.

When I returned to the bedroom, Ian was trying to put a handkerchief into the child's mouth to prevent her from making a noise. Several times on the tape, the words 'Put it in your mouth' are heard.

This point would be strongly taken up by the prosecution who would go on to suggest that it was something very different to a handkerchief…

9

What has continued to be ignored is the fact that my voice is recorded as saying, 'Bite hard on it.' I would hardly have suggested such a thing had it been anything other than a handkerchief.

By making the point that it was a handkerchief and nothing else she had in her mouth does not mean I am glossing over the fact that it was shameful treatment of a young girl anyway. It was, and I have never tried to deny it.

I can only say that I was acting under stress and out of character, that I behaved disgracefully, but that the whole situation, as bad as it was, was a far cry from what it has been alleged to be.

She stated that Lesley Ann eventually relaxed and while Brady prepared to take the photographs, she switched on the radio to ease any lingering tension, and that's what was picked up on the tape recording. She claimed she did not know that Brady had turned the tape recorder on, but that when he had switched it off, Smith then went into the room and the photo session began.

At this point I had had enough and just wanted it all to be over. I had nothing at all to do with the photographs. I was there because Ian had asked me to be.

I was both ashamed and embarrassed and stood with my back to the room, half behind the window curtain. I heard David Smith telling the child to take her clothes off, which she did herself and without objecting. It was obvious that she had some kind of trust in him. For whereas Ian and I frightened her, he didn't…

The radio was still playing and stood on the window ledge, so that while I could hear their voices, I couldn't distinguish what was being said. The whole thing lasted only ten minutes, after which the child dressed herself.

Hindley insisted that Lesley Ann left with Smith in a dark-coloured van and she never saw her again. She said that later that evening Ian told her that a tape recording had been made as 'insurance' as he didn't like the set-up, with a man waiting outside in the van whom he did not know. Brady then apparently told her that Smith had contacts who would buy 'blue photographs' and he had agreed to take them for his share in the money. Hindley claims that she told him she was worried and frightened about the events of earlier that evening and asked him to destroy the photographs and the tape, which he assured her later that he had.

Shortly before the trial, Brady and Hindley were taken to meet their solicitor, Mr Fitzpatrick, in an oak-panelled meeting room. A stack of pictures lay on the table in front of them. Myra told her mother that their solicitor had arranged a special viewing of all the photographs seized by the police so that they could pick out those pictures that were 'special' to them. They selected just a few and Mr Fitzpatrick told them that he would do his best to get these back after the trial.

# 2

# The Trial

On 19 April 1966, at Chester Spring Assizes, the trial of Ian Brady and Myra Hindley began. The courtroom had been specially adapted to accommodate the case and a bullet-proof screen had been erected around three sides of the dock to protect the defendants from possible assassination, while everyone who entered the courtroom was searched by the police.

The bullet-proof screen had been erected because Patrick Downey, Lesley Ann's uncle, had bought a .32 Webley-Scott handgun from a gypsy in Denmark Road, Moss Side in Manchester. Two days after he bought it he handed it in at his local police station and later explained his reasons:

> My wife talked to me about it, telling me that if I didn't hand it in she would go to the police herself. I realised, too, that if I took a shot at Brady, there might be serious consequences for someone else. I might have injured an innocent person if the police had used a decoy again. I had every intention of taking a shot. I didn't want to kill him. A quick death would have been too easy for him. My idea was to maim him for life. I was so incensed, knowing they were not going to hang.

The Trial of Ian Brady and Myra Hindley. This photograph was taken illegally.

Patrick and his brother Terence had been warned that if they went to the trial they would each be guarded by a detective. But he said: 'It would have taken more than a detective to keep me away from Brady if I had heard the evidence. I forced myself to stay away.'

There were no charges brought against Ian Brady or Myra Hindley for the murders of Pauline Reade and Keith Bennett as there was not enough evidence against them. As Chief Superintendent Arthur Benfield said: 'There was no question of capital punishment in the Moors case. Brady and Hindley were not fools, so why should they admit any more? If they did, there might be no possibility of release in the future.'

Before arraignment (in the absence of the jury) Mr Hooson, for Ian Brady, made three submissions, with Mr Heilpern, for Hindley, concurring:

1. As a rule of practice, in a case of murder two or more persons should not be charged in the same indictment
2. The second and third counts in the indictment (the murders of Lesley Ann Downey and John Kilbride) were not founded on the same facts as the first count (the murder of Edward Evans), and were not a series of offences of the same or similar character
3. If the judge ruled against the first two submissions, he should still hold that Brady would be embarrassed in his defence by reason of being charged with three offences on the indictment, and as a matter of discretion should order that there should be a separate trial on the first count.

The trial judge, Mr Justice Fenton Atkinson, gave his ruling:

> I am satisfied that the Kilbride and Downey evidence is admissible in the case of Evans, and vice versa, and the evidence in any one of the three deaths is admissible in the other two; and having considered it, I can see no sufficient reason for the exercise of my discretion in directing that these charges should be tried separately.
>
> I have a further application from Mr Heilpern for a separate trial for his client, Hindley, on the ground that a lot of the evidence against Mr Hooson's client, Brady, is not admissible against Hindley. I have thought about that a great deal, but giving the best consideration I can, considering the evidence and the interests of justice as well as the interests of the accused, I think it right that these two charges should be tried together as one trial.

The court then adjourned and reconvened in the afternoon.

The Clerk of Assize read out the charges against both Brady and Hindley, those of murder against Edward Evans, Lesley Ann Downey and John Kilbride, to which both of them replied 'Not Guilty'. Myra was then also asked to enter a plea on a fourth charge, that of 'knowing that Ian Brady had murdered John Kilbride on a day unknown between the 23 November, 1963 and the 7 October, 1965, you did receive, comfort, harbour, assist and maintain the said Ian Brady.' She replied: 'Not Guilty'.

As the jury were sworn in, Brady's defence QC, Mr Emlyn Hoosen, and Hindley's defence QC, Mr Godfrey Heilpern, had the four women that had been chosen replaced by men, so it consisted of a twelve-man jury. The Attorney General then opened the case on behalf of the Crown. The speech was a straightforward narrative of prosecution evidence in depositions taken at the committal proceedings.

The following day, the Attorney General finished his opening speech and the first witnesses for the prosecution gave their evidence. DC Derek Leighton was the first witness and his evidence was read from deposition. He was the official photographer for the Cheshire Constabulary and he testified that he had taken the photographs of the exterior and interior of 16 Wardle Brook Avenue, the body of Edward Evans before and after the coverings had been removed and of various items, including the hatchet in the immediate vicinity of the body in the bedroom.

The second witness was Harold Beswick, surveyor in the employ of Manchester Corporation, who gave evidence as to the plans he had made of 16, Wardle Brook Avenue and of the whole Hattersley Estate, showing the position of Underwood Court (where David and Maureen Smith lived) and the telephone box (Hyde 3538) from where David Smith had telephoned the police. His evidence was also read to the court.

Leslie Wright, Assistant Street Lighting Superintendent for Hyde Corporation, then provided plans of the street lighting on the Hattersley Estate. His evidence was also read and quoted: 'If anyone were making a journey from Underwood Court to Wardle Brook Avenue at 23.30, the road on which they would travel would, generally speaking, be in darkness.'

The first person to be called to give evidence in person was Myra's sister, Maureen. She was called out of order as she was more than eight months pregnant and could have gone into labour at any time. The police had made special emergency plans to get her to the maternity wing of Chester City Hospital, more than a mile away, within ten minutes if the need arose.

Maureen told the court about her relationship growing up with Myra and how she found out that she was seeing Ian Brady. She said that she saw quite a lot of the couple,

Maureen and David Smith make their way to court.

as she worked for about a year at Millwards, from June 1963–64. She then confirmed that during 1963 she saw Ian Brady at her gran's house almost every night.

Replying to questioning, Maureen told the court that Myra went to Ashton Market every Saturday and would buy items such as tinned food and diamond-patterned nylons. She told the court that Myra stopped going there when she moved to Wardle Brook Avenue. At this point the court was adjourned because Maureen suffered a bad nosebleed. When it reconvened, Maureen confirmed that the day after she married David Smith they were taken to the Lake District in Myra's car, and after that the couples would often see each other and that there were occasions when she and David stayed the night.

She stated that they would go up to Saddleworth Moor, on average, every three weeks and that on most occasions David and Ian would go for a walk, leaving her and Myra in the car.

She then told the court that on Boxing Day 1964 (when Lesley Ann Downey was abducted and murdered) David was with her the whole day and that there was no way he could have gone out and over to Wardle Brook Avenue without her knowing (as Ian and Myra were claiming in the defence).

Maureen then told the court that on New Year's Eve 1964, Ian and Myra visited her flat where Myra told her that they had been up to Saddleworth Moor during the day and that they had taken blankets with them in order to spend the night up there, but they had changed their mind as it was too cold.

Maureen then told the court about the conversation she had with Myra in early 1965 regarding Lesley Ann Downey: 'It was about Mrs Downey offering a reward of £100 to anybody who could give any information as to where her daughter, Lesley, was. I said to Myra: "Her mother must think a lot of the child," and she just laughed.'

Maureen was questioned about a trip they all took to Greenfield Reservoir. She said they went there at about 23.30 on the 24 April 1965 and Brady wanted to show David Smith the reservoir. 'He said it looked nice with the moon shining on it…'

Court was then adjourned until the following morning and Maureen Smith was warned not to discuss the case with anyone.

The following day Maureen continued to give her evidence, stating that towards the end of October 1965, after Ian and Myra had been arrested, she was driven in a police car along the A635 to a spot where she, David, Myra and Ian had stopped off on rare occasions. (This would be Hollin Brown Knoll).

Maureen then gave evidence about the evening of 5 October 1965. She told the court that her husband was at home until around 20.00, when he went around to Wardle Brook Avenue with some books wrapped up in newspaper and returned home about half an hour later.

At around 20.00 the following evening, she sent David over to her grandmother's house at Wardle Brook Avenue for his tea, along with a letter they had received from the housing authority about rent arrears. David returned around fifteen minutes later. They then stayed in the flat for the rest of the evening and went to bed at around 23.00.

They had only been in bed for about half an hour when the telephone buzzer for the front door rang. She got up and answered it and, realising that it was Myra, let her in. Myra then told her that she wanted Maureen to give their mother a message – 'Tell her I'll see her at the weekend as I can't get up there before.' She asked Myra why she had come around so late and Myra said it was because she had forgotten to do so earlier and had only just remembered. Myra also told her that she had walked to the flats because she had already locked the car up.

Maureen then said that Myra asked David if he would walk her home because all of the streetlights were out; David finished getting dressed and told his wife that he would be back in two minutes. Maureen recalled that he took his stick with him, which was nothing unusual, but couldn't recall Myra ever calling at their flat so late before.

She then told the court that she next saw her husband at 02.45, when he was pale and scared. She made him a cup of tea while he had a wash, but heard him being sick. He then told her what he had seen, and they left the flat at around 05.50, with David arming himself with a knife and screwdriver. They made their way to a telephone box and called the police.

Maureen was then cross examined by Mr Hooson. His questioning began by asking her about how she and David made their money. He made the point of showing that David Smith found it hard to hold down a job as he was always taking time off and asked how they came to owe the rent man £14 12s 6d. She replied that she had a job but it didn't pay very well, her husband wasn't regularly attending his job and they were paying off other debts. When asked how they intended to pay the rent arrears, she replied that they were going to ask David's dad. She was then forced to admit that David had not been to work since the 6 October 1965.

**Hooson:** But are things much easier, money-wise?

**Smith:** Yes

**Hooson:** He has a great deal of money now, has he not?

**Smith:** Yes

**Hooson:** Where does he get it?

**Smith:** Must I answer that question?

**Judge Fenton Atkinson:** Yes

**Smith:** Well, he has been getting it off his dad

**Hooson:** How much off his dad?

**Smith:** About £10 a week

**Hooson:** Is that the only place where he was getting money?

**Smith:** No

**Hooson:** Where else has he been getting it?

**Smith:** From a newspaper.

Mr Heilpern then took over the questioning:

**Heilpern:** Are you part and parcel of this financial arrangement with the newspaper?

**Smith:** Yes. Whatever we get we share.

**Heilpern:** What are you getting?

**Smith:** Sometimes £10 a week, sometimes £15, sometimes £20.

**Heilpern:** Who decides?

**Smith:** David

**Heilpern:** What does he do?

**Smith:** He just asks, can he have a bit more.

**Heilpern:** Does the financial arrangement stop there, or is there going to be a very large sum of money coming?

**Smith:** There is going to be a very large sum of money. It depends on syndication.

Mr Heilpern then questioned her about her evidence regarding Myra going to Ashton Market. He suggested that she was confused about where Myra got her tights from and asked her why she would travel over six miles to Ashton Market when that brand of tights were available closer to home. She replied: 'No, she used to tell me she had gone to Ashton Market.'

Following a midday adjournment, David Smith was the next witness called to give evidence. He told the court of his previous addresses and of the honeymoon trip to the Lake District with Ian and Myra.

He told how in early 1965 Ian had asked him what he considered to be the ideal robbery and David told him a large supermarket using a removal van, to which Ian laughed, disagreed and said that a bank was the only real big job going after. David mentioned how the subject of robbery was brought up many times and that after a while he got interested in it:

> We agreed on robbing a bank, the three of us. He instructed me to keep a watch on one certain bank ... I was driven down to a specified bank and told what to do, and I had to take notes of certain things – of arrivals and departures for a good three hours – and then meet him again and tell him what I had taken down.

David was then asked about his trip in a police car in October 1965 up to Hollin Brown Knoll. He said that he could only recall being to that spot once before, and on that occasion:

> It was Ian and Myra, myself and my wife Maureen. We were in the mini driving down the road, and Ian told her to stop the car. He said: 'It's only the reservoir but it looks nice with the moon shining on it. Shall we get out of the van?' Ian and myself walked off towards this reservoir. He told me to stop and he pointed out the reservoir, and we stayed there about ten minutes ... he was falling all over, but he seemed to know where he was.

He told the court that they drove past the same area on their way to test guns. At this juncture, the jury was asked to retire while the admissibility of the evidence was argued.

When the court reconvened, David told the story of him and Ian having a conversation where they discussed what type of robbery they would carry out and Ian told him that he and Myra would be armed as an insurance and that they would be carrying live ammunition. He said he did not object to them carrying guns but did object to them using live ammunition. Ian had just laughed.

He was asked to tell the circumstances of the conversations where Ian had told him that he had killed before. David said Ian told him of his two methods and which one he preferred, and also that 'they' had been buried on the moors and that he had photographic proof. He then recounted what happened the day before Edward Evans was murdered. He had wrapped up all of his books (these were the pornographic and sadistic books written by Marquis de Sade and others that Ian had lent him to read) at Ian's request and taken the parcel over to Wardle Brook Avenue, where he handed the parcel to Myra. Ian had come downstairs, Myra told him that David had brought the books over, so Ian took the parcel off the living room table and took it upstairs. A couple of minutes passed before Ian re-emerged carrying two suitcases, where they 'were taken outside and handed over to Myra and placed in the mini-van. Then they drove away.' David was then asked about the books that he read, some of which were given to him by Ian, including *The Life and Ideals of the Marquis de Sade.*

Questioning quickly moved on to the events of the night of Edward Evans' murder. David told the court that he went over to Wardle Brook Avenue with the note about the rent arrears but when he got there Ian and Myra were getting ready to go out. He said Ian told him that 'there is nothing you can do about it', and that they then went out in the car, leaving him to walk home.

He agreed with his wife that they went to bed at around 23.00 and that the intercom rang about half an hour later. Maureen got up and answered it and, as he was getting dressed, she told him that it was Myra. He said that the two sisters were mainly talking among themselves as he sat stroking his dog. He said that Myra then asked him to walk her home as the streetlights were out.

Then he described in detail what happened when he got to Wardle Brook Avenue and the murder of Edward Evans. He added: 'I have seen butchers working in shops showing as much emotion as he did when they were cutting up sheep's ribs. He was very calm indeed. He was not in a frenzy – no frenzy at all.'

David Smith then stated that he had been nowhere near Wardle Brook Avenue on Boxing Day 1964, the day Lesley Ann Downey was abducted and murdered, and said that he hadn't even heard her name before pictures appeared of her in the newspaper.

He also stated that he had never seen John Kilbride.

Mr Hooson said he would prefer cross-examination to be conducted in one sitting, starting the following morning.

On Friday 22 April, Mr Hooson assured David Smith that he would not be prosecuted in respect of any offence disclosed in his statements. Questioning immediately started in regard to his relationship with the media. Mr Hooson succeeded in showing that if Ian Brady and Myra Hindley were convicted, then David stood to make a significant amount of money. When he was asked to name the newspaper involved, David refused to do so. Even when the trial judge, Mr Justice Fenton Atkinson, told him that he must name the newspaper, David refused and replied: 'I refuse to answer the question unless I have the sanction of the newspaper.'

This attitude enraged the judge, who told the Attorney General that the matter needed investigating, before telling Mr Hooson: 'It seems to me that there is no point in taking steps against him for contempt of court in refusing to answer, because you have got to ask him about a lot more relevant matters.'

Mr Hooson moved on to how David had been earning his money since the arrest of Ian and Myra, to which David replied that he had been living on hand-outs from his father.

David was then questioned about the books on sadism and crime that had been found in Ian Brady's possession, which he admitted he had read, and Mr Hooson asked him about certain passages that he had copied out.

Mr Hooson then switched back to how David had been earning his money at the time of Edward Evans' death and David replied that he had often been unemployed and that it was mostly due to bouts of tonsillitis.

Questioning moved on to the night that Lesley Ann Downey was abducted and murdered, as Ian and Myra's defence story implicated him strongly. It was put to him that he had been the one to suggest to Ian Brady that they could make some money by 'rolling a queer' and selling pornographic photographs, which David flatly denied. It was then put to him that he took Lesley Ann Downey to Wardle Brook Avenue with the help of his friend Keith so that Ian could photograph the girl, and that when the photographs had been taken, she left with David.

David replied that this was the first he had heard about pornographic photographs being taken and that he couldn't have been at Wardle Brook Avenue that evening as he was in the Three Arrows pub in Manchester.

**Hooson:** How do you remember where you were that night?

**Smith:** Because it was Boxing Night.

**Hooson:** You had a small child then?

**Smith:** That is correct.

**Hooson:** And your mother-in-law had not got that child that night?

**Smith:** My mother-in-law is a liar.

**Hooson:** When did you decide that?

**Smith:** She is a liar if she said that. My father saw us walking round from my mother-in-law's with the baby on Boxing Night.

Questioning then moved on to the bank robberies. David admitted that Myra was never present when the conversations took place between himself and Ian and that the talks took place over many months.

It was then put to David that the evidence he offered up regarding Ian having photographic proof of the murders he had committed was false, as was his evidence suggesting that Ian had told him he had killed 'three or four'. David said that both conversations had taken place.

Questioning went back to the night Edward Evans was killed, and David denied that the night before the murder he had taken a cosh to Wardle Brook Avenue and told Ian to put it in with the suitcases. David said that the cosh had once belonged to him, but that he had given it to Myra some time before.

David said that he went to see Ian and Myra the following evening and that he showed them the note regarding the rent arrears. He said that he wasn't so concerned about the money, but more concerned about what to do with his dog. He then denied that a conversation took place where he suggested to Ian that they 'roll a queer' so that he could use the money to pay off the rent.

Mr Hooson moved on to matters later that evening. He put it to David that when Ian opened the front door to him, he nodded to David to indicate that there was someone in the living room and that he had responded by nodding and tapping his stick in the palm of his hand. David flatly denied this.

Mr Hooson suggested that the noise David heard while in the kitchen was not a scream, but a shout. David again denied this.

Mr Hooson suggested that when he ran into the living room and saw Ian and Edward Evans struggling, it was he who hit Edward on the back of the head with his stick, before Ian hit him with his hatchet, and that this explained why there were head hairs and blood from Edward Evans found on his stick. David denied this and said that when he ran into the room Ian was already hitting Evans with the hatchet. David said that the only way he could explain the head hairs and blood getting on his stick was because he dropped it on the living room floor in shock when he ran into the room.

David said he could not swear that Myra was in the room at the time Edward Evans was killed, and then denied that he had put the flex around Evans' neck. Mr Hooson suggested that it was David who had put the flex on to tie the cushion cover over Evans' head, to which David replied: 'I saw him [Brady] use the flex to strangle him.'

It was then put to David that it was he who took Evans' wallet out, went through it, and said: 'Christ, it's empty', and that as he took out the green card he said: 'He's only earning £4 a week. He's an apprentice.' David said that this never happened and that at this point nothing at all had been said.

David then went against his own evidence given to the police by saying that even when they were all cleaning up after Edward was dead, no one was talking and that 'I just cleaned up'. He stated that he said nothing at all the whole time that the body was moved and during the clearing up afterwards.

David was then forced to admit his further dealings with the press and told the court that he and his wife Maureen were being put up in a hotel in Chester during the trial and that their stay was being paid for by the same newspaper that was paying him for his exclusive story, as well as them paying for their trip to Paris. When it was put to him that this paper was the *News of the World*, David Smith replied: 'I am not denying it and I am not confirming it, sir.'

Mr Heilpern, acting on behalf of Myra, was absent on this day due to the murder of his sister-in-law in a shop robbery, so Mr Curtis took over the cross-examination of David Smith.

He also questioned David on his deal with the newspaper and asked: 'Will you be in contact with them over the luncheon adjournment?' To which the judge, Mr Justice Fenton Atkinson, interrupted and said: 'They are probably standing him lunch!'

**Curtis:** Take your mind back to November of last year. How do you say contact was made between you and this newspaper?

**Smith:** There were many reporters round where we live, at the flats, and all of them paid me.

**Curtis:** Paid you? What for?

**Smith:** That is what I would like to know. Usually nothing. Usually they just left their cards and there would be a £5 note or something just tucked underneath it. This happened on a number of occasions, but not with the newspaper I am dealing with.

**Curtis:** Were you really holding an auction for your services in this matter?

**Smith:** No.

**Curtis:** What made you decide to make an arrangement with the particular newspaper?

**Smith:** They offered me a great deal of money.

Mr Curtis moved on to the books read by Ian and David, including *Mein Kampf* and *The Last Days of Goering*. He spoke about David Smith's violent tendencies and David agreed that he could be violent. He said: 'If provoked, yes, if not provoked, very calm.'

He was asked similar questions to those asked by Mr Hooson about the bank robberies, the evening Lesley Ann Downey was murdered and the trip to the moors where Ian took David to see the moonlight shine off the reservoir. Questioning moved on to the night Edward Evans was murdered but was very much on the same level as that which he had faced from Mr Hooson.

David was re-examined by Mr Mars-Jones. He was asked why he went to the police after the murder of Evans, to which he replied: 'Well, I had to. I couldn't hardly keep it to myself.' He was then dismissed, and court was adjourned until the following Monday.

Court reconvened on Monday 25 April, and Dr John Bennett, a General

David and Maureen Smith leaving court.

Practitioner at Hyde, was called to give evidence in relation to Brady's claim that his ankle had been injured by Evans during the fight, and this was why the body had been kept in the house overnight, rather than being buried up on the moors. Dr Bennet had examined Brady at 14.30 on the 8 October 1965. 'I found a small, superficial abrasion on the dorsal of the foot just in front of the lateral malleolus. I would describe the injury as trivial.'

Dr Charles St Hill, Home Office Pathologist for the Liverpool area, was later called to give evidence. He described how he was called to Wardle Brook Avenue and found the body of Edward Evans 'in a large bundle beneath the window in an upstairs bedroom'. He confirmed that he:

> opened the bundle and saw inside the body of a man later identified … as Edward Evans. The body was bent up with the legs brought up to the chest and the arms folded across the body. The legs and arms were kept in position by two cords. It was further secured by two loops of cord which kept the neck bent forward towards the knees; these cords passed round the neck and were attached to the other two cords which bound the legs and arms. [He] found a blood-stained cloth wrapped round the head and neck, and a piece of electric light cable was around the neck but not tied. The body was enclosed in a white cotton blanket which had been knotted. A polythene sheet lay outside this and was itself covered by a grey blanket.

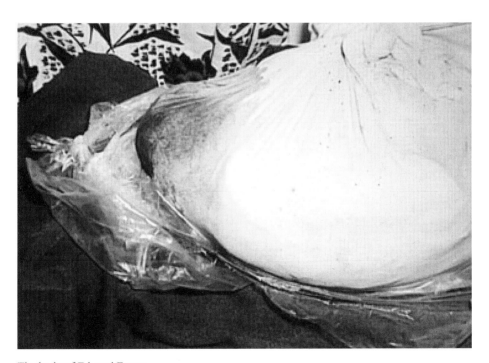

The body of Edward Evans.

Colin Bancroft, a biologist, then identified more than fifty exhibits – mainly clothing and personal belongings of David Smith and Edward Evans, as well as articles removed from Wardle Brook Avenue, which he had examined for blood, saliva, semen and hairs, etc.

> All the blood which was found in the living room was of the same blood group as that of Edward Evans. I examined two fibres taken from the anus of Edward Evans. I would say they were animal hairs. The stick belonging to David Smith was very heavily bloodstained for almost the whole of its length; there were also head hairs similar to those of Edward Evans generally distributed over the surface together with animal hairs. On the three carpets from the living room I found numerous animal hairs but no bloodstaining.

Next to take to the stand was David Noel Jones, Director of the Home Office Forensic Science Laboratory at Preston.

> I have compared the two fibres taken from the anus of Edward Evans with hairs taken from the deceased's home and can find no adequate agreement between them. I have also compared the fibres taken from the anus with samples of hair taken from 16 Wardle Brook Avenue; the latter are largely animal hairs which have the appearance of dog hairs. The majority of these hairs show no agreement with two hairs taken from the anus, but I was able to find some hairs which showed complete microscopic agreement with the two hairs.
>
> I have examined the spots of blood on the two shoes of the accused Hindley. These would be quite consistent with spattering from a wound or a series of wounds such as were present on the head of Edward Evans. As to the suggestion that these spots of blood may have fallen from the head of the deceased while the body was being carried after death, I would think that it is unlikely but not impossible. The spots are small and I would expect blood dropping from a bloodstained head to be somewhat larger than these spots.

Then it was the turn of Detective Chief Superintendent Arthur Benfield. He presented the court slides showing the couch where the murder took place, and it was also where Ian and Myra slept. There were three cigarette ends, which were examined by the forensic scientists and were shown by the saliva test to be positive in respect of the three people (Hindley, Brady and Evans). The wastepaper basket also had blood stains on it, along with hairs from Evans, and it could be seen that one of the blows took a piece out of the fireplace.

The following day the Attorney General read from a transcript made by Leonard Milner, a shorthand writer of the Supreme Court, of tape recordings found in the brown suitcase. It was the recording of the abuse of Lesley Ann Downey. He also referred to another tape recording of Ian, Myra and Pat Hodges discussing the disappearance in the newspaper of Lesley Ann Downey.

According to John Weeks, a BBC recording engineer, to achieve the two copies of the recording containing the voice of Lesley Ann Downey, two recording machines must have been used; the third copy had clearly been made from the second. He also told how a record-player found at Wardle Brook Avenue was capable of playing a Ray Conniff record which contained the same music as that on the tape recording.

When cross-examined by Mr Hooson, Weeks said the tape had not been stopped while it was recording but added:

> I think the music was played from a second tape machine. I think it had been pre-recorded, probably long before this particular recording was made. I think that at the end of the first bit of music the machine stopped, the next record was put on the gramophone, and therefore you have continuity.

The Attorney General wanted to clarify: 'No doubt that while whatever was being done to that child was taking place, there was background music provided?' Mr Weeks then replied: 'Yes, it was being played in that room.'

Detective Sergeant Roy Jarvis of the Fingerprint Department at Manchester City Police was next to give evidence and told the court how fingerprints found on three of the negatives of Lesley Ann Downey were Myra's, but that he had not found David Smith's fingerprints on any of the photographs or any of the negatives.

Detective Chief Superintendent John Tyrrell of Manchester City Police (DCI at the time of the inquiry) was examined by Mr Mars-Jones, but Mr Hooson objected to the admissibility of the evidence concerning his interview with Brady. The jury then left the court as Mr Hooson stated his grounds:

> The grounds for my objection are that the interview which followed … occupied a period of six hours twenty minutes; that the accused was being continually pressed during this period and questioned about these events; that there was no caution given at any time and that the whole interview was oppressive and rendered any answers given not of a voluntary character.

The Attorney General asked him what kind of matters he was trying to get information on, to which DCS Tyrrell replied 'My particular interest was the missing boy, John Kilbride. There were other missing people, sir: a boy and a girl.'

**Mr Justice Fenton Atkinson:** Lesley Ann Downey?

**Tyrrell:** Yes. And another boy as well.

**Attorney General:** Is that the sum total of the matters you were investigating?

**Tyrrell:** There was one other missing person.

**Mr Justice Fenton Atkinson:** Four missing children at that stage?

**Tyrrell:** Kilbride, Downey, and two others, all of whom had vanished without trace.

Mr Hooson wanted to call his defendant, Ian Brady. Brady had told his defence team that he believed he had been interviewed illegally and, as such, the evidence gained from that interview should be inadmissible in court.

23

Brady said of the interview in question: 'There was no break. When Mounsey and Tyrrell stopped questioning, Mattin and Leach came in. They continued to question during the meals.' He said that in the last two hours of questioning there were four detectives questioning him; Mounsey, Tyrrell, Mattin and Leach.

> The interview was Mounsey at one side, Tyrrell at the other, Mattin and Leach at the front. I was being asked simultaneously questions from each side. If I gave one answer to one question, I could be answering three questions at the one time. They were shouting from a foot from each ear from both sides.

Brady said that he was not cautioned during the interview and by the end he felt he had lost his temper. He was then cross-examined by the Attorney General. He said that after he was charged with the murder of Edward Evans, he found it 'amusing' to be questioned about other missing children. The Attorney General said: 'You were aware that you were being questioned about what was thought to be the murder of missing children. Did you find that amusing?' Ian Brady replied: 'I found it amusing, yes.'

He then told the court that what the police claimed he had said in their interviews was fiction, and that what he had said was taken out of context. Questioning of Brady at that time finished and the jury returned.

The following day DCS Tyrrell was recalled to the stand and examined by Mr Mars-Jones. He told the court that he had interviewed Hindley at Risley Remand Centre on the 14 October regarding Brady telling officers he had talked in general terms to David Smith about committing bank robberies, killing people and burying bodies on the moor, all of which Myra denied had happened. He then told of an interview with Brady shortly after, to which Brady told them that a photograph taken of him standing near some rocks was taken in Whaley Bridge, but was later proved to have been taken on Hollin Brown Knoll and within yards of Lesley Ann Downey's grave. He then described to the court how he had found the counterfoil of a left-luggage ticket wedged in the spine of Myra's prayer book.

DCI Mounsey then took to the stand and told of how he had interviewed Ian Brady and asked him questions about John Kilbride. PC Bob Spiers then told the court how he had discovered the body of Lesley Ann Downey, and DS Leslie Eckersley spoke of the excavation he took part in to recover her body.

Inspector John Chaddock told the court that he had spent Christmas Day and Boxing Day 1964 up around the moors on his patrol and said that the roads were in a good condition and that snow had not made driving difficult, as claimed by Myra when she made her grandmother stay with her uncle in Dukinfield. He said that he later saw the body of Lesley Ann Downey in the ground and accompanied her body to Uppermill Mortuary and was present when her mother, Ann, identified her body.

On the 28 April, the prosecution turned to the case of John Kilbride. The court heard from his mother, Sheila, and from the women who had given clothes to her for John, which he was wearing when he disappeared and also when his body was discovered. The court also then heard from 14-year-old John Ryan, who was the last person to see him alive.

Various detectives were called up and confirmed where the exercise book containing the name of John Kilbride had been found in Wardle Brook Avenue and how they had come to discover his body on the moor.

Abdul Letif Chaudhiri, a stall holder at Ashton-under-Lyne market, then gave evidence confirming that he sold similar stockings to those shown to him by detectives. Following him was Professor Cyril Poulson, who had performed the autopsy on John Kilbride.

Detective Policewoman Margaret Campion was then recalled and gave evidence regarding Myra's dog, Puppet, and the handing over of the dog to James Gourley, a vet practising in Ashton-under-Lyne. Gourley then told the court he had sedated the dog so he could perform an X-ray to establish its age; he noticed the dog had stopped breathing while under sedation and tried to revive it for forty-five minutes but without success.

The jury was cleared from the court and Ian Brady was called up to the witness stand where he again disputed certain interviews with the police. Again, he told the court that he was never cautioned during these interviews and that the detectives refused to call his solicitor. He also stated that the detectives intimidated him into talking about subjects that he didn't want to discuss in the absence of his solicitor. Answering to a question from the Attorney General, Ian Brady told the court: 'I am saying that Mr Mounsey's whole statement is lies from beginning to end. Every answer – he's not just changed it, he's manufactured it. Except for a few little pieces of truth at the beginning of the statement.'

Mr Justice Fenton Atkinson listened to legal argument by Mr Hooson, then ruled against the defence submission:

> On the evidence that I have heard, I am quite satisfied that these answers, whatever they may have been, were free and voluntary and are admissible, and I do not believe that the solicitor was asked for and refused. But it is a matter, of course, for the jury ultimately to decide what weight they give to it.

The jury returned to the court and Detective Chief Inspector Joseph Mounsey was recalled; he told the court about his interview with Ian Brady, and later Myra Hindley, on the 28 October 1965.

The following day, once again in the absence of the jury, Mr Heilpern submitted that there was no case for Myra Hindley to answer in regards to the charges brought against her for the murder of John Kilbride and for the alternative charge of being an accessory after the fact, but Mr Justice Fenton Atkinson ruled that there was sufficient evidence to proceed and that it was for the jury to decide on these counts.

At 11.43 Ian Brady took to the stand. He knew that he was going to be given a life sentence, but he was determined that Myra should not and had instructed their counsel not to ask any questions that could damage Myra's defence of knowing nothing about any of the murders. He was also determined to implicate the man who had turned on him: David Smith.

He told the court about his early life in Scotland and how he came to live in Manchester. He admitted his previous convictions and that he had been sent to Borstal in his youth. He said that he first met David Smith in October 1963 and saw him on and off until April 1964. He said that the two of them had not specifically talked about robbing a bank but had talked about robbing payrolls. He said that there was never a discussion about using blank bullets and that Smith was fully aware that they would be using live ammunition.

Questioning then moved on to the night Edward Evans was murdered. Ian agreed that Smith had turned up at his house with a note regarding his overdue rent, but that it was earlier in the evening at around 18.15. He said that David was agitated and kept asking him about the 'job' they had been planning for the following Saturday. That job was to rob the Electricity or Gas Board on Hyde Road.

He said that Smith had also mentioned 'screwing' (housebreaking) as a way of getting the money but that Smith then said the best way to get it would be to 'roll a queer'. Ian agreed with him because:

> if anything did go wrong this person would be unlikely to complain to the police, so there was no real risk ... I told him that Myra and I were going to Glossop and to be prepared, anyway, for that night. There was later discussion after we left the house to go to the car. He left with Myra and I. Myra entered the car and switched the engine on. I was stood outside the car with Smith and I didn't shut the door of the car – I held it to, closed, but not completely shut. Smith and I continued to talk about whether, if something did take place, when it did take place, we would come back to Hattersley. Myra interrupted by tooting her horn. I asked her what was wrong and she said she was cold. As soon as I got in the car, I bawled Myra out for interrupting the conversation, and we went towards Glossop, about one or two miles.

Brady said that Smith went back to his flat and that he and Myra went out on one of their night-time trips. He said that they first went to Gorton to get some wine, where Myra spent fifteen minutes inside talking to the other women while he waited outside. They then drove to Manchester Central Station to see if the buffet was open but arrived two minutes after it had closed. Myra remained in the car while he went off to see if he could get some bottled beer and it was then that he saw Edward Evans, who he said he had met before, standing at the side of a milk-vending machine. Ian told the court:

> Evans said the buffet was closed, but I tried the door just the same. Then we got into conversation. He kept saying there was no place to get a drink. I knew Evans was a homosexual because he went to one club especially, called the Rembrandt, in Manchester, which is a homosexual hang-out. I invited him back to the house.
>
> Before I got to the car, I had decided he would do for what Smith and I had been talking about earlier on that night. I told Evans that my sister was meeting me in the car. We got to the car and I told Myra this was a friend who was coming back to Hattersley. She was surprised at first, then annoyed afterwards, because she would not take part in the conversation.

26

Brady said that he introduced Edward to Myra and said that Myra was his sister. They then drove back to Hattersley and went into the house at around 23.30, when he told Myra to go and fetch Smith. Myra asked if it couldn't wait until the following day, but Brady ordered her to fetch him now and 'while she was gone, Evans was talking mostly about clothes. I wasn't taking an interest; I wasn't listening.' He said that he and Edward were in the living room and the only time Edward left was to go upstairs to use the toilet.

When Hindley arrived with Smith he asked him in a loud voice if he had come round for the miniatures. 'This was in a loud voice for Evans' benefit, nobody else's. Smith stood there with his mouth open. He did not know what I was talking about.' He saw that Smith was carrying his stick and then:

> I said in a low voice 'There is a queer in the living-room. I will ask him for the cash. If he tries to leave you stop him.' When I said that Smith nodded and smacked his hand with his stick. He said: 'Just the job.'
>
> I went back into the living-room and Evans was sitting upon Grandmother's chair with his back towards the door. I stood by the fireplace and said to Evans: 'There is another bloke at the door does not like queers. All you have to do is put your cash and valuables on the table and then you can go.'
>
> Evans was surprised and then he started swearing out loud. He got up from the chair and kicked at me. I grabbed him by the lapels to pull him towards me. Myra shouted 'Dave, Dave'. Myra wasn't in the room. Then, almost simultaneously, there were two thuds or vibrations passed through Evans into my head. Perhaps I had my head against him. Evans was swinging round, his hands were flailing all over the place. He was shouting at the top of his voice and Smith was hitting him – I won't say hard – he was hitting him. It was just a struggle.
>
> I was telling Evans to shut up but he would not shut up and kept shouting. I turned to the fireplace for something to hit Evans with. The axe was by the side of the fireplace. I picked it up and hit Evans with it with the blunt side of the axe.
>
> The axe just bounced off his head. It did not seem to have any effect. It just bounced and then he kept shouting. I hit him again but his shouting continued, only louder. Smith was hitting Evans.

When asked whether he knew how many times he had hit Evans, he replied:

> No, the point was, when I hit him I thought he would shut up. I hit him again and it was not having any effect. There was blood appearing and after that it was just a question … I did not know anything. I just kept hitting him until he shut up.
>
> …
>
> He fell on his knees, facing the table … I was behind him … Smith hit him a couple of times with the stick as he was on the floor. Smith was contributing to this all the way through with kicks and with the stick.

At this specific part he hit him two or three times with the stick as he was going under the table. As he was under the table he was kicking him about the head and shoulders. Evans ended up under the table lying face downwards.

There was blood all over the place at that time. It was on the walls and there were pools on the floor. He was gurgling. Myra was in the room then … Evans was alive. He was gurgling – blood, I suppose. He was lying face downwards, and Myra kept asking: 'What's happened? What did he do? What did he do?' I told her there was an argument. 'Get out. Keep out.' Then Smith dragged Evans out and turned him on to his back parallel with the table. Smith took out his wallet. As Smith was rifling through the wallet, the contents were falling out. He says: 'I don't know why I called him a bastard. I don't even know him.' I didn't actually hear Smith call Evans anything during this. He then showed me a card – a green card. He said: 'He isn't anyone. He's only an F-ing apprentice.' I didn't touch the card.

[At this point Evans] was still alive. I was sitting rubbing my ankle [which he claimed had been kicked by Evans] and I made some comment regarding the blood. Smith picked up a magazine or newspaper and shoved it under Evans' head. Then shortly – within half a minute, I suppose, if that – Evans stopped gurgling and Smith was at the boy. I was almost two foot away. Smith felt the pulse. He says: 'He's a goner' or 'He's gone.' 'I got up from the couch and looked at Evans. He wasn't breathing – completely still. There was no gurgling. I then said we would have to get him out of the house.

Later I told Myra – I think she was at the door – that Evans was dead. She became overwrought or hysterical, whatever you want … I wanted to take Evans out as a drunk between us, an arm each … as if he was drunk. Pick him up an arm over each shoulder.

Smith said he would leave a blood trail along the way. He suggested tying him up in a wrapping of some sort. He then asked Myra for some string; she brought back this. [A piece of flex was shown to the jury and to Brady]

He took it, picked up Evans' legs and folded them towards his chest. He then lay on top of Evans' legs and put this round the back of Evans' head – I don't know how he put it round – and began to pull it up. I then came over to the side of Evans and started pressing down his legs to get this flex round them.

This flex was too short to tie. Smith made a joke then. He said: 'He's got no control.' This was referring to the fact that there was a smell. Evans had soiled himself. I then suggested getting the place cleaned up. The blood was being walked in all over the floor. I asked Smith to get some mops and buckets. He went for them. I picked up the cushion cover and wrapped it round Evans' head, partly to hide his features, partly to soak up the blood. There was no string in the house. The stick was lying on the floor.

28

He tried to undo the knots [in the string tied to the top of the stick] but he couldn't. He handed it to me and said, 'Your nails are better.' I tried to undo the knots but couldn't. I cut the string with scissors or a knife. It came off in small pieces. I handed it to Smith and he tied it together into different lengths.

…

I asked Myra for something – a blanket – and she looked for a white sheet. After we put the white sheet on, the blood was coming through, soaking through, from Evans' head. I asked her for some rag. I think she went upstairs and got a blanket and a piece of polythene, which we spread out on the floor. Smith and I put it over a second time and tied it up exactly the same way as we did the sheet.

[It was my idea to take the body upstairs] because I couldn't put any weight on my ankle. Myra was again going off her head because of the fact that the body was left in the house. Both Smith and I carried the body upstairs. I told Myra to go upstairs and hold grandma's door shut so she wouldn't come out.

[Smith was] reeling off different jokes [and his actions were] theatrical, jocular. He was going out of his way to crack jokes. I don't know if he was trying to prove something, but he was just reeling off different jokes at all stages.

He and Smith cleaned up downstairs, while Myra 'cleaned up a few spots'.

When asked if he had had any intention to kill Edward Evans, Brady replied: 'No. To me it was a bit of practice for the following Saturday or the Saturday afterwards.' He then elaborated and said that he hadn't intended on there being any violence involved at all that night.

I didn't think there would be any violence at all. That was why I kept Smith interested – because if there were two people present, a person would be less inclined to make a show. If he did have an audience, he could stand a lot of humiliation. He would give over the cash easily, whereas if there wasn't two, he would put up some sort of show, some sort of resistance.

He said that both he and Smith discussed where to get rid of Evans. 'I suggested the road which leads from Hattersley to Stockport: it's a rural road. I suggested stripping Evans completely at the spot.' He said this was 'To take traces of dog hairs, fingerprints, everything, off Evans.' He said he wanted to dispose of the body,

To get away with it. Smith suggested taking him up on to the moors where we shoot. We had been up dozens of times shooting, not once or twice. Then Myra came in with the tea. Just before that, when the question of tea – Myra said she could do with some whisky because she was feeling faint, and she had been sick earlier on.

He then said that he had suggested burying Edward's body at Penistone Burn. He had started to write the disposal plan just after 02.00 and finished it around 03.50. They talked about how to move the body and 'Smith wanted to use a wheelbarrow; he didn't want a pram used because it may leave traces of blood on it. I thought it was ludicrous to think of stealing a wheelbarrow to dispose of a body.' He again brought up the 'lists' and said:

> Smith and I have made dozens of these lists in the past, between us, all based on jobs, the principle being that no trace of the starting point was left at the destination and no trace of the destination was taken back to the starting point. He's seen these lists dozens of times.'

He agreed that it would have been him who selected the spot to bury Evans: 'Myra Hindley and Smith were to drive round every five minutes past the spot on the moors where the grave was to be, this was so we would not be detected.'

Questioning then led on to Lesley Ann Downey, Ian Brady was asked by the QC 'How did Lesley Ann Downey come to be in your house at Wardle Brook Avenue?' Brady:

> The discussion started on the 23 or 24 December between Smith and I. Myra and I went to Myra's mother's house in Eaton Street, Gorton. I was sitting in the van. Smith entered the van. Almost immediately the conversation got round to photography. He asked me if I was willing to take pornographic photographs.
>
> I asked him about the financial aspect and who would pose. He said he would get a girl called Madeleine, a girl he knew in Gorton. They were to be taken on the Saturday at Wardle Brook Avenue… On the Saturday about 18.15 Myra and I were having tea. There was a knock on the door. I answered it. Smith was there with a young girl.
>
> Myra had no knowledge of the arrangement and she did not know that Smith was bringing the girl with him.

Smith asked him who else was in the house and Brady told him that it was just him and Myra. Smith told him that he couldn't get 'Madeline' to pose so he had got a girl called Lesley Ann Downey to pose instead. 'Smith told me the girl had agreed to pose for ten shillings. I said the girl was too young. He said there was a market for that sort of thing.

> I went into the living-room and told Myra what was about to take place. She asked why, and I said 'money'. She objected to it, but I insisted that she would be present. I wanted her as a witness to what took place in case something went wrong, either with the fellow or the photographs and it led back to us.
>
> I agreed to take the photographs. He made reference to a boy called Keith who was in the van. He said he was the person who would take the photographs. We then had an argument because I had told him never to mention our association in criminal activities to anyone.

He said that he then told David that he would take the photographs and that Myra would be present. He went upstairs and prepared the bedroom. He got his camera, tripod and photo-flood lamps out and put a white sheet over the bed. He then plugged his tape-recorder in at the end of the bed because 'I wanted to make a record of what took place in case again anything happened afterwards. If either Smith or Keith interfered with the girl or she made a complaint I would have a record of what took place while she was in the house.'

Brady said he asked Smith, in front of Lesley Ann Downey, if she knew what she was there for, and Smith said she did. He then told her to get undressed; she kept saying that she had to be home by 20.00 and that when he reached out to take her coat 'she stiffened and stepped back and then began to shout … I put my hand over her mouth to stop her shouting. She kept trying to shout. I kept my hand over her mouth.'

Brady said that the handkerchief shown in the photographs 'was the girl's handkerchief. I put it in her mouth to keep her quiet.' When asked how the scarf got around her mouth, for the first time Brady slipped up in his evidence, replying: 'It was put on at a later stage. I think it was while the music was on, just before the end…' The Judge asked: '"Just before the end"? – What do you mean by "the end"?' Ian Brady stuttered, 'The end of – just before the – or it could be just after the tripod being opened.'

He said that it was Myra who had switched on the transistor radio to ease the tension in the room and that was how music came to be on the tape. He said that at this point, Smith was stood on the stairs outside the room.

Brady was then shown the photographs he had taken of Lesley Ann Downey naked and said: 'There are two poses on the photographs which are suggested by Smith.' He then slipped up again in his evidence by revealing the fact that he and Myra were also naked, leading to speculation that they had indeed sexually assaulted the young girl. He stated: 'After completion we all got dressed and went downstairs.' This was the only time he had said this.

He then said Lesley Ann took the scarf and handkerchief off herself, before getting dressed and leaving with Smith at around 19.30. He was then asked what he and Myra did for the rest of the evening:

> Towards 21.30 we were going to collect Myra's grandmother. I didn't want to go because of the weather conditions, but Myra insisted. The side roads were bad, but when we got to the main road, there is a hill running down. On the way down there was cars slewing from one side of the road to the other and cars stopped on the hill with their wheels spinning. At the bottom of the hill we meant to turn right and had to turn back on to the main road because we couldn't get up that hill. About a mile or three-quarters of a mile from Dukinfield, Myra had trouble controlling the skids on the road. She eventually stopped the car because I said she couldn't go any further. She went to her uncle's house and I sat in the car. She was gone about three-quarters of an hour. When she came back I said to keep her mouth shut and we started off as slow as she wanted to drive. We got down one hill by using a zig-zag, but we couldn't get up the other hill. The car was abandoned and we walked the rest of the way.

Questioning then moved on to John Kilbride, but Ian denied knowing him or even having heard of him until the police had arrested him and asked him questions in interviews. He said that on the day he went missing he and Myra had hired a car but went to Leek and not to Ashton-under-Lyne.

When asked about the exercise book found at Wardle Brook Avenue in which he had written the name of John Kilbride (among others) he said that he had used the book for exercises that he was doing when he applied for the job at Millwards and therefore the name had been written long before John Kilbride had been abducted. He said that in his police interviews he had written the name because he knew an Irishman called Kilbride or McBride at Hull or Salford and had met with him afterwards.

Mr Heilpern asked Brady about his relationship with Myra. He said that she was in love with him and that if they had differing views on where to go or what to do, it was generally his view that would prevail. He said this was:

> Because she was my typist in the office. I dictated to her in the office and this tended to wrap over … when I argued with her, when she did, it just made me worse. She argued so little – I had to tell her to argue at times. When she did, it had the opposite effect – it was worse.

On Monday 2 May, Ian Brady was recalled to the witness stand and Mr Heilpern questioned him in regard to the photographs taken in the vicinity of Hollin Brown Knoll. Brady admitted that it was he who had chosen the places to be photographed.

The Attorney General then began to question Ian and he asked him questions about answers he had given during police interviews regarding John Kilbride and managed to strike home a huge blow in Ian Brady's defence.

**Attorney General:** Do you know, if you deny killing John Kilbride, who did kill Kilbride?

**Brady:** No

**Attorney General:** You told Chief Inspector Mounsey when he asked you that question: 'It is one of two men. I have given their names to my solicitor.'

**Brady:** I did not tell him that.

**Attorney General:** You do not like being landed with that answer now, do you?

**Brady:** I did not tell him that. I know what I told him.

**Attorney General:** Because it is very difficult to blame Smith for Kilbride. Smith was about fourteen or fifteen when Kilbride was murdered.

**Brady:** I haven't the slightest.

The questioning then moved on to whether or not certain photographs taken by him were markers for graves, but Brady said that they were simply 'snapshots', and others were taken purely to use up the end of the film. The Attorney General then moved on to the murder of Edward Evans:

32

**Attorney General:** The truth is, Brady, that you hit that youth the first blow with the axe when he was sitting on the settee and you struck him from behind. That is how this murder started, was it not?

**Brady:** No

**Attorney General:** And after that initial blow, although he obviously struggled for his life, he never got on his feet again, did he?

**Brady:** He was on his feet the whole time, falling on to the couch and up again. Shouting at the top of his voice. All I was worried about was the noise.

**Attorney General:** You were hitting to stop the noise. But can you account for the area of twelve inches square of bloodstaining on the top edge of the back of the settee?

**Brady:** When he fell on the settee

**Attorney General:** That is where you struck the initial blow?

**Brady:** No

**Attorney General:** And from this position he slid down to the floor?

**Brady:** No

**Attorney General:** That accounts for the blood staining on the front edge of the settee cushions, does it not?

**Brady:** I wouldn't know.

Later on, Ian Brady fell into another trap.

**Attorney General:** What were your feelings when you were striking this boy on the head with the axe?

**Brady:** All I remember was this hitting, how to stop the noise. I just kept hitting him. It was just panic.

**Attorney General:** Panic? You claim to have a very clear idea of everything that was going on in that room. You say Hindley was not there, you say Smith was there, and you claim to have given the court a detailed account of what Smith was doing?

**Brady:** That was after. I cannot say about during the assault. The only thing I had in my mind during it was the noise.

**Attorney General:** Do I understand that you may not be very clear in your recollection as to who was and was not there during the assault? Is that what you are saying now?

**Brady:** I know who was there.

**Attorney General:** The fact is, Hindley was there the whole time, was she not, or most of the time?

**Brady:** The only time I seen Myra was when I sat on the couch – in the doorway. After Evans was lying on the floor.

The Attorney General then trapped Brady again, by suggesting other ways in which he could have chosen to keep Evans quiet.

**Attorney General:** Let me suggest how it could have been done. By gagging him as you did Lesley Ann Downey. That is a very effective way, is it not?

**Brady:** I suppose so…

Brady was then questioned about the tape recording of Lesley Ann Downey.

**Attorney General:** Towards the end, the accused Hindley says: 'Put that in your mouth again, packed more solid.' Of course, you appreciated, did you not, that the more solidly the handkerchief was packed into the mouth of that little girl, she could be suffocated in a matter of seconds by merely putting your hand over her little nose?

**Brady:** No

The cross-examination continued the following day and Brady said that Myra was aware of his criminal activities but did not know any of the details. The Attorney General immediately challenged this and asked him about one of the letters found in the suitcases, dated 16 April 1963. It was written by him to Myra and read: 'I have sprained my ankle … Let's capitalise on this situation. I shall grasp this opportunity to view the investment establishment situated at Stockport Road next Friday. I will contact you before then to give other details.' Astonishingly, Ian said: 'That was a reference to buying a car at a used car lot on Stockport Road.'

The judge then wanted to go over Ian's story regarding Lesley Ann Downey and asked: 'Is it right that you kept a recording, or wanted to make a recording, in case she made a complaint and you were taken into custody for assaulting the girl? The recording would be of some assistance in your defence?' Brady replied: 'That was the idea before the recording, but not after.' He was then asked why he had kept it, as he could not understand. Brady's reply was odd: 'Well, because it was unusual.' He was then released from the witness stand.

Throughout his testimony, he had said that Myra had only helped to clean up after the death of Edward Evans, that she knew nothing at all about John Kilbride and that the only reason her voice appeared on the tape of Lesley Ann Downey was because he had told her that he wanted her in the room to act as a witness in case the girl later went to the police and accused him of things he had not done. He had been in the dock for eight-and-a-half hours.

Next to give evidence was Myra Hindley's mother, Nellie. Her evidence was somewhat tainted as she had disowned her daughter Maureen for believing Smith and giving evidence against Myra. Nellie had refused to believe that her daughter was capable of the charges against her. Under examination from Mr Heilpern, she said that Maureen was frightened of her husband David. 'I don't know if she still is, but she used to be very frightened.' She also said that David could be a bully towards Maureen, 'If he wasn't getting his own way all the while.'

When cross-examined by the Attorney General, she said that Smith could be responsible for her daughter Myra being in the dock. 'He is that kind of person,' she said, but that he could be good 'when he wants to be'.

Nellie had given evidence on when she had looked after her granddaughter, Angela Dawn, which differed to the days given by David and Maureen Smith and which they had both used as evidence of where they were on the night Lesley Ann Downey was abducted:

**Attorney General:** I suggest you are mistaken, and that it was Boxing Night when the baby was brought around so that Maureen and her husband could go and have a short visit to the pub?

**Nellie Hindley:** No, I didn't have her on Boxing Night. I can remember that very well, it was my step-brother's birthday. I had the baby with me on Christmas Eve and Christmas Day, not Boxing Night. Then I had her for a short time on the next two nights, and then I had her again on the following Thursday.

The last witness to give evidence was Myra Hindley. When she took to the stand she was asked about her relationship with Ian and she replied: 'I loved him, and I still … I love him.' She then told the court when she passed her driving test and said that since then she and Ian had been 'all over the place; Leek, Whaley Bridge, the Boston area, Glossop, Snake Pass, all over Yorkshire. We have been practically all over the place.'

She said that shortly before Edward Evans was killed in October 1965 she knew that something was in the pipework involving Ian and David Smith because the suitcases were taken out of her house and she thought that a robbery had been planned and was soon to be executed. She said that neither Brady nor Smith would tell her why they wanted the suitcases removed and that David told her not to ask any questions if she didn't want to be lied to.

She said that if Brady asked her to do something that she objected to then she would argue her corner but would always eventually give in to him. She was then questioned about the night Edward Evans was killed and said that Smith called at her house when she and Brady were having dinner, which was 18.00–18.30, backing up Brady's claim. She said that he went home but returned again at about 19.30 and left again, and half an hour later she drove Ian to Manchester Central Station. She said that everything seemed normal that evening and that they went out because there was nothing of interest on television.

She said that she was sat in the car alone for about ten minutes before Brady returned with Edward Evans, and that Brady told her: 'This is a friend of mine. We are just going back for a drink.'

She said that when they got back to Wardle Brook Avenue Ian asked her to go and get David. She denied that she said anything to him about miniature wine bottles. She also said that it was Smith who opened the door to her at Underwood Court and not her sister Maureen. She said she told him: 'Please slip round a minute. Ian wants you.'

She then spoke to her sister while Smith put his shoes on and was shown the note about the overdue rent. She said that Maureen had told her: 'We will have to get it from somewhere because Page, the caretaker of the flats, wants the slightest opportunity to get rid of us.' Hindley had suggested getting a loan of the money from their father 'who had just had a compensation award from his firm. It was a standing joke that you could not get a tap off the old man.' Hindley said she then asked David about borrowing the money from his own father, but he told her that he didn't have the money to give to them. Smith then told his wife: 'I am going round, Maureen. Don't wait up.' Hindley then said that she caught David in the hallway and told him: 'Hang on, and I will walk along with you in case the lights go off.'

When they reached her home she knocked on the door and Brady opened it. She said that Smith was lying when he had claimed that she told him to wait across the road for the lights to flicker.

Hindley said that when they went indoors, she was in the kitchen opening a tin of dog food when she heard a door bang and a shout.

> I went into the hall and momentarily saw Ian and Evans grappling with each other. I thought they were fighting. When I shouted 'Dave', he came running past me and as soon as he ran in, there was a loud cry and I ran into the kitchen. There was a terrible noise and I put my hands over my ears.

She said that she later went to go into the living room but stopped at the door because she saw a pool of blood. Edward Evans was lying on the floor half under the table and she saw David kicking him and jabbing at him with his stick. She said at that point she was 'sick at seeing the blood … I was crying … I was horrified … I was frightened.'

Conveniently, she said that she didn't see Brady and that she then went back into the kitchen. Smith followed her and asked her for some string. Brady asked her to help to clear up the aftermath, which she did. She said that she did not help to tie up the body and did not help to carry it up the stairs, but she did hold her grandmother's bedroom door closed.

She denied that Brady had said: 'It's the messiest yet', and denied that she had said: 'You should have seen his face. The blow registered…', as she was not in the room to see any blow. She said that at the time the only person she was worried about was Brady.

She then claimed that after the body of Edward Evans had been locked in her bedroom, all three of them went back downstairs and she went into the kitchen to make a cup of tea. Ian and David went into the living room and sat on the settee, with a coffee table pulled up in front of them. 'There was a shorthand pad, papers, and pencils about. They were talking and Ian was writing.'

Hindley said she couldn't see what was being written down so she asked Ian, who told her that it didn't matter.

> I asked what they were going to do, and Smith said the best thing to do was to bury it. I said, 'Where, in the back garden?' He said: 'No, not in the back garden, you fool … what about the place where we were shooting? It is as good a place as any.
> …
> If they did bury it up there and it was discovered, too many people knew we had been up there. I said it would be stupid to contemplate going

up there. I said, 'What about Penistone?' and Ian said, 'There's police patrols up there'.

She said that Brady was still writing on the notepad when Smith left their house at around 03.00. She was then asked how she and Ian spent the next few hours up until the police arrived at her door. She replied: 'Up until 5 o'clock I was walking in and out of the kitchen trying to tidy up. I finally lay down on the divan.' But she could not sleep. 'I was worried and thinking what would happen, and how the hell it had happened, and things like that.'

She then tried to cover up the discrepancies between the stories both she and Brady had given to the police when they were originally questioned. Hindley admitted she had lied when she said they had gone to Glossop on the night Evans was killed, and Brady had said they had gone in the opposite direction to Manchester, 'because I was still frightened … it was stupidity, but that was the original intention.'

Hindley was then questioned about Lesley Ann Downey and told the court that on that particular Boxing Day she had taken her grandmother in her Mini-van to her uncle's house in Dukinfield. She backed up Brady's story and said she knew nothing of the arrangements that he and Smith had made about bringing anyone to the house.

She said that at about 18.30 that evening Brady answered a knock at the door and told her 'Dave has brought a girl and he wants me to take a photograph. But she is a bit younger than I expected and I want you to be present when I take them.' She said she did not want him to take the photographs. 'Money was mentioned. That was what Ian wanted to take the photographs for.' Hindley said she now knew the girl's name was Lesley Ann Downey and had heard the tape recording, of which she was 'ashamed'. She was asked why she took part.

> Because Ian asked and Smith kept saying 'We have come all this way', and 'Don't start poking your nose in.' This was because when I saw the girl, I saw how young she was. I said again, 'She's too young and this is not right.' Smith said it was not right for me to start arguing. He said he had just had an argument with Ian about it and he didn't want another. Ian said, 'I want you to be there.' So I agreed.
>
> …
>
> The child was quiet downstairs. I took her upstairs and told her to go into the bedroom and I came down again. Ian was ready, so I shouted 'Ready, Dave.' Ian went upstairs and Smith stood in the garden. Then the girl screamed…
>
> As soon as she started crying I started to panic because I was worried. That is why I was so brusque and cruel in my attitude because I wanted her to be quiet. I didn't expect her to start making such a noise … The front door was wide open. The bedroom door was open and the bedroom window was open. I was frightened that anyone would hear. I just wanted her to be quiet and I said, 'Be quiet until we get things sorted out.'
>
> The girl sat on the bed. I switched on the radio then because I was hoping that she would remain quiet and that the radio would help to

alleviate her fears. Two photographs were taken and Smith told the girl to get dressed again, which she did.

When asked whether Smith was in the room when the photographs were taken, she replied:

> Just in the doorway. He couldn't get into the room because Ian was there with the tripod. He was in the hall just outside the door.... Smith's mate was waiting outside in the van. I saw Smith talking to somebody but did not see who it was.

Hindley said the girl got dressed and walked out of the house with David Smith.

The cross-examination by the Attorney General continued the following day and Hindley stated that she did not know that Brady had recorded the session until about an hour and a half after the girl had left with Smith. She said that Brady played it to her and she didn't like what she heard so she told him: 'It sounds terrible. Get rid of it or wipe it off.'

She claimed that her fingerprints came to be on the photographs because Brady showed them to her a couple of days after they were taken and told her that he wasn't going to give them to Smith. 'I looked at them and said I was glad that he had not given them to Smith.'

She then flatly denied that she had had any conversation with her sister regarding Lesley Ann's disappearance and that she had laughed when Maureen had told her about the £100 reward.

The Attorney General then went back and asked Myra why she didn't get the girl out of the house before the photographs were taken, to which she replied: 'I should have done and I didn't. I have no defence for that. No defence. It was indefensible. I was cruel.'

Attention then switched to the transcript of the tape and Myra denied that the first voice heard on it apart from Lesley Ann's was hers. She said that when the child was told to 'Shut up' it was not her voice, but Brady whispering to the child. This was such an obvious lie that the judge intervened and said to her: 'This is very serious. Just think. Are you telling the jury that when this transcript shows it was a woman speaking, it was not you at all, it was Ian Brady?' She replied: 'No, in the beginning it is all in whispers. It is not my voice at all, I am sure.'

**Attorney General:** Further on, the woman says: 'Shut up or I'll forget myself and hit you one.' Was that you?

**Hindley:** Yes, I remember saying that.

**Attorney General:** You were then trying to force the gag into the child's mouth, were you not?

**Hindley:** No, I was trying to move her hand so Ian could put the handkerchief in her mouth.

**Attorney General:** If she had not moved her hand, you would have had no compunction in hitting her?

**Hindley:** I wouldn't have hit her much. I never touched her. I never harmed her.

**Attorney General:** Do you still say, in the light of that terrible sentence, that you were reluctant to take part in what was going on?

**Hindley:** I was reluctant originally, but when she started crying and shouting and screaming, I just wanted her to be quiet.

Questioning then moved on to John Kilbride and Hindley denied knowing anything about his disappearance. She said she had passed her driving test at the fourth attempt and hired a car from Warren's Auto on the day John Kilbride went missing because 'as soon as I passed it I wanted to hire a car to get some driving practice'. She claimed that she drove up to Whaley Bridge with Brady that day and on all other occasions when she had hired a car too. She denied that the car was taken back to Warren's Auto's in a muddy condition and said that no one mentioned it to her at the time. (This part of her testimony is probably true).

Hindley then claimed her sister was lying again in regard to her going to Ashton Market and said that she had only been there twice in her life – once when she was 15 years old and then again in August 1964, just before they moved to Wardle Brook Avenue. She said that she normally did her Saturday shopping nearer home in Gorton.

Hindley was then stood down having been in the dock for almost six hours, and this brought an end to the evidential part of the case. Throughout, Brady and Hindley had looked bored and disinterested in what was being said, but once or twice exchanged secret smiles when something was said that they found amusing. They shared sweets and at times whispered to each other and on one occasion, as Hindley was being led out of the court at the end of the day, she poked her tongue out at the reporters who were sat watching. She even wrote copious notes to her solicitor which were passed on to the barrister. One of them had said: 'I told you, no cross-examination that damages Ian.'

The Attorney General then gave his closing speech on behalf of the crown. He pointed out eight main common features of the case:

- The victims were all young people, aged between ten and seventeen
- All three victims disappeared from a public place without trace – in the cases of John Kilbride and Lesley Ann Downey, on a Saturday.
- All three vanished from places in the same general area within comparatively easy reach of the home of Brady and Hindley
- There was evidence of 'some abnormal sexual activity' involving each of the three victims shortly before they died
- A motor vehicle was an essential requirement in all three cases
- The method of killing in two cases was almost certainly asphyxia and the jury might come to the conclusion that asphyxia was at any rate attempted in the case of Edward Evans. The difference there was he may well have died before the strangling ligature was applied to his neck
- The preservation of records relating to the murders. John Kilbride's name appeared in an exercise book – 'a strange, remarkable piece of evidence'. Then there were the tape recording and the photographs of Lesley Ann Downey; the 'macabre and

remarkable photographs' taken in the vicinity of the graves and photographs of the accused. 'The difference arose in the Evans case, but that was an unfinished work. The perfect murder did not come off. The Smiths had gone to the police.'

- 'Finally, you may think this is the most dramatic feature of all – in each case the actual burial place was a lonely moorland grave. Two graves, three hundred and seventy-three yards apart … the clear intention was that Evans should join them there. It is inconceivable that two unconnected and unrelated child killers were using that tiny area in that great moorland to dispose separately and independently of their child victims.'

Following the Attorney General, Mr Hooson gave his closing speech on behalf of Ian Brady. Of Maureen Smith's evidence regarding Hindley's visits to Ashton Market, he said that it was evidence against Myra Hindley, not against Brady. 'How reliable a witness was Maureen Smith? If I follow the example of the Attorney General and use plain words, she told lies in the witness box without any doubt at all.'

Of the photographs taken of Lesley Ann Downey, he said that it was absolutely disgraceful, but: 'of these photographs, one would say there was a grave suspicion of Brady and Hindley, but that does not amount to proof of murder.'

He then turned to the Edward Evans case:

> It has never been doubted that Brady wielded the axe, and I cannot suggest to you, on Brady's own evidence, that in law this could be other than murder. … Smith is facing no charges. It cannot, and should not, be suggested by the defence that Smith went to the police because he had an arrangement with that newspaper. He went to the police on 7 October, before he had seen anybody from any newspaper. Thereafter, in a short time he acquired a financial interest in the conviction of both Brady and Hindley. I am not suggesting that a newspaper man would improperly get Smith to change his evidence, but there is great danger in a long conversation between a witness and an outside person interested in the case. It may well be that in the course of those conversations a witness may see different ways of strengthening his evidence, improving his case.

Mr Heilpern then gave his closing speech on behalf of Hindley. He said that: 'It is my submission that the prosecution case against Hindley is an insubstantial structure.' In regard to the Evans charge, he said that there was no evidence that she knew of the plan to pick up and rob anyone, or that she knew that anyone was to be brought to the house to be killed and there was no evidence that she took part in the compilation of the body disposal plan.

When he moved on to the Lesley Ann Downey case, he said:

> No one, least of all those appearing for the defence in this case, could listen to that tape recording, that transcript that was read out, and see the photographs of that little girl, without the most intense feelings of abhorrence and revulsion. You must not allow your natural and human

feelings of indignation and horror to cloud your judgement about the real issues in this charge.

He said that Myra Hindley's case was simple: she knew nothing of the child's death, she had no hand in it and no hand in burying the child. 'I suggest there is no evidence in relation to Myra Hindley.'

Mr Heilpern then moved on to the John Kilbride case and said that it could be summed up in half a dozen words: 'I know nothing about it.'

Mr Justice Fenton Atkinson then began his summing-up. Of the Evans case:

> As he [Brady] advances no slight justification or excuse for what he did, that would on the face of it be a plain case of murder. The intention to kill is really the necessary inference from the nature of the violence employed and the wounds inflicted.
>
> The other two cases, of course, are different. Those two children's bodies had been buried so long they were decomposed to the state they were in when they were found, and it is not possible for the doctors to ascertain any definite cause of death…
>
> From first to last in this case there has not been the smallest suggestion that either of these two was in any way mentally abnormal or not fully responsible for his or her actions. That leads on to this, does it not – that if (and I am saying that, so to speak, underlined) – if the prosecution is right, you are dealing with two sadistic killers of the utmost depravity. There is no escape from that, and, as was said in another very well-known murder trial some years ago, they are entitled to the unusual incredulity which such terrible offences must raise in the mind of any normal person. Could anybody be as wicked as that? This is what the prosecution are setting out to prove…

The following day, 6 May, Mr Justice Fenton Atkinson continued his summing-up. He said that of the photographing of Lesley Ann Downey: 'When the photographing was over we have that answer: "We all got dressed." It possibly casts a flood of light on the nature of the activities that were going on.'

Of the part played by Hindley, he said:

> You have a picture of her being very closely in Brady's confidence … Brady was quite dependent upon her for transport. That must lead to this, members of the jury, that if you were to conclude, for example in the Downey case, that Brady had buried Downey's body on the moors, the prosecution can say this, can they not, that he could not very well have done that without motor transport available, and nobody has suggested that he had anyone with whom he would have shared such an operation other than Hindley…
>
> You may take the view that the really crucial case from her point of view is the Downey case. There the prosecution have a strong case against

her, because you heard her voice speaking on that recording and know so
much of what was going on on that occasion, and if you are satisfied that
she was guilty there and has really told a lying story to try and put the
blame on to Smith, that may throw light in your minds on the Kilbride
case, having regard to the marked similarity between those two cases.
If you think she was a party to both of those, it may colour your view as to
the Evans case – as to whether she was in on that with Brady as a willing
participant or whether it was a complete surprise to her and she was in the
kitchen when it all happened, covering her ears, with no sort of advanced
knowledge of what was being planned by Brady and by Smith.

Of David Smith, he said:

Mr Hooson has told you that the prosecution case is founded upon Smith,
and that a case founded upon Smith can be likened to a house built on sand.
Is he closing his eyes to the reality of the situation? No words have been
too strong for the defence to apply to Smith. They have used such terms
as 'unprincipled', 'without scruple', 'without mercy', and so on and so
forth, and, of course, a lot of that was clearly justified … He had previous
convictions for violence. He was asked for details, and it appeared that
if some young man had called him a bastard, his reaction was a violent
one and he retaliated in no uncertain manner; but as yet he has not killed
anybody with an axe, or anything so extreme as that…

Then there is this unfortunate affair with the newspaper. I am sure they
did not intend to do so, but they have handed the defence a stick with which
to beat Smith and his wife Maureen. You have heard that this youth at the
time was pretty desperate for money, and he has been promised £1,000 for
his story. I understood him to say it was going to be something like a series
of articles about his times with Brady – something of a defamatory nature
which could only be published if there was a conviction … It is the sort of
temptation to which he should never have been exposed for a moment …
I do not think it is really suggested that the substance of his evidence has
been substantially affected by this quite extraordinary arrangement that he
had with this newspaper.

Something further about Smith is this: on his own saying, he is there in
the room when Evans was killed. He does nothing, says nothing; he helps to
clean up the mess afterwards; he helps to tie and wrap up the body. It is the
string off his own stick which was used to tie the boy's legs to his chest. There
was apparently just as much blood on his clothing as there was on Brady's.

There is blood on that stick, and he says that that must have happened
when he dropped his stick on the floor … You will have to consider the
question as to whether he did take some part in that attack. And in that
case he is what the law calls an accomplice … If you think he was in on
it, he would have the temptation to minimise his share and exaggerate
Brady's … Knowing so much of his background, that he was planning a

bank robbery and had a lot of unpleasant views which you have heard, you will probably think it is safest to say: 'We will not act upon his evidence unless we can find something outside it to support it.'

The jury retired at 14.40 to consider their verdict. At 16.20 they returned to ask two questions: 'When did Myra Hindley purchase the guns?', and 'what was the date of the letter referring to the investment establishment?' When they were given the answers they again retired at 16.27.

At 16.56 the jury returned from their deliberations and gave their verdicts. Ian Brady was given a life sentence at Chester Assizes for each of the murders of John Kilbride, Lesley Ann Downey and Edward Evans.

Mr Justice Fenton Atkinson: 'Ian Brady these were three calculated, cruel, cold-blooded murders. I pass the only sentences which the law now allows which is three concurrent sentences of life imprisonment. Put him down.'

Myra Hindley was convicted of murdering Lesley Ann Downey and Edward Evans and harbouring Ian Brady after John Kilbride's murder. She was given two life sentences for the murders and seven years for harbouring.

Mr Justice Fenton Atkinson:

> In your case, Hindley, you have been found guilty of two equally horrible murders and in the third as an accessory after the fact. On the two murders the sentence is two concurrent sentences of life imprisonment. On the accessory charge a concurrent sentence of seven years' imprisonment. Put her down.

Myra swayed forwards slightly before a woman prison officer caught her arm and took her below. It took the jury just two hours and fourteen minutes to reach their conclusion. They were both taken to spend the night at Risley Remand Centre.

Myra's prison notes state:

> Throughout the trial has shown no emotion or reaction, has remained expressionless the whole time while XXXXX have been in charge. When sentenced didn't show any emotion. When we got downstairs she asked what concurrent meant. When told, she said it didn't make any difference & smiled. <u>Hard faced.</u>

Mr Justice Fenton Atkinson, wrote to the Home Secretary two days after the trial:

Dear Home Secretary,

<u>Brady and Hindley</u>

I did not make a recommendation in passing sentence because the only possible one would have been at that stage that neither of them should ever be set free again.

*Above*: Brady and Hindley are driven through the streets back to the remand centre.

*Left*: Brady (third from left) and Hindley (second from right) are driven away from court.

Myra Hindley is taken from court.

Though I believe that Brady is wicked beyond belief without hope of redemption (short of a miracle), I cannot feel that the same is necessarily true of Hindley once she is removed from his influence. At present she is as deeply corrupted as Brady but it is not so long ago that she was taking instruction in the Roman Catholic Church and was a communicant and a normal sort of girl.

One watched them day after day, looking for the smallest flicker of an expression indicating some shame or regret or realisation of the horror of what was being unfolded in the evidence, but it never came. There can be no doubt they tortured and later killed children because they enjoyed it and I am convinced that they regard those who are horrified by such conduct as 'morons' and beneath contempt.

I hope Brady will not be released in any foreseeable future (assuming his fellow prisoners allow him to live) and that Hindley (apart from some dramatic conversion) will be kept in prison for a very long time. Indeed I would not expect to be available for consultation when any question of release comes up for consideration. But I do not claim sufficient prophetic insight to venture to suggest any terms of years.

Yours Sincerely
Fenton Atkinson

Front page of the *Daily Mirror*.

# 3

# David and Maureen Smith

On 9 May 1966, just three days after the trial finished, Myra's sister Maureen Smith went into labour and gave birth to the couple's first son, Paul. Back at their flat at Underwood Court in Hattersley, the council were turning up on a regular basis to scrub graffiti off their front door. 'Child Killers Live Here' and 'Murdering Bastards' was constantly being daubed on the door and walls, following Brady and Hindley's defence that David Smith had abducted and killed Lesley Ann Downey. The press also continued to hound them, despite *The News of The World* paying out the full £1,000 of their deal, but there was no extra money to follow as David had been led to believe.

The young family survived on the pay-out for a while, but no one would give David a job and their friends didn't want to know them anymore. David was soon unable to support his young family. When employers found out who he was he was either immediately sacked, or, if a manager was prepared to give him a chance, then his co-workers would refuse to work with him. On one occasion he turned up for his first day in a new job and was met by his co-workers waiting for him at the gate and they gave him a choice – leave and never return or take a beating. He walked away to shouts of 'Murdering Bastards' and 'They should've hanged the fucking lot of you!'

Explaining the situation to the dole office, he received a letter a couple of days later from Social Security telling him that 'Due to exceptional circumstances' he was no longer required to seek employment and that he was entitled to unemployment benefit.

With no job to go to and no friends to hang around with, David spent most of his time drinking and physically fighting with his father, who still lived with him. By the end of January 1967 Maureen was heavily pregnant again and her life consisted of housework and shopping for food. When she went out of the flat she was always abused in the streets and people would shout 'Hindley bitch!' and 'Whore!' at her. She even had to shield baby Paul from other women who would spit at them both. Every day brought hate mail through their door. Years later, Maureen would recall that:

> 'Don't let the children play outside – we are going to take them away and bury them on the Moors' was a constant theme. I'd open them and scream with horror. Can you imagine any mother in England getting letters like that through her own front door? I couldn't let my children out of my sight when they were little. They were too young to tell them why they had to stay in, to explain why they couldn't go out to play like all the other children.

## David and Maureen Smith

David and Maureen often took the stress of the situation out on each other. David could be vicious and cruel, especially when he was drunk and upset. After one argument he screamed at Maureen: 'Myra's a cunt, your mother's a cunt and you're a fucking cunt. Maureen fucking Hindley, these are your people, you're all fucking rotten,' before she stormed out of the flat.

A couple of hours after this fight, David took the dog out for a walk but when he reached the bottom of the stairs he heard a cough and a noise coming from underneath them. When he took a closer look he found Maureen trying to hide under her coat. She had taken an overdose of aspirin and Lucozade and had vomited on her blouse. He quickly took her back to the flat and made her drink salt water until she could vomit no more and then put her to bed.

Things didn't get any better between the couple, even when their second son, David, was born on 18 April 1967. David recalled that at this time he was tired from fighting and had a permanently broken nose and damaged knuckles from where he was forced to defend himself from attack after attack by strangers who were convinced he played a part in the Moors Murders. He recalled that the relationship between himself and Maureen had turned toxic and that they were by now merely existing.

During 1968 Maureen tried to get in contact with Myra, perhaps because she felt so isolated, but Myra didn't reply. She even sent pictures of her two children in letters to Myra, but again didn't get a reply. She even contacted HMP Holloway, where Myra was imprisoned, to get a Visiting Order, but she was denied one and told that her sister did not wish to see her.

David, Maureen and their children.

On 22 December she gave birth to another son, John, despite David spending most of his days and nights getting drunk and into fights. By now they had moved, to Slater Way in Hattersley, hoping maybe that a change of scenery would help their faltering relationship. David's father again moved in with them.

They became familiar with some of the Afro-Caribbean residents around the estate and would go off to parties with them around Moss Side. David said they took him at face value and him and Maureen grew close to them as friends.

While David and Maureen were out getting drunk and stoned, David's father was left to look after the three young boys and David admitted later that the children were neglected. When they woke up and realised that they were back to reality, David and Maureen often had physical fights and David would hit her.

On some evenings he and Maureen would go out separately but would usually end up at the same house party. It was on one of these occasions when David caught Maureen kissing someone else. They had both met up at one of these parties and were high on marijuana and alcohol and dancing together. After a while Maureen disappeared and David was dancing with a friend of his called Joyce.

When the music stopped he went searching for Maureen and was told that she was in the toilet. David wanted to leave and was headed towards the front door when he looked up the stairs and saw some couples on the stairs kissing and fondling each other. Then he saw Maureen, at the top kissing another man.

He exploded in anger and leapt up the stairs, putting his hands around her neck and slamming her head into the wall. He threw her down the stairs before throwing her out into the street and screaming obscenities at her, striking her over and over again.

Still, they would go out drinking together, and one night found themselves at the Underwood Court Social Club. They began drinking and soon one man began to stare at David. He heard the odd comment, and then as the night wore on there was the 'accidental' bump into him and then later the man called him a 'murdering bastard'. David made the mistake of reacting and smiled at the man. As he went to turn away the man punched him and as he staggered, more men pounced on him. He was then carried outside where the men carried on beating him before withdrawing for the women to kick and claw at him. He heard Maureen scream but was then kicked unconscious. When he came too, he realised that he was bleeding profusely and the pain made him vomit. Just then he saw Maureen sitting on the kerb with blood pouring from her nose. She also had a split lip, a cut and blackening eye and her clothes had been ripped to pieces. They managed to stumble home together.

About six months after that attack, on 8 June 1969, they ended up going back to the Underwood Court Social Club and met up with two of their Jamaican friends, Joyce and Lloyd. After a while David went to the bar and a man started shouting obscenities at him. When David looked, he realised that it was the same man who had started the beating last time. David noticed that a group of women got off their feet and yelled 'Fucking do the bastard!' David felt a woman's hand grab at his hair and the rest of the women jumped on him, kicking, scratching and screaming at him. After a while, the women's partners grabbed them off of him before landing a few of their own punches.

Before the situation could turn out like last time, with both he and Maureen bloodied and battered, Lloyd grabbed David and shoved him outside, while Joyce did the same with Maureen. The four of them walked off to Joyce's home in silence.

When they arrived, Joyce gave David a beer and, as she put a record on, there was a loud bang on the front door, followed by another and another. Soon enough the front door had been kicked in and stood in front of David was the man from the Social Club. There was a group outside on the street shouting: 'Get him out, get the bastard out here!'

At that, David picked up a knife and took a swipe at the man, who staggered back out into the street with blood pouring from his face. Joyce took the knife off of him and told him to leave, and Maureen grabbed him by the hand. They quickly made their way past the crowd outside, who stared in shock at what had just happened. The man that David had stabbed was called William Lees. Unsure of how many times he had stabbed Lees, David and Maureen went straight to the local police station and he handed himself in.

On 16 July, aged 21, David was sentenced at Chester Assizes to three years' imprisonment after he pleaded guilty to wounding William Lees with intent to do grievous bodily harm. The judge, Mr Justice Veale, said he accepted that since the Moors trial David Smith had been 'subjected to a great deal of open and sustained hostility', but he could not ignore Smith's four previous convictions for assault.

He was sent from Risley Remand Centre to Walton Prison (now HMP Liverpool) on 21 July and immediately put on Rule 43 – solitary confinement – by the Governor.

The investigation into the disappearance of Pauline Reade and Keith Bennett was still continuing, and in January 1970 David Smith was visited by Detectives Mattin and Tyrrell. They asked him to look through an album of photographs and to point out if he saw anywhere of significance. None of the pictures looked familiar to him but he did agree to return to the moors with the detectives and also to go with them to Derbyshire in the near future.

A short while later David was woken up in his cell at 05.30 and told to get dressed into his civilian clothes. Two policemen took him to meet detectives Mattin and Tyrrell and the three of them drove off in an unmarked police car up to Saddleworth Moor and to other places that David had visited with Brady and Hindley. David realised the detectives were looking for a particular area of interest, but was unable to help locate it. They then returned to the police station and David looked through some more photographs before being taken back to prison.

He was still on Rule 43 so he could only see his visitors through a sheet of glass in a small cubicle. He would be visited by his friend Joyce, and then his dad and Maureen would both visit him together.

Maureen, the three boys and David's father had been rehoused again but this time to Moss Side. David was upset by this, and suspicious because as it meant that Maureen was now living closer to the man he had caught her kissing, a Jamaican named Tom.

After a short while, David's father began to visit alone and kept making excuses for Maureen. Sometimes Maureen went months without visiting, and eventually Joyce broke it to him that Maureen and Tom were seeing a lot of each other but that it was none of her business. When David's father turned up on his own on the next visit David managed to get the truth out of him. He told David that Maureen had stopped coming home and that just a few days previously he had met Maureen and Tom in the street and that they were 'all over each other'. He told David that he dragged her home, smashed the place up and tried to point out that the children were her responsibility, but all Maureen could say was 'Please, don't tell Dave.'

Maureen had been neglecting the children and spending her time getting drunk and high at parties with Tom. The children had often been left to fend for themselves, despite the oldest, Paul, being just 6 years old. David's father grew tired of coming home from working a night shift to find the three boys at home alone and soon moved out to stay with a friend.

Maureen's mental health soon deteriorated with having to look after the three boys on her own and the situation was soon with the Welfare Department. This angered David and he put in a request to be taken off Rule 43 so that he could talk to Maureen properly. He was sent to Lancaster Prison and when he arrived he sent his wife a Visiting Order.

David then received a letter from Maureen, telling him that she wouldn't be using the Visiting Order. She told him that they needed a break and that she was fed up of arguing with his father. She told him that she had been going out a lot with Joyce and that she was seeing Tom. She then asked him not to write to her anymore as she would burn any letters.

Maureen abandoned the children and never had any intention of getting back together with David. With his father having moved out it was easier for Maureen to get her belongings together and she moved in with Tom.

She admitted to the Welfare Department that she could not cope alone. When the case worker arrived to collect the children, the front door was wide open and Maureen was nowhere to be seen. The boys were all seriously underweight, riddled with lice and their bed sheets hadn't been changed in months. David was kept up to date with the boys' progress in the care home while he was in prison and the boys even visited him. Meanwhile, after abandoning the house, Maureen broke up with Tom and got herself a one-bedroom flat.

David continued to be visited by his children and his father, who had been diagnosed with cancer, in early 1971.

David was released during the second year of his three-year sentence. After a short while he met the woman who was to become his next wife – and with whom he would stay for the rest of his life – Mary. She was just 15 years old when they first met; she used to mind his sons when his father took them out of care for the day and he and Mary's father would pop to the pub for a drink.

Not long after they had begun to date, David was informed by the Welfare Department that he had won custody of the three boys which Maureen was not at all happy about. She had begun to visit the children while they were in care and had also applied for custody, but her living arrangements had been deemed inadequate so the boys went to live with David.

Shortly afterwards, Maureen received a telephone call from her aunt informing her that her mother wished to see her. They had not spoken since Nellie had disowned her for giving evidence against Myra at the trial. She later recalled: 'It was just as if we'd never been parted. After all, your mum's your mum! We talked about everything.' She moved in to live with her mother, who was by now married to Bill Moulton, and had a modern council maisonette in Gorton, only a few hundred yards from where Maureen had been brought up.

It was while Maureen was out having a drink with her mother in the Hyde Road Hotel that she met the man she was to marry and spend the rest of her life with, Bill Scott, who was 22 years older than her.

## *David and Maureen Smith*

They moved into a house together in 1972 and Maureen gave birth to their daughter, Sharon. Eighteen months later they married.

In October 1972 David Smith, his father and the three boys were moved to Lloyd Street South, Moss Side, as their current accommodation had been earmarked for demolition. Not long after moving there, David was visited by a Welfare Officer and told that Nellie Hindley, Myra and Maureen's mother, wanted to see the boys. He was fine with this, but worried that Maureen would soon follow suit.

David's father was by now severely crippled with cancer and when David got home from work one day his partner, Mary, told him that his father had fallen out of bed. He went upstairs and picked up his skeletal body before putting him back in to bed. By now his father didn't recognise anyone and was unable to communicate with him. David went back downstairs and boiled some milk, before crushing around twenty Sodium Amytal tablets and putting the powder into the milk, which he took upstairs and gave to his father.

After giving the tablets a short time to work he called for a doctor and told him what he had done. The doctor called for an ambulance and David and his father were taken to the hospital where David was told that his father was very close to the end. David didn't want to be around when his father passed away and left the hospital, before calling from a phone box on his way home where he was told that his father had passed away, aged just 52.

Because he had told the doctor that he had crushed up the tablets and given them to his father, David was arrested and charged with murder. The detective in charge of the case, however, treated it as a mercy killing and didn't question David too intensely. The following morning, in front of the Magistrates, David was granted bail and allowed to return home, but at his next appearance, in front of a different Magistrate, he was refused bail and taken into custody, leaving Mary to look after the three boys at her dad's house.

The boys' case worker had been in touch with Mary and told her that Maureen had requested access to her children. Mary recalled:

> I was already worrying because I was still only 15 at the time and didn't want anyone else to know about me and David. So, when Mrs Delaney turned up, I panicked a bit. But then something terrible happened: the boys were handed back to Maureen. David was on bail then and there was nothing we could do. But the whole thing was resolved very quickly because Maureen decided she didn't want the boys after all. Less than a week after demanding them back, she abandoned them on the steps of Hyde Town Hall. They brought the boys home to us and we thought that was an end to it, but then David had his bail taken from him and Maureen insisted on having the boys back again.
>
> The boys didn't want to go. Paul was very upset. He clung to my neck and Mrs Delaney had to physically pull him away. He was screaming for me. She got angry, telling me off for not handing them over properly. But I was deeply upset, too. Then exactly the same thing happened again: Maureen decided she couldn't cope. Mrs Delaney turned up at my door

and said flatly: 'She doesn't want them.' So, thankfully, they brought them back to me.

David Smith's solicitor was successful in an appeal against the withdrawal of his bail and after a while he was allowed to return home to await the trial.

It began on 8 November at Manchester Crown Court. Mr Justice Kilner Brown heard David's counsel describe his appearance at the trial eight years previously as a searing and blistering experience which had had a profound effect on him. He sentenced David to two days' imprisonment, which meant his immediate release.

'I accept your admission of manslaughter. There will be no further trial – I shall sentence you today. I sentence you to two days' imprisonment but take into account the time you served on remand. You are free to go.'

On 6 April 1973 David Smith's partner, Mary, gave birth to their first child together, a girl called Jody. Within weeks David had also officially divorced Maureen on the uncontested grounds of 'unreasonable behaviour'. A custody battle ensued and Maureen was again granted access to their three children once a week.

Maureen would arrive at David and Mary's house with Nellie and take the boys out; after a while they started to spend the occasional Saturday night with her too. Unfortunately, the arrangement ran into trouble when Maureen started to miss appointments with the children, and when she did turn up Nellie wasn't with her. Her behaviour started to become odd; David and Mary remember how she would walk into their house, flop down in a chair and throw one leg over the arm of the chair while talking rubbish. Mary recalled:

> She was actually quite dismissive of the boys. She brought presents for them, but I never saw her cuddle Paul, David or John … It was as if she had no genuine motherly feelings for them at all … This went on for about three months until the visits dried up completely. She disappeared from their lives and never came back. Only Paul ever saw her again.

On 15 February 1975, David Smith married Mary Flaherty in Flowery Field Church, Hyde.

David and Mary rented a house in Dukinfield Road, Hyde, but when locals realised that they were trying to move into the area, a petition was started to get the council to move them to somewhere else. Mary recalled:

> Hardly a day went by without some form of abuse. There was always *something*. A young builder who didn't like having David Smith as a neighbour used to get tanked up and then start effing and blinding outside the door. Weekends were the worst: we'd often get drunks banging on the door, wanting 'a word'. Bricks were thrown through the windows and the kids' pet rabbits were slaughtered – someone slit their throats and slung the bodies out in the garden. Once Paul was on his way home from walking the dog when a gang attacked him. We were in bed when we heard a commotion on the street. Dave raced outside and punched one of the lads

who had hold of Paul, knocking him to the ground. The lad lay still and people were leaning out of their windows, screaming, 'Them Smiths have murdered somebody again!' But Paul was the one who had his arm broken.

David was still being beaten up at times in pubs and recalled an attack that almost proved fatal:

> Mary and I were stood at a taxi rank when a gang approached us. One of them recognised me and, before I knew it, they were beating me to a pulp. I was dragged out into the road and into the path of oncoming cars. Mary was screaming, but no one came to help us. They beat me until I was unconscious.

David and Mary Smith.

# 4

# Ian Brady's Prison Years 1966–1972

Having been found guilty of the murders of John Kilbride, Lesley Ann Downey and Edward Evans, Ian Brady was sent from the court to Risley Remand Centre and then on to HMP Durham that evening, where he was noted by those that received him into the prison as 'a fairly tall person with a tendency to break into a cold smile without apparent reason …Quite unemotional.'

It only took a couple of days for his fellow inmates to get to him. He was walking through the kitchen when a saucepan full of boiling water was thrown at him. Those accused of this attack claimed that the saucepan had been 'accidentally' tipped over as he happened to be passing. Scared by this, Brady requested to go onto Rule 43 – solitary confinement.

His new cell was in the top security 'E' Wing, which housed some of Britain's most dangerous criminals. Such was his notoriety, he was guarded by three warders on his walks to and from the exercise yard, despite all other inmates being locked in their cells at the time. He also ate alone and quickly found work sewing mail bags in his cell. He also wrote his weekly letter to Myra alone in his cell. Brady later commented:

> I wrote to Myra every Friday morning so that she would receive the letter in Holloway on Saturday morning. Myra wrote to me every week. The prison authorities copied all our letters, of course. We wrote the criminal bits in code. I kept all of Myra's letters received from her over a six-and-a-half-year period.

Of the letters that are available to the public, the first was written by Brady to Hindley six days after the trial, where he told her about his job sewing mail bags and that it was an injustice that she received the sentence that she had:

> Well, Myra, I hope you've now gotten over the initial shock of your sentence. I at least got what I expected but you should never have been on any charge except harbouring.
>
> Keep your chin up. The day you are released will be the happiest day of my life. I expect none happier.
>
> So clear your mind of well-justified hate and bitterness and approach each day in hope and each person as an individual; never express despair,

you have a future and I will see you begin life anew, and so, I'll dwell once more in freedom as seen through your eyes…

Ignore the grimy ground till you again tread grass underfoot. I'm counting on you, by gaining your freedom, to bring me back to life. So don't let me down, Kiddo…

I wish I knew where you are and how you are feeling. Only a week since I saw you but it seems an age. Absence makes the heart grow fonder – or breaks it!

Let's make sure the latter does not apply to us. I know that I will love you more as time passes. I know I can never love you less.

Where my love is, there I will be. That and little else is certain. So much has been lost; our love for each other is all that remains and will always remain. Everything else was only an accessory to our love.

So, when one looks at life from that angle, we really have lost little. However, cynical logic does not wipe the realities from our minds, but it makes them easier to accept.

Funny, but when I write of our love my letter tends to read rather sombre; whereas I am in excellent spirits…

Ich werde sie nicht vergessen [German for 'I will not forget you'] I love you.

Xxxxxxx

In early January 1967, DCS Nimmo and DCI Butcher went to see Brady, enquiring about two missing children of whom there was still no trace – Pauline Reade and Keith Bennett. His reply was succinct: 'Fuck off!' Despite this, in one of his letters to Myra, he told her that she must see the detectives.

Brady was also desperate to get hold of the photographs that the police still had possession of and had his solicitor attempt to negotiate the release of them.

He was given permission to have photographs of Hindley put up in his cell and when interviewed by his Probation Officer he was noted to be 'distant and not inclined to talk about himself'.

On 11 May, he was seen by Dr Westbury to see if there was any form of mental illness present. Dr Westbury noted that he 'differentiates himself from the norm and considers himself to be unique'. He went on:

> Some of the superficial manifestations of his personality, particularly his apparent lack of affection and vagueness about his planning, carry the suggestion of a possibility of schizophrenia at first sight, but I found no evidence of the existence of any psychotic or neurotic illness and am firmly of the opinion that at the moment there is no mental illness.

Despite that report, his Probation Officer noted a couple of months later that Brady 'still had that cold, long smile at times', and that he was in his cell twenty-three hours a day, either reading, working on his German course or working sewing mail bags.

This went on until October, when the Assistant Governor wrote a statement: 'I am concerned about Brady's state of mind as his mental ability appears to be beginning to deteriorate.' Brady had complained of hearing noises in his cell. He was moved to a different cell where he should have been free from any noise but continued to complain that he could hear the talking. Brady later recalled in a letter:

> I had become so obsessed with studying, partly for the sake of keeping my mind active in solitary, partly intellectual pride, that when the environment in the wing suddenly changed and became more organised and ordered, and consequently more free, there was a great increase in noise, i.e., TVs on each landing blaring the whole day, from test-card music to racing commentaries, personal radios blasting out pop music from the ever-open cells, groups of people talking or shouting in the wing (the wing then held about 60 prisoners, before the Mountbatten lot ground the number down to 12), I got to such a state that I was willing to do almost anything to stop the least distraction of concentration.

He then gave up his studies and instead began to read and reread all of his books. Another reason that staff were becoming concerned was the way that he was treating his mother. Despite having lost her husband recently, Brady was cold and mean towards her. His Probation Officer noted that: 'His mother visited recently and he has requested her not to come again – he felt "irritated" by her, although he will continue to write to her … He wishes to "be cut off completely" from the outside world. His "whole world" is Myra Hindley and her letters are "everything" to him.'

The Probation Officer also noted that: 'I feel on this occasion that he was less mentally alert than previously – any answer requiring much thought took a long time … Feels that the police are being "bloody minded" about not returning the album of family photographs.'

Because of those reports, Brady was seen again by Dr Westbury on 20 November 1967 who concluded:

> Brady was attaching at the best undue significance to them [noises] and at the worst they could have been hallucinations. I formed the opinion that at times his speech showed disconnection of thought and that his answers to questions were vague and circumstantial. The impression that I have is that these have become more pronounced since I last examined him on 11 May 1967. In addition, the apparent flattening of affect and unreality about some of his thinking, that as I said in my report of 11 May 1967 were suggestive of schizophrenia, are still present.
>
> In my opinion, this man has changed for the worse during the six-month interval May–November. It is not possible without observing more objective signs of mental illness to make a firm decision whether this is a schizophrenic process or the result of his isolation.

Towards Christmas, Brady was seen by his Probation Officer who noted that: 'Brady is acutely aware of the hostility of other prisoners towards him – they continually shout threats and bang his door and he is afraid of being attacked. I noticed that every time there were footsteps outside his door, which was ajar, he was apprehensive.'

Brady also told the Probation Officer that he hoped arrangements could be made where those in prison 'after committing child crimes' could be separated from 'normal' criminals. By now Brady was refusing to take exercise and his Probation Officer noted that:

> I think it is because he is scared of violence on his way to the yard and sick
> of the abuse hurled at him. He feels he has deteriorated mentally but this
> is not evident to me – in fact he looks exactly the same as when I first saw
> him a year ago.

He also noted that Brady was reading a wider range of books, whereas 'before he concentrated on exotic, masochistic and sadistic literature'.

Just two days later, Brady was seen again, and it was noted that: 'He is not very concerned about his environment beyond a very reasonable request that he be completely isolated from others and completely shielded from their abuse and also protected from the real danger of violence.'

Brady then decided that he wanted to study for an O-Level in German and was visited by a lecturer from Durham University once a week. He told Hindley, in one of his letters, what he was doing, and she decided to study the same course. To aid each other, some of their letters to each other were written partly in German and partly in English.

Just six-months later, both Brady and Hindley passed their exam. Annoyed that they couldn't celebrate together, they pressed on with the idea of being allowed to see each other. They were told by the prison authorities that this would not be allowed as they were not married, but they argued that they had lived together as common-law husband and wife and that as such they should be allowed to visit each other.

It was in September 1968 that both Brady and Hindley were first visited by Lord Longford. He was a penal reformer and had visited Myra first after she had written to him to see if he could help her in her campaign to see Brady. Lord Longford recalled at the time:

> Ian Brady is a man of natural intellectuality. It is almost incredible that
> someone brought up in a very poor area, not knowing who his father was,
> packed off at one point to Borstal, should, by the time he went to prison,
> have developed such an impressive knowledge of writers like Dostoevsky,
> Tolstoy and Blake. When I look back at his earlier letters, I am still
> astounded at the contrast between this young man of genuine culture and
> idealism and the author of such dreadful crimes.

In March 1969 Brady's Probation Officer wrote that: 'Physically and mentally there appears to be little change. He is still extremely sensitive about the publicity and "brew ha ha" surrounding everything he does. He is obsessed with his campaign to get permission for "his girl" Myra Hindley to visit him in prison.'

He also noted that there had been many instances of Brady 'deliberately provoking' two other child murderers on his landing and picking on them. The note was finished off with him saying: 'Apart from my good relationship with him, I see absolutely no change in Brady. He deliberately isolates himself from VIPs and any other visitor, because he refuses to become a "peep show".'

Brady was also threatening to petition Parliament if his attempts to have Hindley visit him continued to fall on deaf ears.

Just two months later, Brady's bullying behaviour continued when he threw hot tea over fellow inmate David Burgess; he was put on report, receiving three days confinement in his cell. The punishment seemed to harden Brady's attitude towards staff, but it was noted that while he was being punished the mood on the wing lifted and that the other inmates 'all now harmoniously share the TV room, etc'. He continued to be 'very hostile to Morris' (another child killer) and that 'a 'punch up' was almost inevitable. It was noted that 'much of his reading material is of a sensuous and masochistic nature. He does not like to talk about his crimes, except that he felt that his murder of the 17-year-old youth was "justified and excusable" because of homosexual advances.'

Indeed, just two months later Brady hit the other child killer that he didn't like, Raymond Morris, and lost seven days of association. The Senior Prison Welfare Officer thought that: 'He shrugs off attempts to discuss the quarrels he sometimes picks with other inmates. These may be done deliberately as a demonstration of his willingness, and ability, to take care of himself, as he is often on the receiving end of abuse and aggression from others.'

At this time, the Governor of Durham wrote a report in which he told that Brady 'is arrogant, abusive and childish in turn, but until now there have been no serious behavioural problems. He has no friends among other prisoners in the wing ... Apart from his studies and reading his sole interest is Myra Hindley.'

The Assistant Governor wrote a separate report to the Home Office in which he described how:

> in the past week or so ... [Brady] has shown interest in translating books into braille, and an experimental scheme has now started whereby he works at translating children's books into braille. These books are used in a local school for blind children...
>
> He states quite openly that he has only two fixed points in his life. One to gain inter-prison visits; the second, albeit many years ahead, Myra Hindley's eventual release. After that, he has nothing.

On 12 December 1969, Brady got into another argument with Raymond Morris and Brady snapped. He picked up a jug of hot tea and threw it over Morris. He got twenty-eight days loss of privileges – including his last remaining freedom: smoking. Upset at the punishment, Brady went on hunger strike. Refusing any food and exercise for a week, he was tube-fed for the final twenty-one days of his punishment. Two days after his punishment had finished, Raymond Morris got his revenge and threw a jug of hot water over Brady. He was also punished with twenty-eight days loss of privileges.

On 28 January 1970, a medical officer who had seen Brady before the trial gave his report in which he stated:

> My view of Brady remains as it has done since I first knew him before his trial. He is physically fit, of reasonably good intelligence and free from mental illness. He is, however, a schizoid psychopath of utter untruthfulness who has the rather unusual ability in this type of personality of dissociating himself from the crimes of which he has been convicted. Increasingly, I feel that it is a symptom of the terrifying intensity of his psychopathy and that he is not defending against recalling his offences but that, as far as he is concerned, they fail to rise above his mental horizon.

The officer went on to advise that the appropriate place for Brady, 'for a period anyway', was a 'special hospital' on the grounds of psychopathic disorder.

He concluded, 'he is a psychopathic personality to an extreme and pathological degree'. This is the first report in which it was suggested that Brady would be better off in a psychiatric hospital.

Brady was seen the following month by Dr P. McGrath who was a Senior Consultant Psychiatrist at Broadmoor Hospital. He referred to Brady's apparent enjoyment of the interview and his manifest regard for himself as intellectually superior to other prisoners. Brady spoke of the noises which he had heard from other prisoners and Dr McGrath commented, 'He did not give me the impression that these experiences had been hallucinatory and the prison staff said that the events could in fact have happened.'

Dr McGrath concluded that he recommended the transfer to hospital as being necessary 'if there is any hope of salvaging what is worth retaining in [his] personality and perhaps modifying it.' This recommendation was supported by a Dr Whittaker but was rejected without comment by the Secretary of State.

Brady's Probation Officer also spoke with him over his failed switch to Broadmoor Hospital and reported:

> Brady has mixed feelings – I think that he saw Broadmoor as a place where visits from Hindley were more likely. He hinted at a further campaign to draw attention to the injustice of the visits business. He says he does not feel mentally 'different' from when he came in … He expects Hindley to be out in 'say 15 years' – but he would not expect her to devote her life entirely to visiting him, 'Why waste 2 lives?'

He was again frustrated in August when the Home Office refused his latest petition to see Hindley and so went on hunger strike for a second time. During the second week of his hunger strike he was seen by his Probation Officer who remarked that 'he looked even thinner than the last time and his memory was cloudy… He sent the birthday card to Myra Hindley and continues to hear from her regularly.'

He gave up the hunger strike on 28 September after beginning a new job as 'duty cook'. It was noticed how remarkably well he was looking and had put on 8lbs in one day. It was fully believed that during this job he was helping himself to scraps to supplement his tube feed and was seen drinking tea.

In December 1970 prison authorities had decided to close 'E' Wing as it was deemed too old for the current needs and slowly the inmates were transferred to other prisons. In the meantime, Brady was informed that his adoptive mother in Glasgow, Mrs Sloan, had passed away in hospital following a long illness.

Two months later Brady's plan to be moved to Broadmoor gathered pace. He was seen by Dr Duggan-Keen who recorded that Brady had become more suspicious and paranoid in his outlook and had become more and more withdrawn.

> In view of the depressive state and the development of what I believe to be an early paranoid schizophrenic illness, it is my view that this man is in need of full psychiatric investigation and active psychiatric treatment as it is my view that there is evidence that this psychiatric illness is developing and that there is a deterioration in his mental state.

In order to aid his move, he went on a third hunger strike and asked for dark sunglasses and ear plugs so that he could block out the world entirely. He was forcibly fed three times a day.

Brady was then interviewed three times by a Dr Scott but he found no signs of mental illness in Brady. In his report he said:

> He has no thought disorder. I found no evidence of schizophrenia. He is not paranoid (i.e. he has no unreasonable or grandiose suspicions). He is not depressed to a psychotic degree … the only positive findings, therefore relate to his personality but these are extremely severe.

On the issue of paranoia, Dr Scott's comments were:

> He often speaks about being scapegoated by the Home Office, by which he means that because of the nature of his crime he is being denied privileges that are rightfully his. This is not in any way paranoid … It has been stated in the past that he has shown paranoid features but these seem more akin to the usual suspiciousness towards authority experienced by any frustrated person e.g. soldiers or seamen on foreign service.

Dr Scott's conclusions were that Brady could be cared for either in the Prison Service (if special arrangements were made) or in Broadmoor. 'In my opinion as things stand at present, it would be better to transfer him under Section 72 [the then relevant provision of the Mental Health Act 1959] to Broadmoor.'

Brady gave up his hunger strike on 10 May 1971, when he discovered that the protest might prejudice his chances of a transfer. The following day Brady was seen by his Probation Officer who again thought that the reason Brady wanted a transfer to

Broadmoor was because it would 'better his chances of getting visits with Myra Hindley authorised. This was in fact the main reason for his application. He is perturbed because of no letters from Hindley for 4 weeks – which is most unusual.'

Brady got his move on 28 August 1971, when 'E' Wing was finally closed. Just he and triple child killer John Straffen had remained, and both were moved to the Isle of Wight. Straffen was sent to HMP Parkhurst while Brady was transferred to HMP Albany. Brady later recalled the move:

> Prison officers arrived at my cell door to tell me I was being moved. They didn't say where. Even the officers driving me South didn't know. They had sealed instructions to be opened en route after calling for refreshments at Gartree Prison in Leicestershire. The buff envelope was opened. It was Albany prison on the Isle of Wight.

He had refused breakfast that morning in protest as he suspected that he wasn't going to Broadmoor. He continued to refuse to eat and thus began his fourth hunger strike in order to be moved to Broadmoor and to be allowed to see Myra. He was moved to HMP Parkhurst on 3 September because he had continued his hunger strike and they were better equipped to force feed him, via a tube, in the hospital.

The hunger strike came to an end on 17 September and he was kept at Parkhurst for observation. The strike may well have come to an end thanks to his new Probation Officer, who told him:

> In not allowing his mother to visit him he was persecuting her, that by continuing his hunger strike he was depriving the blind people of his Braille work and, furthermore, as his hunger strike has registered his protest, I felt it was jolly well time he started to eat in the normal way and not cause so much unpleasantness to the staff who had to forcibly feed him. I continued to discuss with him along these lines and before I left he shook me warmly by the hand, thanked me for bringing him up with a jerk as he put it, and promised to eat his dinner.

Brady himself wrote to Tom Driberg MP at the House of Commons and told him:

> A doctor here has suggested to me that I may have a better chance of receiving consideration from the Home Office if I request an annual allocation of telephone conversations with Myra. This, if granted, would at least be a substantial improvement in personal communication and a slow step in the right direction towards the future possibility of visits.

Brady was transferred back to HMP Albany on 6 October due to the lack of suitable accommodation in the hospital at HMP Parkhurst. Upset by this, Brady immediately asked to go into solitary confinement and chose neither to associate with anyone or to exercise.

On 7 December, Brady's Probation Officer received a telephone call from HMP Holloway saying that Myra had made a book marker for Brady but would like it to be handed to him on Christmas Day, rather than have it sent into his possessions and him have to apply for it. In return, Brady was granted permission to send hand-painted Christmas cards to Hindley, his mother and Lord Longford.

In January 1972, Brady discussed with his Probation Officer his efforts to see Myra.

> He was now petitioning to see if he could have three telephone conversations with her [Myra] as visits had not been allowed ... He stated that a telephone conversation would be to him like release. He did not expect to be released during his lifetime. If he was, because of his name and history, he doubted whether he would be long out of prison. He then mentioned his trial and the fact that in order to protect Myra he had denied they had been living together for three years. The reason for this is that the prosecution had wanted to use their three years association to prove her implication. This now had backfired on him and they were using this to say she was not his common-law wife and therefore could not have visits under prison regulations.

Hindley made Brady another bookmark for Valentine's Day, which she had sent to the prison for him. It was passed on to him in the Segregation Unit and was embroidered with 'Carpe Diem'. The letters from Myra had begun to dry up and when the book-mark was handed over to him and he was told that Myra did not feel like writing to him,

> There was no emotion ... he talked about Myra and that Lord Longford was seeing her regularly. The reports were that she was alright. He implied that he knew differently; that when a person was interviewed they brightened up but the depression came later. I asked him about the embroidery on it and he said that Carpe Diem was a poem. He had had it about 5 years. He could not remember the meaning of the poem.

On 24 May, Brady was visited by his Probation Officer who noted:

> He hadn't heard from Myra for some time and he had written four letters, one of which would bring the reply he wanted. I gained the impression that there was a lot of anger underneath his attitude about not hearing from her ... I then went on to say that had he thought that she may feel it better for them both to go their own ways and he said 'yes'. In the end he asked if I could ring Holloway to find out what the position was and how she was.

The Probation Officer did as he was asked and spoke to his counterpart at HMP Holloway the following day. He noted: 'A letter from their Governor had gone to our Governor with a letter from Myra to be handed to Brady and that she had in fact asked that no letters from Brady be issued to her.' The Probation Officer later visited the Governor:

he gave me the letter from Myra and said I could hand it to Brady. I also saw the letter from the Governor of Holloway which said that Myra has officially requested that no letter from Brady be issued to her so the Governor said he would be grateful if this correspondence no longer is allowed. In the letter it also mentioned Myra Hindley's suggestion that in the past Brady had apparently threatened suicide should this happen.

He later visited Brady 'and gave him the letter from Myra. He read it. There was no deep show of feeling. He said he would now have to alter letters he had already written and which he had been holding back until I had got him some information.' The following day the Probation Officer again saw Brady:

> We talked at length and he said that when they had been living together she had threatened to sever the relationship on several occasions. He also said he felt it was pressure from her own family which had caused this rift and blamed Lord Longford too for influencing her.
>
> He then went on to talk about her family and that contrary to the reports about her family they were an unstable family. Her sister had had to be married to the main prosecution witness, Smith, Myra's brother-in-law and he seemed to have strong feelings about Smith. He then went on to show me the photograph he had of Myra and a younger girl and two dogs. He said that was taken the previous day to them being arrested…
>
> It is apparent that the only person he has any feelings for at all is Myra. I suggested that perhaps this was her way of hoping that she may eventually be released when he said that he felt that might be so.

Brady refused to believe that things were over between him and Hindley and even during June his Probation Officer was noticing this. He even wrote to their joint solicitor, Mr Fitzpatrick, asking him to find out what was going on with regard to Myra.

Brady's Probation Officer saw him again on 26 June:

> He went on at length about Myra … He also went on about photographs which had been on his agreement released by the police to Myra's mother. He said that Myra's mother had been granted a divorce while the trial was pending and had remarried. He could not understand why she wanted to hang on to the photographs.
>
> We discussed the various reasons for photographs and their value. He said the police had had all the photographs. He said he knew that some photographs of Myra had been sold to the press but they had not been published … He again talked about the day prior to his arrest and slides which he had taken. These slides were the ones which Myra's mother still had. If he could not get them back by reasonable means he would take legal proceedings in order to find out where they were. He appears to have an obsession about these photographs.

Just after Myra had turned 30, he asked his Probation Officer to contact Mr Fitzpatrick to find out if he had heard from Myra. He wanted to know if then Myra was:

> definitely finished with him he would instruct Mr Fitzpatrick that he must not send on information any more to Myra and that he, Brady, would not be prepared to pay out any more money on her behalf ... He also went on again about photos and that if Myra was finished he would then take legal steps to obtain them back from her mother.

The Probation Officer then telephoned Mr Fitzpatrick

> Who said that he had been in a dilemma. He had had confirmation that Myra definitely did not want any more correspondence from Brady and that she wanted the association to end. I asked specifically if he had a personal letter written by her to him. He had delayed answering Brady's letter as he felt that he would be upset at receiving the news. I told him that I didn't think so. I would prepare him. Then he could write to Brady the full facts. I mentioned his obsession about Myra's mother having these photographs. He felt that he ought to let sleeping dogs lie and not bother about them and could not understand the reason why Brady wanted them. I pointed out they must have some significance to him.

On 8 August Brady requested to be allowed out on general association with the other inmates on Rule 43 and this request was granted. There were problems, however.

Raymond Morris had also been transferred to HMP Albany and was in the same Segregation Unit. It was feared that there would be a continuation of the violence between the two from their days in HMP Durham, but initially Morris refused to leave his cell when Brady was out on the landing. After around a week, Morris began to emerge from his cell at the same time as Brady and on 5 September it was noted that 'The staff have remained vigilant at all times. Brady and Morris mix freely with the other Rule 43 inmates, but they do not communicate with one another, thereby lending strength to the theory that these two men must be closely supervised at all times.'

On 3 October, Brady again assaulted Raymond Morris – this time with a pair of scissors – and was re-segregated. His Probation Officer visited Morris and stated:

> When talking to Morris I asked him why this should have occurred. He said it all stemmed back to when they were in the top security wing of Durham Prison. It was over something quite trivial but he said Brady was the type of man who would harbour hatred for ever and would take the first opportunity to get revenge. [The attack was obviously pre-meditated by Brady as he had wrapped up the scissors in order to take them into the association room so that he could perpetrate it].

He then went on his fifth hunger strike which lasted until 10 November and was transferred to HMP Parkhurst.

His Probation Officer was contacted by Brady's mother and recorded that: 'She said that she knew he was upset about the photographs that Myra's mother still had. She had been in touch with his solicitor several times but could never see the solicitor personally.' On 14 November she asked him to pass on a message to Brady:

> She had visited his solicitor last week and that Myra's mother had now agreed to hand over the photographs to the solicitor. She just didn't know where she had put them at the time but as soon as she found them she would do this. This in fact would stop having legal action taken against her. Mrs Brady was relieved about this.

The following day Brady was sent back to HMP Albany and promptly went on his sixth hunger strike because Raymond Morris was still in the same Segregation Unit. He also opted to go back on Rule 43 and was almost immediately returned to HMP Parkhurst as the Home Office was not prepared to upset the unit for Brady's sake.

# 5

# Myra Hindley's Prison Years 1966–1972

After spending the night at Risley Remand Centre, Hindley was taken to HMP Holloway in London and she later recalled the journey: 'My first impression of London was of trees. I looked and looked and looked and mercifully didn't see the yawning gates of Holloway until we were locked inside them.'

She was led across the courtyard to the maximum security 'E' Wing, where she was housed with other child murderers, two Russian spies and Bunty Gee, who was in prison for Treason. Three days after arriving Myra had new mugshots taken.

HMP Holloway.

As she was crossing the courtyard, she was subjected to a torrent of abuse from the other inmates in the cells that overlooked, and she was left in no doubt that she would be a marked woman from then on.

She ran the daily gauntlet of insults and threats such as 'Slut', 'Cow', 'Bitch', 'Child Killer' and 'We're gonna get you!' whenever she was in ear shot of the other prisoners. When she wasn't being insulted, she was being ignored. A fellow prisoner who was sweeping the stairs even attacked her with a broom.

The other women noticed that all she was interested in was Brady and one commented:

> She just lives for that letter arriving …it's the only thing that seems to keep her going. That and the hope that she'll be able to marry him one day. You can tell. She's still madly in love with him … She just stares straight ahead when she walks around with the screws. She ignores everything that's shouted at her.

She was shocked to receive an invitation one day to go and play cards with her fellow inmates and went along, thinking that finally she might be accepted by them, but after just a few minutes the cheery mood suddenly changed and the ten women who were present jumped her. She was punched, kicked and clawed at, and it took quite an effort from the prison staff to break up the attack. Following the beating, Myra requested to be put on Rule 43.

On 21 May Hindley wrote to Brady and mentioned her appeal against her sentence:

> I don't for a minute, think they'll grant it, but I've nothing to lose by trying, and what's a year, with sentences like ours? Anyway, I've been convicted and branded a murderess, so I'm not just sitting back and accepting it. We know each other, and one day, in the fullness of time, the truth will out. It must be so! I dreamed last night that Smith had died, or left Maureen, and she came forward and said she'd lied about … Ashton

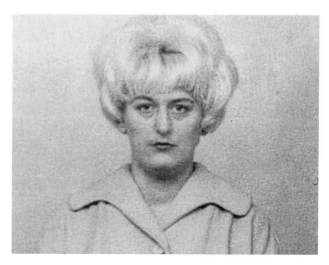

Myra Hindley mugshot at HMP Holloway.

Market, etc. She had her baby last week, a boy, I think her conscience will start bothering her pretty soon.

I feel desolately … Not because I'm on my own of course, but because you aren't here. I miss you all the time, but sometimes more than others.

She had appealed against her sentence on the grounds that she should have been tried separately from Ian Brady.

After a short while, she was persuaded by a prison doctor to come off Rule 43 as she had been sentenced to spend a long time in prison and it wouldn't be healthy for her to serve her sentence in solitary confinement. It didn't take long for Hindley to find herself in trouble with the authorities, however. She was fined three days' earnings on 30 June after a search by prison officers found two unauthorised letters that she had written to another inmate. This was usually how Myra tested the water with other inmates, to see whether or not they could be of use to her. If the letter was replied to and the contents favourable, then she would have someone on her side to help protect her and to do things for her.

On 17 October 1966, at the Criminal Division of the Court of Appeal, Lord Chief Justice Parker turned down Hindley's appeal on the grounds that Brady had, at all times, sought to exonerate her during the trial. To that degree, it was an advantage for her to be tried with Brady.

THE LORD CHIEF JUSTICE:

The Court is quite satisfied that there is no ground for saying that the Judge erred in the exercise of his discretion or that any miscarriage has resulted. The evidence complained of, of course, was very damaging evidence against Brady; but the important thing to observe is that it was not evidence which directly at any rate sought to implicate this appellant; indeed Brady has at all times sought to exonerate this appellant from any part in his activities. To that extent it has been a benefit for this appellant to be tried with Brady who has given evidence seeking to exonerate her.

It may be said that that inadmissible evidence does impliedly implicate the appellant in that it quite clearly shows for instance the taking of bodies to the moor and the confession that he could not drive. It is certainly not implicating her in any matter which is in dispute, because she throughout has said that he could not drive and that she drove the car. At any rate any implication against the appellant that is to be found in this inadmissible evidence could certainly be put right by an adequate direction from the Judge. There is no doubt in this case a danger of grave prejudice from the fact that this man is really a triple murderer, and that she has throughout admitted very close association with him, taking part in all his activities, and indeed being in the house, if not in the room on the occasion of two of the murders. There is no doubt grave prejudice, if nothing more, to an appellant in those circumstances, but that is a prejudice which is inevitable and is there just as much, if not to a greater extent, if she is tried separately than if she is tried jointly with Brady.

Finally, this Court is quite satisfied that there has been in this case no miscarriage of justice. If one reads through the latter part of the summing-up of the Judge when he is dealing with the case against this appellant on evidence which was clearly admissible against her, it seems to this Court that the case was overwhelming.

This appeal is dismissed, as is the application for leave to appeal against sentence in regard to the fourth count.

As Christmas approached, Myra wrote a letter to Brady:

Dearest Ian,

Hello my little hairy Girklechin. It was with profound relief I received your letter today … It was a lovely, soothing, nostalgic letter which comforted me almost as much as if you were here yourself. I had a beautifully tender dream about you last night and awoke feeling safe and secure, thinking I was in the harbour of your arms. Even when I realised I wasn't, the thought of your presence remained with me, leaving me tranquilly calm and strong.

I pictured your face and said your name to myself over and over again and imagined the arms of the chair I was clenching to be your hands, lovely strong 'insurance' hands (remember?).

Each day that passes I miss you more and more. You are the only thing that keeps my heart beating, my only reason for living. Without you what does life mean? Nothing, absolutely nothing. Freedom without you means nothing too. I've got one interest in life and that's you. We had six short but precious years together, six years of memories to sustain us until we're together again, to make dreams realities.

In the letters swapped between them, and as noted earlier, they had both decided to study 'O' level German and would use the language for certain parts of their letters to each other. One letter, later decoded, was from Brady to Hindley, in which he told her that she would have to find a lesbian lover in order to survive in prison, and in her reply to him she told him not to worry, as she already had.

In other letters, written between Hindley and fellow inmates whom she believed she could influence, the theme was often admiration and love. Prison officers at the time said:

We were always overworked. There were always fights and trouble. If two women were getting on well we chose to ignore just how well. It was better than having them screaming and tearing each other's hair out.

We would shine a torch in and if they were both there and quiet, we wouldn't worry too much if they were in the same bed.

The first object of her desire was a teenage blonde girl called Rita, but the relationship was quickly ended as Hindley was moved away from the girl.

Sensing that Hindley was still struggling to gain allies, she was attacked by one of the Russian spies on her wing, Helen Kroger, who smashed a teapot over her head. At the time, Hindley was working in the kitchen handing out dry rations such as tea and sugar, and Kroger believed that she was deliberately giving her short rations. Hindley staggered around dazed before Kroger pushed her to the ground and started kicking her. She was pulled off by prison officers but carried on spitting and screaming while she could still see Hindley.

In a letter to her mother, Hindley wrote: 'Remember the record you bought down one week, 'It's All Over Now Baby Blue?' Can you get me another copy of it some time and keep it for me?' This was in fact the song that Brady had bought for her on the morning of Edward Evans' murder, and her request for a new copy suggests that she was intent on reliving the murder.

By now, Hindley had ditched her bleached blonde hair and gone back to her natural dark hair.

On 23 May 1967, Hindley asked to be put on Rule 43 as she was still getting abuse from most people on her wing and further out in the prison. Her latest lover, Norma, had had previous relationships inside and one of those women, Bernadette, worked with Hindley in the kitchen. She was jealous and the situation exploded into a fight. They were both taken off kitchen duties but Bernadette, who was mentally unstable, threw urine over Hindley's clothes and put excrement into her bed. Hindley's wish was granted and she stayed in solitary confinement for the rest of the year.

On 4 August, Hindley petitioned to be allowed to move to a prison closer to Manchester, either Styal or Risley, as she had only seen her mother on four occasions since the trial. She also claimed in her petition that her grandmother was disabled and that this was another reason why she should be allowed to move closer to home. The Governor at HMP Holloway, Dorothy Wing, described her as 'Superficially a "good prisoner", Myra

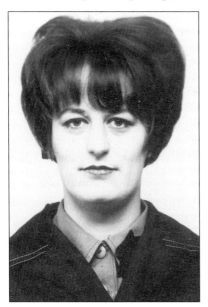

is far from trustworthy and in my opinion would require secure conditions if transferred to Styal or Risley.'

In February 1968, Hindley's grandmother, Ellen Maybury, was taken seriously ill and she was allowed to spend a week in Risley Remand Centre, visiting her grandmother twice. She later passed away in a care home in 1971 suffering from dementia. They had had very little contact since the trial but had exchanged a few letters, with Hindley finding out later that her grandmother had had her letters written for her.

Shortly afterwards, Hindley was given Category 'A' status in prison. Those given this status are prisoners 'whose escape would be highly dangerous to the public, the police or the security of the state'. As such they were deemed

Myra Hindley with her natural, dark hair.

to need escorts of officers when they moved around their prisons, and their visitors were more keenly vetted. All of her visitors who had travelled to Holloway to see her would now have to be photographed by the police and their identities corroborated.

On 21 March, Hindley was given permission to change her name by Deed Poll to Clare Stewart, but she changed it to Myra Spencer without official permission. She was allowed by the authorities to do so provided she continued using her birth name in prison. She changed her name in the event she was ever released.

A *Daily Express* photographer scooped a picture of Hindley on her way back to prison.

Soon afterwards, at a discussion group for women on the wing held by a magistrate, she met a woman named Carole Callaghan who recalled that Hindley was:

> very up her own arse I'd say… She shouldn't have been with people like us – we were scum … She considered herself a step or two up from us.… I walked in and they were all sitting in a circle. Myra stood up and told me it was a private group. I swore and said, 'Who's going to throw me out then?' She said, 'I'm Myra Hindley', as though I was supposed to kowtow to that. So, I said: 'Let's see how hard you are with me, I'm not a little kid.' I attacked her, and the magistrate grabbed me and pulled me off.'

Shortly after this, Hindley's lover Norma was moved to Styal prison and Callaghan enrolled in English classes but discovered that her only classmate was Myra:

> We soon discovered that we'd got the same sense of humour. When you're in prison you don't worry about what other people are in there for, you just care about whether you can get on with them. On that wing, with only thirteen prisoners, it was especially important that you found some you could be friendly with. Myra and I were soon good friends. She told me that she had felt very threatened by me at first, because I was so self-confident and seemed to her glamourous.

They were in adjoining cells and Callaghan recalled: 'We used to stand at the windows of our cells when we were locked in at night, talking for hours and dreaming of what we would do when we got out. She was confident then that she'd be out after seven years.'

A tapestry room was opened in the summer of 1968 and Hindley proved to be a gifted worker. She worked with two other inmates on a carpet which had been commissioned by the Polish Embassy and in the hem, she tucked a cigarette paper with the words 'Myra Hindley made this carpet' written on it.

71

Her next lover was a girl from Rochdale named Alice. She became devoted to Myra and did all of her washing and ironing, as well as cleaning her cell and cooking her breakfast. They would climb beneath Hindley's bed (which was propped up on jam jar tins to make it higher) and make love several times a day while Callaghan or Alice's friend May stood guard outside the door.

That summer the Governor of HMP Holloway wrote a memo regarding Hindley's position towards Brady and for the first time discussed a forced break with Brady:

> Throughout her sentence Myra Hindley has been well-behaved, self-effacing and entirely cooperative. It would be no exaggeration to say that her determination to be a 'model' prisoner, and in fact the entire pattern of her life in prison revolves about her regular communication with Ian Brady, her persistent hope that visits with him will be allowed, and that ultimately they will be reunited on release. If she were to be told now that meetings are not to be permitted and that correspondence is to cease, her morale would be very severely disturbed and her stability would be shattered.
>
> In the past she has resisted suggestions of psychiatric help, but with persistent encouragement she has at last, very recently, requested to see XXXXX regularly. It seems that she is motivated largely by her determination to score another good mark for cooperation. On the other hand, although she still absolutely denies the main offences for which she was convicted, she does often speak of her troubled conscience for the 'many terrible things' which she has done... If she were to be told now that visits were to be denied and correspondence to cease, this would undoubtedly jeopardise the prospects of her cooperating with XXXXX.
>
> She has often expressed suspicion that the authorities are trying to separate her from Ian Brady. If it appears that her ultimate rehabilitation can best be achieved by excluding Brady from her future, it may be that to force a break at the appropriate time may be useful...
>
> If, however, it became apparent that she is unwilling to contemplate any future without Brady in her life, (and this would certainly be her reaction now) then imposing a break with him would increase her suffering during a long sentence, to no useful purpose.

In August 1968, Mr Fitzpatrick, Brady and Hindley's solicitor, succeeded in reclaiming Brady's photographs, negatives and slides in Brady's 'Tartan Album' from the police. Hindley's mother, Nellie, originally took possession of them and Hindley insisted that there were three slides in particular which Brady wanted returned, together with several photographs.

She wrote to her mother: 'I told Neddy you were having those 3 of me developed, and he's pleased, for he feels you will get them done quicker than his mam. Post them direct to him, right away.'

She told her mother that once she had done this then the rest of the photographs could be destroyed, but just a week later she wrote to her mother asking: 'Have you sent the slides to Neddy yet?' But Nellie was concerned about the photographs that she had been asked to pass on, and many years later Hindley wrote in a draft of her autobiography that the photographs in question were of the Waterhouse children (who lived on their estate) that had been taken at Shiny Brook.

The following month, Lord Longford entered Hindley's life. He was a penal reformer and visited her at her request as part of her campaign to be allowed to see Brady. This was the beginning of Hindley's split prison personality. To Lord Longford, and the other supporters she would later gain, she was either a woman not guilty of her crimes or one that was fully repentant of her crimes and so deserved forgiveness.

To her prison friends she was only interested in getting out of prison no matter what it took, and she would use whoever it took to achieve her goal.

It was noted in early 1969 that there was resentment from prison staff towards Lord Longford's visits to Hindley. One memo observed: 'The already existing feelings of superiority in this very dominating woman are being augmented by his encouragement.' Another, recorded by the Governor, said: 'Myra is a forceful, dominating woman at any time and is adept at manipulating any circumstance to her advantage.'

The Governor wrote a letter on 24 March 1969 regarding Hindley wanting to be transferred to a prison closer to her family:

> In view of the troubles experienced by Risley Remand Centre when she was transferred there for a visit with her grandmother I would think that, apart from the lack of a Security Wing at Styal, transfer would be inadvisable. The offence was committed in this area and aroused extremely hostile emotions in the vicinity of Styal.

A second letter from the Governor, this time to the Category 'A' Committee, written on the 2 July, told how Hindley was a well-behaved inmate who had begun to show some signs of interest in Catholicism. She noted how Hindley 'although outwardly a model prisoner I do not think that Myra has basically changed very much... She is still obsessed with Brady and her solicitor is preparing a petition to parliament on their behalf to secure visits for them.'

Just before her 27th birthday she began to reply to letters from her sister, Maureen. She told DCS Topping in 1987 that she had never hated her sister but was hurt by some of the things she had said at the trial. Hindley told him that: 'She was almost as dominated by Smith as I was by Brady.'

Later in the year, and in letters from Lord Longford, he had told her that if she gave up wanting to see Brady then it would be entirely possible that she could be released from prison and could apply for parole after serving seven years. Buoyed by this, Hindley did all she could publicly to show that she was a reformed character and had only been acting under duress from Brady. She went back to Mass and told the prison vicar, Father Kahle, that she wanted to re-establish her Roman Catholic faith. Privately, however, she still wanted to see Brady and in letters to him she mocked Lord Longford.

As well as mocking those trying to help her, in December 1969 a plot to escape from prison while she was on remand was unearthed through 'ingeniously coded letters' between her and Brady. A document states: 'She was detected at an earlier stage employing a code about escaping in her correspondence with Brady. Hindley and Brady made some arrangement for escaping before they were convicted.'

It was in July 1970 that Carole Callaghan returned from a visit to the dentist and told Hindley that she'd seen someone who was just her type, but this one was different to the rest. This one was a Prison Officer named Patricia Cairns.

Myra recalled years later that she was sat outside the canteen when the door to 'A' Wing opened and a brown-haired officer emerged. She said that 'something happened' deep inside her and that, just like with Brady, it was love at first sight.

Patricia Cairns was a 30-year-old from Ashton-under-Lyne in Manchester who had left school at 16, after which she worked as an Accounts Clerk before spending six years as a Carmelite Nun. She left the convent as a result of illness and after working for a short time as an Accounts Clerk again, she had joined the Prison Service.

Several days later Cairns caught Myra with her 'special friend' Alice in Myra's cell. Alice was sprawled across the mattress watching Myra, who was naked after a bath, apply 'intimate' body lotion. An argument between Myra and Cairns ensued, though eventually Cairns let Myra know that they were from the same area and that she used to teach Sunday School at Gorton Monastery when she was a nun.

On Hindley's 28th birthday, she was asked to go to the sports room where Cairns was alone practicing table tennis. Cairns gave her a record – Rachmaninov's 'Rhapsody on a Theme of Paganini'. They both walked down to the music room and listened to the record in silence before Cairns gave her a note which let her know that Cairns fancied her too.

One night soon after, Hindley heard a knocking on her cell door and got up off her bed to find a rose bud in the centre of the spy hole. She took it and found Cairns staring at her. That was the first time they both told each other that they loved each other.

Cairns later said that Hindley had begun to dread getting letters from Brady and she was faking love in her replies to him. 'She had been struggling to reply to his letters for about a month before we met. His grip was loosening, and her world view broadened ... she needed a push to get rid of him. I was a sort of replacement.'

Over the next six months Hindley's friend Carol Callaghan drafted and dictated her replies to Brady. He had been critical of her return to Catholicism and would ask her questions about whether it was just Catholics who made it into heaven and what happened to the souls of millions of Chinese. Despite this, on 24 July, she asked for permission to send six photographs to Brady.

Patricia Cairns.

Hindley was now fairly comfortable in prison. Although still subject to taunts and threats, she was reasonably safe with her group of minders, various lovers and now a Prison Officer looking out for her. Most of her minders she had bought by supplying them with cannabis.

At the beginning of February 1971 Hindley lost three days earnings after a cell search in which a number of unauthorised items were found, including an unauthorised letter and envelope, stuffed animals and clothing, and she was then left feeling more vulnerable when her closest ally, Carole Callaghan, was released from prison.

Despite Hindley and Prison Officer Cairns having declared their love for each other, both women were involved in other relationships. Cairns was living with her partner, Debbie, who was also a Prison Officer, and Hindley used the opportunity to make her jealous by having an affair with a woman known as Bibby.

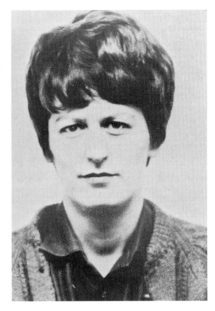

Myra Hindley.

As Hindley decided to try what was, for her, a radical new look, with her hair trimmed, allegations were made to the prison authorities about her affair with Pat Cairns.

On 26 March 1971 inmate Violet 'Pat' Ali told the prison authorities that in around August 1970 Hindley had approached her and asked her to pass letters between herself and Cairns, which she had agreed to do. Hindley had asked her to do this as she knew that she could not read or write and so the contents would remain a secret.

According to Ali, one of the notes from Hindley to Cairns contained a £5 note for Cairns to buy things for her on the outside and smuggle them into the prison. Ali said that they were to be hidden in the dining room, and Cairns had spoken of getting a key cut for Hindley so that she could access them illegally. She also said that there was a sexual relationship going on between them. An enquiry was held by the Prison Governor, in which Cairns denied the allegations:

> I wish to state for your information that I deny categorically, all that this woman has accused me of. Ordinarily, I would have no contact with 'E' Wing, [where both Myra Hindley and Pat Ali are located] but approximately eight months ago, officers were invited onto the wing to practice for a table tennis tournament, which I volunteered for. Several weeks later the Principal Officer on 'E' Wing advised me that she had heard a rumour among the women on 'E' Wing that a relationship had grown between Myra Hindley and myself, and suggested that I drop table tennis for a week or two, until the rumours had died down. On learning this, I not only accepted her advice, but have never since that day, played table tennis on 'E' Wing.

Myra herself wrote a nine-page response to the allegations. She accepted that she had asked Ali to pass letters, but they were between two different prisoners who had since left the prison, and not between herself and Cairns.

> I think I will explain that I have in fact given to Pat Ali letters to take to the workroom and have received ones in return, but they were for a very close friend of mine, an ex-inmate, to another ex-inmate, between whom there was an association. This relationship was known to the staff, who disapproved of it because the person to whom my friend was writing was younger than she was, and they thought it was an unhealthy friendship and some of them went to considerable lengths to prevent contact between them.
>
> When I first began to give Pat Ali letters, I tried to make sure she was alone in her room, but as there were usually other people in there, if I walked in when anyone else was in, I used to make some excuse about borrowing some sugar or something, but she used to say 'It's alright Myra, you can give it to me, they're alright, they won't say anything.' And this went on for some time.
>
> Table-tennis was played quite a lot on 'E' Wing, and the then Deputy Governor helped to arrange a singles tournament; the inmates against the staff; (she herself played in it) and officers who didn't work on 'E' Wing were allowed to come over in off-duty times to practise. This tournament was such a success, for we combined it with a social evening, that we decided to practice for a doubles tournament, and Miss Cairns was one of the officers who used to come over and practise quite often, for her friend, Miss Harber, was an 'E' Wing officer and a keen table-tennis player.
>
> I used to spend quite some time 'coaching' Miss Cairns, who wasn't then a very good player, and this was noticed by women on the wing, and eventually I began to hear rumours that there was 'something going on' between Miss Cairns and I.
>
> I subsequently heard of another rumour circulating the wing that Pat Ali was telling people she was passing letters between Miss Cairns and I, and that we were having an affair. I challenged her with this, and she denied it, saying that the women had probably jumped to this conclusion, since a few of them knew I was giving letters to her, Pat Ali, and seeing Miss Cairns and I together.
>
> As the wing began to fill up with 'F' Wing women and our 'E' Wing 'way of life' began to change, we played less and less table-tennis, and I only ever saw Miss Cairns on the wing when she came over to take her tea break with Miss Harber.
>
> I would now like to list my disputations as far as possible point by point, firstly regarding the letters, and my supposedly asking her if she could keep a secret. I would no more believe she could keep a secret than a bottomless bucket could hold water, for she is known to be one of the most untrustworthy, unscrupulous women in Holloway, and I don't think there

is one 'fiddle' in the prison that she hasn't been involved in, according to the prison grape-vine.

She then mentions a key, and in the ludicrous event of my having one, nothing would be more noticeable than my using it to open the door, which is more or less adjacent to the wing kitchen, which is almost always in use by somebody; and since the officers can observe practically the whole wing, and since I am a Category 'A' prisoner and am naturally observed more diligently than other prisoners, Pat Ali's remark is quite ridiculous.

Furthermore, if it were true that Miss Cairns and I were in love with each other, as Pat Ali alleges I said, and the fact that we were supposed to be writing two and three letters per day to each other could also suggest it similarly, I hardly think it credible to believe I was having to pay for goods when it is reasonable to assume that I would be given them. I completely and categorically deny that I ever received any goods off Miss Cairns or that she ever received money from me.

I have single visits, (meaning I do not have them with other prisoners, or haven't had for more than almost 18 months,) supervised by an officer, and … my mother is supplied with a grant from the prison to visit me because of her limited means.

I happen to earn a good wage in the canteen; over 12/- and as I don't smoke or buy many sweets I find it quite within my means to purchase whatever I wish, even if it means saving for a few weeks … Also, during my 5½ years in prison, I have learned to be so economical that I can save up money from my earnings and put it to private cash for other items which cannot be purchased from the canteen.

I am deeply sorry that Miss Cairns' name has been linked with mine in such a callous and calculatedly cruel way, for I have much respect for her, both as an officer and a person (as opposed to her official position, I mean by person,) since, when she was coming on the wing to play table-tennis, knowing she was a Catholic I asked her advice about a particularly painful religious struggle I was having, and she (like the Priest, and other members of the staff I discussed it with) was of considerable spiritual help to me.

The result of the complaint put before the Visiting Committee was released on 2 June. They had believed Hindley's and Cairns' version of events. Ali's allegations were found 'not proven' and as punishment she lost 180 days remission and was confined to her cell for fourteen days. She was also put on report 'Contrary to rule 47 making a false, malicious allegation against an officer i.e. Officer Miss Cairns after receiving an official warning on 23.3.71 and was unable to provide evidence to substantiate this at the enquiry held by the Governor on 13.4.71.'

'Pat' Ali stuck to her guns though and we now know that she was telling the truth. She had told the Visiting Committee that she had kept a letter from Hindley to Cairns (and vice versa) and given them to her sister so that she could sell them once she was out of prison, but failed to produce the letters when requested at the hearing. She also said that she had two witnesses in the prison who could back up her claims about the sexual relationship but failed to give them their names.

She later claimed that these two witnesses were called Pat Clarke and Mary Scorse and that they had found Hindley and Pat Cairns having sex in the corner of the record room that was adjacent to the table tennis room. Ali claimed:

> We were ashamed that we could not play records, or table tennis – they were always there being nice to each other. I like Miss Cairns. I've never had much chance at knowing her as we don't come from the same wing. I bear her no malice, as she did nothing wrong to me. I have got nothing to gain by telling lies and no reason to make false statements. It would not get me out before my time.

Hindley and Cairns had dodged a bullet this time. But with Ali out of the picture, they now needed someone else to pass their notes to each other, and that woman was called Gail Payne.

Just seven weeks later, on 27 July 1971, a complaint was made against Pat Cairns and Gail Payne, by Prison Officer T. Briggs. Her letter to the Prison Governor read:

> On 27.7.71 I was in charge of the stoking party when my suspicion was aroused by the behaviour of Miss Cairns and Gail Payne.
>
> At approx. 9.55 am in the passage outside the visiting boxes Gail Payne deliberately bumped in to Miss Cairns, who was coming from the centre and walking towards the Staff Toilets. About 2 mins later Gail Payne also walked towards the Staff Toilets. I asked her where she was going, she replied: 'To wash my hands.' I watched her continuously, she came out and stood behind the door near DC Office until Cairns passed her and gave her a note which I saw in her left hand.
>
> I decided to let Gail Payne finish her work, then take her back to 'E' Wing and straight into the office.
>
> When I asked her in the presence of Senior Officer Miss Watson and Prison Officer Miss Clinch, to hand me the note which was passed to her, she replied 'what note?' She was told to turn out her pockets which she did.

Gail Payne then pulled a piece of paper out of her bra, put it in her mouth and tried to run out of the office. She was restrained and Prison Officer Clinch held her throat and hit her on her back in order to make her spit the piece of paper out but it was too late and she had already swallowed it.

Gail Payne said that she did swallow a letter, but it had nothing to do with Hindley or Cairns. When Pat Cairns was asked to make a statement regarding this incident she said:

> Besides denying this allegation, I can only suggest that Officer Mrs Briggs was mistaken. If I was in the toilet at the time, I had no knowledge that Gail Payne was in the washroom. I am unable to assist further, since I have no reason to recollect the incident on July 27.

Once again, Hindley and Cairns had narrowly avoided being found out and as Cairns denied it and the evidence had been swallowed, there could be no proof in the allegation. They now needed to come up with a new method of being able to keep in touch with each other and decided that they needed a go-between outside of the prison.

On 4 August Hindley requested a meeting with the Prison Governor and stated that she wished to start writing to her cousin but only under the following conditions:

- That no Police or Probation enquiries were made at the cousins' home address or in the vicinity
- That all correspondence was conducted through her mother's address. The reason she gave was that gossip had caused her cousin to move on three occasions and that even a letter with just the Holloway postmark could cause further upset

The Governor thought this odd, and rightly so, but for the wrong reason. She believed that the address that Hindley gave her was extremely close to that of a family of another life sentence prisoner with whom Hindley was extremely friendly. The Governor stated:

> I have seen letters from Myra's mother stating that her aunt and cousin would correspond with her if no local check by anyone were made but in view of the friendship between these two lifers and the similarity of address I would like to know if this correspondence for Myra Hindley should be allowed in the unusual channel of using Myra's mother as a go-between.

Astonishingly this was allowed, but it wasn't for correspondence with another inmate. Hindley and Cairns had decided that they would use Hindley's mother's address to send letters to and Hindley's mother would forward them on. Between 25 September 1971 and 27 November 1973 Hindley sent seventy-four letters to 'Glennis Moores' and received fifty-one letters in reply. The letters to Hindley were all typewritten in case someone recognised Cairns' handwriting, and on three separate occasions a £5 note was included.

Janet Harber, a fellow Prison Officer at Holloway who lived with Cairns at their prison's official quarters in Flat 26, 18 Collingham Gardens, SW5, later recalled visiting Cairns' bedroom, 'when I noticed in her bedside locker there was a letter which I recognised as being Myra Hindley's. I showed Pat the letter and she agreed it was from Myra Hindley but said it was an old one she had received a long time ago.'

Myra had recently been reduced to a Category 'B' prisoner for good behaviour and was now afforded greater freedom within the prison, but she was also eligible for supervised days outside of Holloway. Myra recalled: 'After they took that ridiculous, farcical Cat A tag off me I had almost the run of the prison – took myself to work, education, library and even worked a couple of afternoons in the garden.'

On 12 September 1972, the Governor of Holloway, Dorothy Wing, took Myra out for a ninety minute walk on Hampstead Heath. She did this partly as a reward for Myra breaking contact with Brady and when she felt that prisoners could be rehabilitated and

Dorothy Wing, the Governor of HMP Holloway.

'deemed to present no risk of escape', they were taken on trips to reintroduce them to the outside world.

Myra and the Governor got on well and they shared an interest in poetry. Myra had even been invited into the Governor's home inside the perimeter walls for poetry readings. Myra recalled later: 'Matthew Arnold was her favourite. She used to say that many a night, when the traffic outside her window kept her awake, she thought of his 'Dover Beach' and the soothing surge of the tide washing away the shingle lulled her to sleep.'

Hindley, Wing and her dog, plus a male friend of Wing's, climbed into her car and they drove to London's Hampstead Heath. There was a national outcry when the press found out about the trip. Bill Palfrey, ex-Chief Constable of Lancashire Police, said that it was 'a bloody scandal' that Hindley had been taken on a day out from prison. He went on:

> What on earth are they going to do next? What they should do to some of the do-gooders is to play them the tapes the Moors Murderers recorded when these children were killed. That would make them change their minds. What possible use can prison sentences be as a deterrent when killers can get away with spending just seven or eight years in prison? I have always believed in the death penalty and I would have said this was a case where that should have been imposed.

The Home Secretary, Robert Carr, publicly admonished the Prison Governor, 62-year-old Dorothy Wing. In a statement, he called it 'an error of judgement' on Mrs Wing's behalf and went on: 'I have given instructions for this not to be repeated.'

Dorothy Wing said:

> The outing was a perfectly simple thing I would do for any prisoner. I took Myra out because I thought it would do her some good to see some grass and trees and have a breath of fresh air. Bless her heart, she enjoyed it very much. She said: 'Doesn't the grass smell beautiful?' She is reasonably happy, but I am afraid that the reaction from the press and television has rather taken the edge off what was meant to be an outing. In my judgement, it seemed to be a good thing to do at the time. I now realise that it was an error of judgement because Mr Carr has said that it was.

Lord Longford took the opportunity to join in the debate and stated that he believed that the walk was a good idea: 'She is no longer the person she used to be. She has changed. She is now very religious and full of remorse.' But Father Kahle, who had left the post as prison chaplain two months earlier due to health problems, disagreed. When asked if, in the six years he had known her, her personality and attitudes had changed, he flung out his arms and said:

> I don't think so. Has your personality changed in ten years? Has mine? I was asked to see her because I was a Roman Catholic and a German with a lot of knowledge of a cruel people. Lord Longford said to me, 'Hasn't she changed a great deal? Hasn't her personality changed?' I told him I did not think so.

A Home Office report gave an update on Brady's condition following the news about Hindley:

> I understand Lord Colville has asked how Brady now is and what reaction, if any, he has shown to the recent publicity about Myra Hindley.
>
> Brady was initially very upset following Hindley's decision earlier this year to stop writing to him and to refuse to receive his letters. He apparently got over this fairly rapidly however and decided in early August, to come out of his cell. He is now going on normal association in the evenings, but not taking exercise. The doctor reports that there is now no concern about his mental deterioration. He is attending group with the psychologist. He continues to work in his cell.
>
> The Governor has spoken to Brady this morning. Brady has taken the publicity very calmly, commenting only that it would open old sores and that this could do no good. He showed no interest in Hindley or her walk.

# 6

# Hindley Wants Out

On 20 January 1973, a 22-year-old fellow inmate of Hindley's named Maxine Croft was made a 'Green Band'. Green Bands were prisoners who could move freely within the perimeter walls on their own but were not issued with any keys. The main duties were making tea for the staff in the admin offices and morning coffee in the board room for the senior officers. As such she also worked in the staff kitchen and kept the staff room clean and tidy.

Maxine was serving a three-year sentence for handling forged £5 notes, but had previously been in trouble for a string of offences, including twice for the possession of an offensive weapon, four counts of theft, two counts of theft of a motor vehicle and an assault on a woman police officer.

She later recalled:

> I wasn't particular friends with Myra Hindley but on speaking terms. Miss K was the assistant governor of the wing. She had arranged for some kind of poetry reading in the Ivory Tower.
>
> Myra Hindley and myself were allowed to come up to the kitchen in the lunch hour to clean the Ivory Tower. At this time I had only heard of the affair between Miss Cairns and Myra Hindley. I had asked Myra if it was true and she had denied it.
>
> On this day Miss Cairns came up for lunch. Myra Hindley went into the sitting room where Miss Cairns was and asked me to keep watch. Obviously she explained after to me that the affair between her and Miss Cairns was still going on. Miss K came back so Myra left the sitting room and we went downstairs with Miss K, leaving Miss Cairns in the sitting room.
>
> The next day I went to work and after the dinner hour Miss Cairns was in the sitting room and asked me would I pass messages. I replied that I would.
>
> I went back to the wing and then in the evening Myra told me that she possessed photographs of Miss Cairns in a small leather pouch attached to her body. She also told me that her and Miss Cairns write legally to each other. Miss Cairns using the name of her cousin Glenis. They had been writing for some time using her mother's address, that is Myra's mother.

Staff sitting room at HMP Holloway.

She also told me that Miss Cairns was living with Miss Harber and that there was some suspicion of the affair going on – that is the affair between Myra and Miss Cairns.

Myra then became very friendly with me and told me that Miss Cairns sent all her clothes in and bought her everything she needed. She had also given Myra the divisions of officers so that Myra could tell her duties.

I then saw Miss Cairns who told me that should any allegations ever arise, coming from me or any inmate then it wouldn't be believed [Prison Officer Angela Glynn later backed up this claim from Croft] and a VC would follow because she stated that an officer is above an inmate but she said this without threats but her attitude gave me some kind of warning.

At first I was only asked to deliver personal messages. After some time I was asked to deliver letters, fruit and other things to Myra. All of these being left either on the shelf in the kitchen or in the clock in the sitting room. By this time there was a lot of pressure and if I refused at any time to carry things across then the attitude of both Myra Hindley and Miss Cairns was I would be fitted up.

Although still being friendly with Myra Hindley I know there was always the threat of being subjected to pressures.

At this time Myra and Miss Cairns would often talk of other officers who suspected their affair. I was told not to repeat anything to any of these certain officers.

83

This went on for some time. At the time all this was happening I had lost parole twice and was considering asking for open prison but was told by Miss Cairns this was impossible as I was needed to pass messages and carry things.

On 14 May 1973, Patricia Cairns began work in the Discipline Office on Legal Aid duties, as well as her other duties. Opposite the Discipline Office were two small rooms which were used by solicitors, which she had access to. Myra had access to a small office adjoining the solicitor's room where she worked on her tapestry. She also had access to the chapel in which she was allowed to have practice on the piano.

In July, Heather Longhurst, another Prison Officer at Holloway, knew Pat Cairns, her partner/flat mate Harber, and Hindley. She recalled:

> Pat told me she was writing to Myra from outside the prison using a false name. I think the name she was using was 'Glen'. Cairns told me she loved Hindley more than anything else in the world, they seemed to have a perfect understanding in every way. This was not only on a physical level but also on a spiritual level and that she thought that this was to be her destiny.
>
> Pat told me she was meeting Myra Hindley in the chapel occasionally. She also said that she spoke to her in an adjoining office through a gap in the wall where pipes ran through.
>
> Pat showed me knitted articles in the form of animals which Myra had made for her. Pat also showed me books Myra had sent her. A couple of these were spiritual books. She also showed me photographs of Myra. These photographs were recent. I knew this by Myra's hair style and clothes and I could also see they had been taken in her cell. These photographs were in colour. There was one of Myra sitting on the bed. One lying on the bed. One of her standing and one full face.

Maxine Croft recalled:

> She [Cairns] used the room next door to where Myra works. They were able to speak and pass written messages through a gap in the wall where the pipe runs.
>
> …
>
> Myra Hindley was meeting Miss Cairns in the church where she went for piano practice in the lunch hours. She went Monday, Tuesday and Wednesday lunch hours and Thursday and Fridays evening practice after tea. Myra and Miss Cairns were nearly caught by Miss Bates who saw someone leaving by the back chapel door. As to nearly catching them she immediately went to the Discipline Office to check if Miss Cairns was there. Miss Cairns was there. She had just managed to reach there in time.
>
> Miss Bates returned to the wing and some period after told another officer whose name is Miss Longhurst, this was on an evening duty, 'I nearly caught them in the chapel. Now I will keep watch'.

Prison Officer Heather Longhurst recalled that incident:

> I was on evening duty with a prison officer named Miss Bates and she
> commented about Myra Hindley having chewing gum. Miss Bates said
> she had a suspicion of where Hindley had obtained the chewing gum.
> She went on to say that Hindley must have had it for some time because
> the person she suspected was on leave. Miss Bates then went on to tell
> me about an occasion she had visited the chapel and had nearly caught
> the person there because as she entered, the door was closing and had
> not been locked behind the person leaving. She saw Myra Hindley in the
> chapel and escorted her back to 'D' wing. Miss Bates then searched around
> for the prison officer concerned and said she had found her very flustered.
> Although Miss Bates did not mention the officer's name I knew she was
> referring to Patricia Cairns because she had already told me she had nearly
> been caught in the chapel with Myra Hindley.

Prison Officer Barbara Bates said in her statement:

> During the course of my duty I have come to know a Prison Officer named
> Patricia Cairns and an inmate named Myra Hindley. Hindley has been
> given permission to have piano practice in the Prison Chapel. The church
> is situated on the third floor of the building. At lunch time on a day during
> the first week of October, I was dinner patrol officer for 'D' wing. Myra
> Hindley asked me if I would take her to the church for piano practice and
> I took her there at about 12.10. I checked the doors to see that they were
> locked and left open the door leading to the centre which is the secure part
> of the prison.
>
> At about 13.20, I returned to the church to escort Hindley back to her
> wing. On entering the church I had a full view of the piano but could not
> see Myra Hindley. On going further into the church I noticed that the door
> between the altar and the side chapel which opens into the church was
> being slowly closed by someone whom I could not see who was outside
> the church. This door had previously been checked by me and I had in fact
> locked it prior to leaving Myra Hindley in the church. The person who had
> left by this door did not lock it.
>
> The next thing I saw was Myra Hindley coming from the side chapel.
> I asked her what she had been doing and she said she had been saying her
> prayers.
>
> I then took her back to 'D' wing and continued my duties there for
> a few minutes. I handed over to a colleague and then went back to the
> church to investigate. I left the church through the door I had been closing,
> it was not locked but I locked it after me. I then went down the back stairs
> and walked past the Discipline Office. I looked through the window of
> that office. I saw a prison officer with black hair, who was wearing a white
> blouse and had her back to me.

On repassing the Discipline Office I again looked through the window and saw Patricia Cairns sitting in the office dressed in the same manner as the person who had previously had her back to me. I looked at her and she looked at me. She gave me the impression that she knew I was checking on her. There was insufficient evidence for me to report this matter.

Subsequent to this I was in conversation with Miss Longhurst, a fellow prison officer and I mentioned the incident to her.

Maxine Croft recalled:

There seemed to be an area of suspicion from many officers. Myra Hindley then told me that Miss Harber who lives with Miss Cairns had knowledge of the affair and was greatly upset. Myra Hindley used to refer to Miss Harber as 'Janet', and said she was worried in case Janet went to the Chief. There was a lot of rows between Miss Cairns and Miss Harber. Also Miss Longhurst was involved in some kind of entanglement between Miss Cairns and Miss Harber. She [Miss Longhurst] phoned Miss Cairns one night and Miss Glyn (who lived in the flat closest to the phone) reported about some disturbance going on about late phone calls to Miss Cairns. Miss Glyn made a written statement which Miss Cairns showed me and said that the Chief Miss Davis had said she would have to reply to the statement.

Miss Cairns said to me at the time 'Now you see that even statements from officers making complaints are laughed at. Can you imagine if an inmate should make one?' I took this as to mean if I should ever have the need to make one myself.

This was all within a few months up to the period when the escape was first suggested.

Later in the same statement she said:

By this time Myra and myself wasn't so friendly but Myra had stated to me that it would seem suspicious if our friendship was to have ended. I told her that I felt the pressures were too great on me but she only replied that something had come up and that I was too involved to get out of it now. She had said there had been searching on the moors by police and she feared that Ian Brady would reveal anything to cause her more charges. She said he had this hold over her and that something would have to be done. She told me she had gone in for a degree but wasn't interested in getting it and almost hoped they would refuse to allow her to take one.

Patricia Cairns said that it was at about the beginning of September 1973 when she and Myra discussed breaking out of jail, with Maxine Croft's help. Only after the court case did Cairns admit 'She just came out with it. I want to escape … I'm going to be stuck in this place until I die. I want you to think about it.' Cairns said that Myra was 'depressed all the time. What I did was to keep her going. I had no intention of springing her. In my mind I was pretending to go along with it. … Various "plans" were discussed between us, over the weeks until I suggested my taking Myra to Sao Paulo [Brazil] where we could do missionary work.'

In order to get Hindley out of Holloway it would've been necessary to be in possession of at least five different keys. Cairns and Croft both admitted making plaster casts and soap impressions of three of the keys, and a soap impression of a fourth. At no time did they have access to the fifth key which was the key to the gate house situated in the perimeter wall of the prison. Their plan was to have keys made to enable Hindley to escape the prison building which would then give her the opportunity of scaling the perimeter wall and thus escaping.

Maxine Croft:

> Miss Cairns had already told me that it was necessary to get Myra Hindley out of prison. She said that Miss Harber was becoming a nuisance and had once or twice threatened to go to the Chief. Miss Cairns said that it could be easily done and an attempt would be made.

Cairns:

> I needed spare keys to release her, at that time of day and Maxine said that she knew someone who could make them from impressions.

Croft:

> She asked me if I knew of anyone to make keys. I replied that I knew people but wasn't interested in the escape and I didn't think that they would be either. Miss Cairns replied, 'Well you're in it now, you have a family outside and you have no protection in here.
>
> She then said she had already made some plans and had seen other people outside of prison. She told me to think it over and left. I went back to the wing and approached Myra who knew of the escape and told me of the night patrols and said that it was critical that I made some kind of effort when Miss Cairns said. She said I would be given instructions on what to do and at no point to show any anxiety. She said that Miss Cairns would talk to me and to wait and see her.
>
> Myra Hindley seemed quite confident that the escape would come off. I saw Miss Cairns the next day who told me she would supply me with an instamatic camera and flash bulbs to take photographs of Myra Hindley. I refused at first, being as it was too dangerous but she said that there was too much involved now and that she would leave the camera and I was to carry it to the wing.
>
> The following day or soon afterwards the camera and flash bulbs were in the clock. I took them to the wing and took twenty photographs of Myra Hindley. I then carried the camera back the following morning.

Miss Cairns picked it up from the clock and said she would take them to a shop to get them developed. She then said to me that things were going well but that Miss Harber was becoming a worry. She then left.

After a few days Miss Cairns came to the sitting room and told me that the film in the camera had come out blank. I asked her if the shop keeper might have recognised the photographs as being Myra Hindley. She said that she had to go back at 17.00–17.30, to see the manager as the camera was new.

I saw Miss Cairns the next day and she told me that the shutter of the camera had been closed all the time. I told Miss Cairns it was just as well as it was too risky. She just laughed. She just said 'wait a while'. She didn't seem to take much notice of me.

The second occasion happened about a week and a half later, when Myra Hindley told me there was some goods to pick up from the clock. When I went down there was a paper bag containing the camera, two sets of flash bulbs and instructions on how to use the camera properly. This was in the lunch hour. There was a lot of activity on the centre so I only carried the camera across to the wing and took the flash bulbs over at tea time.

I took another twenty photographs of Myra Hindley, destroyed the flash bulbs and took the camera back the following morning.

Miss Cairns collected it from the clock. She told me she had collected it. She took the camera with the film to the same shop where she gave a different name. A few days later she came to the sitting room and showed me the photographs. She said she had run into a fish and chip shop nearby to look at them. She then told me I would be given the camera again for other purposes. I asked what purposes and she replied she'd tell me in the future. She then left.

In the meantime, Myra Hindley told me things had been prepared for her escape. She indicated that there was a lot of outside help. She told me that the room she was in was too dangerous to escape from as the night patrol officer could see her room from the centre.

She then said she would have to move.

Photo of Myra taken in her cell.

Myra on her cell bed.

Myra in her cell shortly before her attempted jail break.

She told me Miss Cairns would be telling me of all the night patrol movements and of the wall areas and that she had some more things she wanted me to do.

I saw Miss Cairns who told me she had thought that some part of the prison wall would be best for escape or there was a hay loft above the chapel. She then said she would be bringing her keys and material to make key impressions. I asked her if she couldn't do the impressions herself. She replied 'No', that I must do them in the kitchen. She supplied me with a seven pound bag of plaster and came up to the sitting room with her keys. I believe she was on dinner patrol that day. We removed the bag from behind a walled door and made some mixture. She removed her keys off the ring but the material proved useless. I believe this was the day she was in possession of the master key. I am not quite sure if she was on dinner patrol. We finally had to make an impression of the master key on brown soap. Miss Cairns left.

The second time we tried, Miss Cairns brought two bars of pink soap, she also had her keys again. I made two impressions of two keys.

On the third occasion Miss Cairns brought two boxes of art plaster and cardboard, left them in the clock and was to use them in the afternoon because she was on dinner patrol. When she came up from dinner patrol she had no keys and had been on a short escort. She went downstairs to collect her keys and came upstairs again. She then mixed the plaster in the sitting room on a plate. She had left her coat in the kitchen.

Half way through mixing a friend of mine came up the stairs. Miss Cairns pushed me out of the sitting room and told me to keep my friend talking. My friend is Carol White. She noticed Miss Cairns' coat on the chair and I told her Miss Cairns had left it there while having lunch. Miss Cairns came into the kitchen while Carol was still with me, washed her hands and returned downstairs with her coat. Carol left shortly after.

I went back into the sitting room. There was some plaster made up and half of an impression in the clock. I went downstairs and saw Miss Cairns near the Discipline Office. She said to me, 'You've messed things up, having your friend up there. You will have to do the keys this afternoon.' She gave me a time.

I went back upstairs, got rid of the half impression and plaster, done my jobs and then got everything ready. Miss Cairns came up. I poured the plaster into three cardboard boxes which Miss Cairns had made up. She then took her keys off the ring and I made the three impressions. She told me she had already made one soap impression herself. She then said, 'You're in it now. If you say anything to your friends or anybody I'll have you nicked.'

I put the impressions, the plaster ones, back in the clock. She washed her keys and went back downstairs.

She collected the impressions from the clock and took them home with her. I saw her the following day and she told me that there had been a terrible row in the flat between herself and Miss Harber. She also stated that the key impressions could not be kept there as Miss Harber had put in her notice and had suspected Miss Cairns even more strongly of the affair between Miss Cairns and Myra Hindley. I was later told by Miss Cairns that Miss Harber had retracted her notice. I told her I couldn't think of where to put the impressions. She said they would have to go and then she went silent and left.

Prison Officer Janet:

I have been sharing a flat with Patricia Cairns for about the last three years. We were very close friends but about twelve months ago this started to change. She mentioned things about Myra Hindley which I would not have expected her to know.

When I put this to her she just laughed. I felt she was either in contact with Myra Hindley or that she was receiving messages from her through a third or fourth person, namely Miss Longhurst or Maxine Croft.

I used to have access to Patricia Cairns' bedroom. About early October this year when I was in her bedroom, I saw a note in her handwriting which seemed to me to be jottings to remind her of messages to give to Myra Hindley. I remarked about this note to Miss Cairns and a row took place.

From that time she refused me access to her bedroom by locking it. I was so upset by Miss Cairns' attitude and the fact that I could no longer discuss work problems with her that on 24 October 1973, I put in my resignation from the prison service, which I later withdrew.

On 10 October Maxine Croft applied for a day's parole, which was granted for 29 October:

I had previously asked for a days parole and was told I could have it on 29 October 1973 but was not allowed to go home to see my mother. When I saw Miss Cairns she told me it's just as well because now I can meet you and we can arrange for the impressions to be delivered to one of your friends. I asked her couldn't she leave them with any of her friends and she replied 'No' they will have to go to yours.

I told her I didn't remember any of the addresses or phone numbers but had them written down in an address book which was at my mother's address. She told me to ask my brother to collect the address book and she would write to him and get him to send it to an address where she could pick it up.

I asked her what was the point of my friends holding the impressions? She just said she wanted the package available outside her flat for her to pick up and get the keys made. I asked her if she had found a key maker and she didn't answer.

Four days later Myra managed to move cells. She had occupied Cell 1 on the fourth floor which was in full view of both the evening duty officer and the night duty officers when they were sitting at the table outside their office. She was then moved to Cell 13, which was on the same side as the office and above it at the opposite end of the landing, meaning that it was no longer visible to the prison officers sat outside their office.

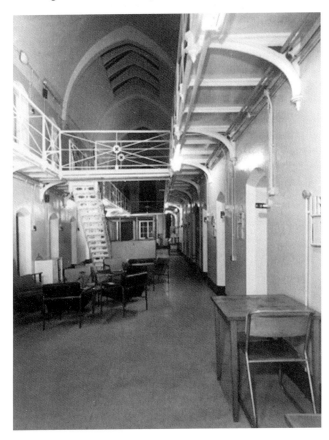

View of the wing from the staff office.

*Hindley Wants Out*

Janet Harber:

> In the middle of October, 1973, Patricia Cairns made it quite obvious that she knew I was again suspicious about what was going on between her and Myra Hindley. I am certain that Cairns told Hindley about this because when I saw Hindley in prison we always said 'good morning' and 'good afternoon' to each other, but from the middle of October when I saw Hindley, although I knew she had seen me she pretended she hadn't. She would look the other way and not speak to me. She had the appearance of someone who was very guilty. This was quite the opposite from her previous attitude.

Harber also said that Cairns had admitted using Miss Longhurst to pass notes between herself and Hindley, which they rowed about and Cairns told her that she would no longer use Miss Longhurst.

Maxine Croft was visited by her brother Dennis. He visited her every second Sunday and during one visit Maxine asked him to collect her address book from her mothers' address in Essex. She asked him to keep it and she would let him know an address to send it to later. The object of this was to obtain a telephone number and an address to which a left luggage ticket receipt could be sent to enable the plaster casts and soap impressions of the prison keys to be collected at a later date.

He told her that he had already received a letter in the post claiming to be from a 'friend' of hers. It was later established that the 'friend' was in fact an impatient Patricia Cairns. Dennis Croft went and collected the address book the following day. At no point did he ask why his sister wanted the address book or why she wanted it sent to someone else.

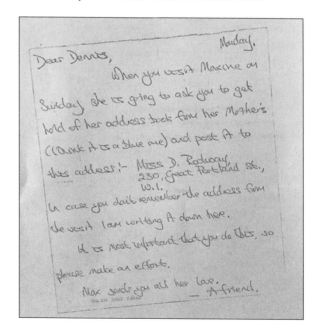

The note from Patricia Cairns.

Deborah Rodway, a 26-year-old hairdresser of 230 Great Portland Street, was a friend of Cairns'. She had previous convictions for obtaining money by deception, obtaining goods by deception, obtaining property by forged instrument, obtaining property by false pretences, attempting to obtain a coat by false pretences, and twenty-five offences of stealing property. Early in October 1973 she took a call from Cairns asking if she would receive some mail on her behalf. In the meantime, Dennis Croft received a telegram from someone he didn't know saying 'Please post the address book urgent.'

Maxine Croft recalled: 'She [Cairns] told me the address book hadn't arrived ... As it had not arrived Miss Cairns got a bit annoyed and didn't believe I had asked him. She said "I will send a telegram to him straight away".'

About a week later a small brown package arrived which was sealed by cellotape. Rodway said in her statement:

> I opened it and inside was a coloured book with addresses in. It meant nothing to me. The same day the package arrived Pat Cairns phoned me about 17.00 and I told her the book had come. She asked me to take the book to where I work on Monday 29 October 1973, which I did.

Maxine Croft recalled:

> She [Cairns] said to me 'I will see you Monday'. I asked her where we should meet and she told me to be at Speakers Corner by 11.45. She said: 'Get rid of your Probation Officer as soon as possible'. I said it would be difficult as it was up to the Probation Officer as to what time she left me. She just replied: 'Get rid of her'. She also added 'If I am on escort Monday I will have to report sick.'

At 06.00 on Monday 29 October, Pat Cairns did indeed phone in sick at work. She should have reported for duty to go to Winchester Crown Court but instead, between 09.30–10.00, went to the Hairdressing Department at the Piccadilly Hotel to meet Deborah Rodway, who gave her the address book. She remembered:

> She had a cup of coffee and I noticed she was carrying a brown paper package about nine inches by four inches by five inches approximately. I said to her: 'What have you got there?' She said: 'It's nothing'. I said: 'It looks like a bomb'. She laughed.

Her reference to a 'bomb' was because, at the time, the IRA were in an active period of bombing London train stations. At 09.20, Prison Officer Sylvia Hurford escorted Maxine Croft from 'D' Wing to reception. She recalled: 'I searched her but did not search her coat which she was carrying over her arm.'

Croft's Probation Officer was called Margaret Powell:

> I have been visiting Maxine Croft in HM Prison Holloway since November 1972. I waited in the Gate House until Maxine was brought down by a Prison

Officer. The Prison Officer handed me an envelope containing £5. This was to buy trousers for Maxine as pre-arranged. My understanding of the situation was Maxine was to have a day out for shopping and rehabilitation purposes…

Maxine and I left the prison at about 09.30 and walked to the office in Penn Road and left there about 10.00 and drove to the Marble Arch area. I parked my car in Upper Berkley Street. We walked through to Oxford Street and looked in a few shops and she bought a pair of trousers. We walked back to Edgware Road and there we separated just before 11.30. I gave her 30 pence for any emergencies and the telephone number of my office. I told her I would be in the Old Kentucky Restaurant from about 15.00 onwards and would expect her to have met me there by 16.00.

Maxine Croft:

I went straight to Speakers Corner and walked around for a while. At about 11.40 I heard a whistle and behind me was Miss Cairns. She was dressed in a brown suede trouser suit and a shirt and was carrying a package which was wrapped up in brown paper in box form [Cairns said that the box contained the key impressions and a written description of the thickness of each key]. I asked her where she had been and she said she had been watching me for some time to see if I was on my own. She then said I have got the impressions and the address book on me. I said the parcel looks a bit 'iffy'. She said she hoped that nobody thought it was a bomb. She then suggested we went for a drink. I said OK.

We walked under the subway to a building on the Marble Arch side and went into a side bar [The Cumberland Hotel]. We asked at the enquiries if the bar was open. It was. I sat in the corner of the bar. Miss Cairns left the package on the seat and went up to the bar and bought two vodka & limes. She came back and sat down and began to talk about the escape. She seemed quite confident that everything was going to be OK. She asked me if visas were needed on 10-year passports to South America. She said she would be taking passport photographs of Myra Hindley in the church later in the week with a wig on. I asked her about money wondering how much all this would cost and she didn't seem to want to tell me just how much she had acquired already. She was explaining to me how expensive all this was to her but seemed confident that it was no problem now.

We talked of prison security, different parts of the walls and night patrols. She asked me if I was prepared to have meetings with her outside the prison once I was released and I answered no. She said that she would see me anyway to get some things straightened out.

She then got up and bought two more vodka & limes while I was looking in the address book for a phone number. When she came back I told her I had found the phone number, she said 'Good'. She then said if the keys were made it might be a good idea for them to be left with me after she had gone. I asked her why as they would be useless. She just shrugged it off.

We left the bar and went to a telephone box where I phoned George Stephens and asked him could I leave a package in Paddington Station for him to collect and that I would send the receipt on. He asked me what was in the package and I just said 'something personal'. He said OK he'd pick it up. He had no idea what was in it.

George Stephens was a Salvage Broker who lived in Ilford, Essex. He had known Maxine Croft for around five years as she used to go into his yard with a lady named Mrs Donovan who was the wife of a friend of his. He recalled:

> Around lunch time, I received a phone call at my office from a woman who said she was Maxine Croft. I was very surprised and asked her how she could make a phone call from prison. She said she was out for the day and that she had some personal effects she would like me to take care of. She said she couldn't get down to me in the time she had and she went on to say if she left them at Paddington Railway Station in the 'Left Luggage' office and sent me the receipt would I hold on to it for her. She said she was due out in a few weeks.
>
> I asked her what the personal effects were and she said it is nothing to worry about but it is stuff I cannot take back with me. She asked me for my address which I gave her. I thought she had been doing a bit of Christmas shopping which she wanted to pick up later.

Croft:

> [After the phone call] We left for Paddington Station and asked a Porter if the left luggage was open. He said 'No' because of the bomb scares.
>
> We then went to a phone booth where Miss Cairns phoned Euston. They replied that the left luggage was open there. She said she would leave the parcel at Euston and that I could write a note to George telling him to pick it up from there instead of Paddington.
>
> We left Paddington Station and went into a card shop just off Sussex Gardens where Miss Cairns bought notepaper and envelopes. We then caught a cab back to Marble Arch and went into a small restaurant [The Quality Inn]. We had lunch and a few drinks.
>
> I wrote the letter to George and passed everything across the table to Miss Cairns. I also addressed the envelope. She then paid the bill. We left the restaurant … She said she was going straight to Euston to leave the package there. We then parted company.

Cairns:

> On arriving at the left luggage office [at Euston] I saw that packages were being thoroughly searched before being accepted. So, I decided to post the impressions, after adding a PS to the letter that Maxine had written to George, explaining why it had to be posted. I then posted it.

# Hindley Wants Out

Linda Summers, a Prison Officer at HMP Holloway up until the end of August that year, knew both Pat Cairns and Maxine Croft. She still frequently visited the prison to see her former colleagues and recalled:

> On one of those visits in October Pat Cairns told me that Maxine Croft was having a day out and wanted to see me. I had been friendly with Maxine while I was working there.
>
> Pat Cairns told me Maxine had a day out on Monday 29 October and would be with her Probation Officer until 14.30.
>
> She said Maxine would like to meet me at Speakers Corner at that time … I met Maxine at 14.45 approximately.
>
> I noticed Maxine had been drinking and she told me she had been drinking with her Probation Officer. I asked Maxine where she wanted to go and she eventually said for a ride and we went to Hampstead Heath. She said she had to be back to the prison by 17.30.
>
> When we got to the Heath we walked for about an hour and at about 16.45, we got in the car. When we got into the car she told me she had not been with her Probation Officer all day but had been with Pat Cairns since about 11.30. She told me she had been drinking vodka & lime when I first met her.
>
> When I heard she had not been with her Probation Officer all day I started shouting at her because I thought she had done a bunk. She then started crying and seemed frightened. She then told me she had seen Pat Cairns. She told me she had left her Probation Officer by arrangement.
> I asked her why she had been with Pat Cairns and Maxine said 'I'm frightened. Pat is going to break Myra Hindley out.' Maxine was crying and was very upset and wanted me to help her.
>
> Then I said, 'You're a bloody fool Maxine. You're still in prison. Why don't you give yourself a chance? What are you supposed to be doing?' She said, 'I am supposed to be getting the passports for them. I have already taken the prints.'
>
> She went on to say when she got out she wasn't going to get them the passports because she wasn't going to get into trouble again.
>
> She did not tell me about her movements with Pat Cairns that day other than that they had been for a drink together.
>
> I said to her as she came out with a Probation Officer she would have to go back with one. I then drove to a telephone box and made Maxine telephone the Probation Officers.
>
> I then drove to a taxi office and put her in a minicab and told the man to take her to 1A, Penn Road, Holloway.

Margaret Powell:

> I went to the restaurant as arranged but she did not arrive and then as a result of a telephone call at 16.55 I returned to Penn Road, where Maxine was waiting for me.

She was in an emotional state bordering on hysterical, she may well have been drinking. I attempted to calm her down and returned her to the prison at about 17.50.

The following day George Stephens recalled: 'About 13.00 I arrived at my office. My manager told me he picked up a parcel for me at the corner shop ... On my desk I saw a parcel wrapped up in brown paper.'

He did not like the look of the parcel because it was addressed to him personally and not to his firm. He was not expecting any parcels. He left it on his desk as he had some customers to deal with.

In a major stroke of luck, DCI Phillip Thomas of Dagenham Police Station was off duty and called at the yard to enquire about getting his car repaired. As he entered the office, he noticed the parcel and Stephens joked to him that he thought it was a bomb. DCI Thomas sniffed it and noticed that it smelt of soap. He opened it and found that it contained key impressions in soap and plaster. He did not know that they were impressions from prison keys at first. DCI Thomas:

> My first thought was they were impressions of safe keys. I questioned Mr Stephens and he told me of the parcel being received through the post and of receiving a telephone call the day before from a Maxine Croft ... I returned to my own office with the parcel and there made a closer examination of the contents. I then realised the impression could be of prison keys and I was aware of the fact Maxine Croft was serving a sentence.

DCI Thomas then contacted the Police Liaison Officer and the Home Office and told them of his suspicions. He sent the parcel on to DCI Hoggarth at the Home Office for further investigation.

Pat Cairns was back at work on 1 November and was on duty at Croydon Crown Court, leaving HMP Holloway at 07.50 and not returning until 17.40.

DCI Hoggarth began enquiries at HMP Holloway, where he met with the Governor, Dr Bull, and other prison personnel. He said: 'My principal concern at that time was to establish whether, or to what extent, the security of Holloway Prison had been breached. I therefore decided that a direct approach to a person with Croft's background would be unproductive.' He enlisted the help of prison officials to ascertain Croft's movements on 29 October.

Valerie Haig-Brown, a Probation Officer and Head of the Welfare Department at Holloway spoke to Maxine Croft about key impressions getting into police possession. She wanted to know Croft's movements on her day out, but Croft refused to tell her and so was allowed back on to the wing. Following that conversation Croft told Hindley that they had been caught. Hindley panicked and said: 'You can't say anything about Patricia because they won't believe you.' Croft told Hindley that Cairns had written notes on the impressions and that it wouldn't be long before they discovered her handwriting.

According to Croft:

> Myra Hindley immediately started destroying all Miss Cairns' letters and said that a message must be got to Miss Cairns … I told Myra that it was all on top and she said that Miss Cairns would get herself out of it and that I was just like Ian Brady. I was then called to the Governor but was still unwilling to say anything.

Prison Officer Heather Longhurst returned to the wing at about 14.00. She saw Croft outside the Discipline Office:

> She came and spoke to me and asked me to tell Pat to get rid of everything as she was having a police visit. I did not pass this information on to Pat.
>
> After leaving Maxine I made my way up to 'D' Wing and as I passed Myra's office she followed me up the stairs … She then asked me to pass a written message to Janet Harber who is Pat Cairns' flatmate. Myra said the message was really urgent.
>
> I did not read the message but gave it to Janet. The message consisted of a folded piece of paper which was not in an envelope.
>
> Later the same day I saw Maxine and she said again to tell Pat to get rid of everything because the police knew about her and Euston. I said, 'What's it about?' and Maxine replied, 'The key impressions.' This was the first time I had heard keys or anything mentioned.
> 'Myra again saw me and asked if I would phone Pat in the evening and tell her in case Janet hadn't passed the note or message on. I didn't phone Pat.

Janet Harber recalled: 'When I left the prison at about 17.00 I met Miss Cairns who was on her way to the prison and gave her the note.'

Somehow, Myra had got word to Cairns and told her to meet her in the chapel. When Cairns got to the chapel she found that it had been security locked. Myra told her, through her door, to get rid of all the incriminating evidence that was in her flat. Cairns rushed to Earls Court and cleared everything out: the luggage she'd bought for their escape, the literature from the Brazilian Embassy, and all the letters Myra had written to her over the past three years.

Maxine Croft was taken to CX (part of the hospital wing) to be segregated and was told the police were coming the following morning:

> In the morning I was allowed out. Miss Cairns was on legal aid and came down to CX. She said to me: 'You'll have to carry this one on your own.' I asked her if the parcel was left at Euston and she said: 'No, I posted it.'
>
> I said: 'I can't carry this one'. She said: 'I'll see you later.' She came down again, walked to the top of the wing and told me to follow her. As most of the people down CX are on lots of medicine and there are only nurses nobody thought this strange.
>
> At the top of the wing she dropped a letter and said: 'Read that. I'll be back later.' The letter was printed telling me what to say to the police.

It was a silly story. It also said tear this up. The story was 'Say that AG [Assistant Governor] who has left the prison now left her keys in the board room one day and made a regular habit of it. I took it in my head to make impressions of these keys hoping that I would be able to sell them, once out of prison.' I tore the letter up.

Miss Cairns came back again. I told her the story was silly that any idiot would realise I would never have had time to make all those impressions in just a few seconds and that AG's just don't happen to leave their keys laying about. Miss Cairns replied 'if you say anything to the police I'll do you for allegations and remember that you have no protection in here'. She left. She said before she left someone will be coming down to have a chat with me. I was then taken up to the police. I have not spoken to Miss Cairns since.

DCI Hoggarth informally interviewed Croft in the presence of the Deputy Governor:

She at first denied all knowledge of the key impressions, but then said she was responsible for making them. When asked how she had obtained the keys she said that an Assistant Governor had once left her keys on a boardroom table, and that she (Croft) had made the impressions from them.

As a result of further questioning, Croft changed her story and implicated a prison officer named Patricia Cairns. Because of this I sought advice, and at about 14.30, DCI McGuinness came to the prison and commenced enquiries.

DCI McGuinness and DS Peace interviewed Maxine Croft. Croft implicated Cairns in the making of some of the impressions:

**DCI McGuinness:** Can you tell me why you made these casts and impressions of three prison keys?

**Croft:** I made them at the request of Miss Cairns.

**DCI McGuinness:** Where did you get these keys from in order to make these impressions and casts?

**Croft:** From Miss Cairns.

**DCI McGuinness:** When did you make these impressions and casts?

**Croft:** A few weeks ago.

**DCI McGuinness:** What was the purpose of making these impressions and casts?

**Croft:** So that somebody could escape from the prison.

**DCI McGuinness:** What is the name of the person you intended to escape from the prison?

**Croft:** Myra Hindley.

**DCI McGuinness:** Why did you wish Myra Hindley to escape from the prison?

**Croft:** It was not my wish. I was just in sympathy and under strain.

**DCI McGuinness:** With whom were you in sympathy?

**Croft:** With a prison officer and with Myra Hindley.

**DCI McGuinness:** Have you ever spoken with Myra Hindley?

**Croft:** Yes.

**DCI McGuinness:** Who suggested to you to make these impressions and casts?

**Croft:** Miss Cairns.

**DCI McGuinness:** Was Myra Hindley aware these casts and impressions were being made?

**Croft:** No.

The interview was suspended and at 17.30 DCI McGuinness and DS Peace interviewed Patricia Cairns. Cairns said that she knew Maxine Croft, but denied meeting her on 29 October, denied ever giving her any keys to make impressions from and denied being in a relationship with Myra Hindley.

**DCI McGuinness:** Maxine Croft has alleged that you supplied her with keys to make three of these exhibits. Is this true?

**Cairns:** No.

**DCI McGuinness:** Did you make one of these exhibits yourself?

**Cairns:** No.

**DCI McGuiness:** She further alleges that these impressions and casts were made at your instigation with the object of assisting the escape of Myra Hindley. Have you any comment to make?

**Cairns:** Certainly. There is no truth in the accusation.

**DCI McGuinness:** Can you think of any reason why Maxine Croft should make these allegations against you?

**Cairns:** No.

**DCI McGuinness:** We're police officers and we have allegations made against us. We usually know the reason why.

**Cairns:** I don't know what she would have keys for she's going home soon.

**DCI McGuinness:** Maxine Croft alleges that the exhibits I have produced were in your possession.

**Cairns:** No.

**DCI McGuinness:** Have you ever posted a parcel for Maxine Croft?

**Cairns:** No. I might have at Borstal.

**DCI McGuinness:** Did you post a parcel for her on Monday 29 October?

**Cairns:** No.

**DCI McGuinness:** Have you any strong feeling about Myra Hindley?

**Cairns:** No. I have been accused of it in 1971. An inmate made an allegation in April 1971. An enquiry was made and was found to be groundless.

The interview ended at 18.07. At 20.25 DCI McGuinness, DCI Hoggarth and TDC Barr returned to HMP Holloway and saw the Prison Governor, Dr Bull. Twenty-five minutes later, along with Maxine Croft, they went to the third-floor staff kitchen, where Croft showed them a packet of moulding powder which had been concealed in a rubbish box outside the kitchen. The officers also took possession of two pieces of brown soap from the kitchen, one metal teapot from the shelf of the kitchen, one green plastic spoon and one brown clock from the staff sitting room.

At 22.10, with DCI Hoggarth and TDC Barr, DCI McGuinness went to Patricia Cairns' flat and with her permission searched her bedroom. In a chest of drawers they discovered a plastic bag which contained a Kodak Instamatic 100 camera and accessories and an envelope containing fifty-nine photographic transparencies. Under her bed they also discovered a box containing four film cartridges.

At 22.25 the officers and Miss Cairns entered the sitting room where they began to question her about the finds:

**DCI McGuinness:** Maxine Croft has told me you took this camera to Holloway Prison for her to photograph Myra Hindley. Is that correct?

**Cairns:** No, I most certainly did not!

**DCI McGuinness:** I'll have these negatives developed. If there are photos of her I will know.

**Cairns:** I can assure you there are certainly not any.

**DCI McGuinness:** This will be a searching enquiry. If there's anything you do know now is the time to tell me.

**Cairns:** There's nothing I can tell you. I just don't know what it's all about.

**DCI McGuinness:** I may have to see you again and the situation could well be different. Get in touch with me if you change your mind.

On 3 November, Prison Officer Heather Longhurst recalled:

> I was on duty. Pat saw me and told me that she had been questioned by the police the night before and that her camera had been taken away and her room had been searched. She said she thought they were looking for the photographs. She said she had taken everything to a friends'. She did not tell me the name or address of her friend.

The following day Prison Officer Heather Longhurst saw Pat Cairns at work and told her that she needed to talk to her, as she was concerned whether her knowledge of the affair between Cairns and Hindley could get her in to trouble. They met at around 17.00 at the Wimpy on Holloway Road. Pat Cairns turned up with her flatmate Janet Harber.

Cairns told her it would only be the criminal act that they would be investigating and as such she had nothing to be worried about. They all left and went to a bus stop where Longhurst got on a bus, leaving Cairns and Harber behind.

Cairns and Harber went back to Wimpy, where they met a woman called Mary McIntosh. She would sometimes go and visit Myra and was clearly being used to pass messages between Cairns and Myra now that Croft had been compromised.

At about 21.30 that evening Cairns and Harber went to visit Heather Longhurst at her flat. She was in her kitchen having a wash when they arrived and so they talked to her flatmate, Kathleen Moores. When Longhurst was ready she said hello to her visitors and went back to the kitchen to make some coffee. Pat Cairns then followed her.

Cairns told her that she was denying everything to the police, and Longhurst told her that she was 'crazy and bloody mad'. Cairns asked her what she would say to the police. 'Then she said if I was going to go to the police she would go and confess and I wouldn't be mentioned. I left it at that. She told me that if I made up my mind what I was going to do would I let her know.'

Kathleen Moores, in her second statement to the police, recalled:

> When Pat Cairns and Janet Harber visited our flat … I didn't tell you all that was said by Pat Cairns and Janet Harber.
>
> During the conversation Cairns said the police had taken her keys for tests but she said they couldn't find anything on them because the keys they had taken were not hers. She had changed them over. She told me she had changed them with Janet Harber's keys and then later changed them with someone else. I believe she said she had changed them the second time with a Miss Summers' keys. Janet Harber was present when she said this.
>
> She also mentioned about some photographs of Hindley and also some letters. She stated she had sent these to America.
>
> She also said she had sent a parcel to Janet Harber's uncle in Maidstone. She said the parcel was addressed to Janet.

Janet Harber recalled that after this meeting:

> Patricia has told me that she has had some photographs of Myra Hindley and she has destroyed them.
>
> I asked her how on earth did she think she could get anyone out of Holloway, I can hardly imagine Myra jumping over the wall. She said she wasn't meant to. If one wanted there is an old gate at the back of the prison where one can just walk out. I said: 'How strange I didn't know about it.' She said: 'Well there is.' I took this remark with a pinch of salt. I haven't looked to see if there is any such a gate.
>
> I asked her what Hindley was going to do when she escaped from prison and Patricia said, 'I don't know what she was going to do.'

I also asked her how anyone in 'D' wing could possibly escape after being locked in. She said: 'It's simple, one has only to walk through the reception door and up the stairs.' I said: 'But 'D' wing is right near the centre and if anyone came from their room they would be heard.' Miss Cairns replied: 'Not necessarily.' I said: 'It would be a bit of a risk and you would be stupid if you tried it.' Cairns just shrugged.

The following day, Dennis Croft, Maxine's brother, received a letter from someone called 'Marie' (known to be one of Pat Cairns' aliases) asking him to burn the previous telegram and this letter and put them in the bin.

Back in HMP Holloway, Prison Officer Heather Longhurst was on duty on 'D' Wing when Hindley approached her. She asked Longhurst to tell Cairns that her (Myra's) fingerprints could be on the camera because Croft had taken photographs of her and she, Hindley, had taken photographs of Croft.

Later, at around tea time, Longhurst saw Cairns in the staff sitting room. Cairns told her that the police had taken her keys and were going to do 'forensic tests on them but she said the keys they had taken were not the keys used. She did not tell me which keys had been used for the impressions.'

Linda Summers was worried about the whole situation and so phoned Cairns and told her that she was going to see a solicitor. Cairns replied 'Alright. Will you let me know what he says?' Summers didn't go to her solicitor and instead went to the prison and reported all that she knew.

At 11.25 on 6 November, DCI McGuinness and DS Peace went to interview Maxine Croft at HMP Holloway:

**DCI McGuinness:** To go to the soap. Is this the remnants from which you made the key impression?

**Croft:** Yes.

**DCI McGuinness:** At the same time you handed me this metal teapot. Is this the one you mixed the plaster in?

**Croft:** Yes.

**DCI McGuinness:** You also handed me this spoon. Is this the one you used to mix the plaster?

**Croft:** No.

**DCI McGuinness:** Why did you hand it to me?

**Croft:** Because it was used at one time

**DCI McGuinness:** Who used it?

**Croft:** Miss Cairns.

**DCI McGuinness:** When did she use this?

**Croft:** On the same occasion that I made the impression of the master key.

**DCI McGuinness:** Did you see her using this spoon?

**Croft:** Yes.

**DCI McGuinness:** What did she use the spoon for?

**Croft:** To mix a different plaster.

**DCI McGuinness:** Did you see her make use of the plaster she mixed?

**Croft:** Yes.

**DCI McGuinness:** What did she do with the plaster?

**Croft:** It was no good. I threw it away.

**DCI McGuinness:** What was she going to do with the plaster?

**Croft:** Make impressions of keys.

**DCI McGuinness:** You mean prison keys?

**Croft:** Yes.

**DCI McGuinness:** The same night you gave me the brown clock which was in the sideboard of the staff sitting room. Would you like to tell me what this clock was used for?

**Croft:** For the purpose of putting things in.

**DCI McGuinness:** Would you like to be more specific?

**Croft:** So many things were put in it. To tell you I would be here all day.

**DCI McGuinness:** Can you tell me what things relating to this case were put into the clock?

**Croft:** Instamatic camera, flash bulbs, were put in the clock by Miss Cairns. Two boxes of art mould, instruction how to use the camera, cardboard to make up boxes. That's all that affects this enquiry.

**DCI McGuinness:** I am showing you an instamatic camera. Is this the camera Miss Cairns put in the clock for you?

**Croft:** Yes, unless it's a double.

**DCI McGuinness:** What was the purpose of her leaving the camera for you?

**Croft:** To take photographs.

**DCI McGuinness:** Of whom?

**Croft:** I don't wish to answer.

**DCI McGuinness:** You told me on Friday night it was to take photographs of Myra Hindley. Were you telling the truth?

**Croft:** Yes.

**DCI McGuinness:** So it was to take photographs of Myra Hindley?

**Croft:** Yes.

**DCI McGuiness:** How many photographs did you take of Myra Hindley?

**Croft:** Twenty-two.

**DCI McGuinness:** Where are the photographs now?

**Croft:** Destroyed I should imagine.

**DCI McGuinness:** To whom did you give the photographs?

**Croft:** I returned the camera to Miss Cairns which contained film after I had taken photographs of Myra Hindley.

**DCI McGuinness:** What was the purpose of taking the photographs of Myra Hindley?

**Croft:** I was told just to take photographs of Myra Hindley.

**DCI McGuinness:** Was this by Miss Cairns?

**Croft:** By Miss Cairns.

Later:

**DCI McGuinness:** What arrangement had you made for having the keys made?

**Croft:** The arrangements for the keys was to be left to me to find somebody. This was in the early stages but it seemed that Miss Cairns was confident she could get them made herself.

**DCI McGuinness:** Did she give you any indication where?

**Croft:** No. She didn't give me any indication.

**DCI McGuinness:** You realise that to get involved in making prison keys with a view to assisting a prisoner to escape is a very serious matter. Would you like to tell me why you became involved in this?

**Croft:** I was pressured. A lot of pressures which affected me to the extent there was no getting out of it. No refusing.

**DCI McGuinness:** Can you tell me about these pressures?

**Croft:** I cannot explain the pressures put on me because of my family being outside. I have reason to believe that there are people who could cause damage to them. I mean my family.

**DCI McGuinness:** Are you prepared to name the people outside involved in this matter who would cause damage to your family?

**Croft:** No.

**DCI McGuinness:** Do you know the names of these people?

**Croft:** I know of certain names but I am too frightened to tell.

**DCI McGuinness:** Have you ever discussed this matter with Myra Hindley?

**Croft:** I don't wish to answer that.

**DCI McGuinness:** When you took the photographs of Myra Hindley what was said between you?

**Croft:** Could you stand 3 feet away from me please and she did. That was all.

**DCI McGuinness:** Did she say anything about this?

**Croft:** She just said carry the camera back.

**DCI McGuinness:** Did she ever mention Miss Cairns to you at this stage?

**Croft:** No I don't wish to answer that. Has Miss Cairns said anything about this?

DCI McGuinness then read over notes taken at the interview with Miss Cairns

**Croft:** The woman is an absolute maniac, lunatic. There must be proof against her. I will tell you all about it and tell you the truth.

**DCI McGuinness:** Do you wish to make a written statement under caution about this?

**Croft:** Yes.

Maxine Croft then elected to make a written statement which was recorded by DS Peace. The statement ended uncompleted at 18.30.

Dennis Croft said that he had a phone call from his sister Maxine, and as a result he handed the telegram and letter to DS Peace at Dagenham Police Station. DS Peace told a different story in his statement. He said that he was following Dennis Croft 'as a result of certain enquiries' to his home address. Croft stopped his vehicle in Reede Road, Dagenham, and handed him a letter. He then went with Croft to his home at 62A Wood Lane, where he searched the waste bin and found a torn letter and envelope. The torn letter read:

Dear Dennis

Please burn this letter, the telegram and the letter giving the address of where to send that address book in case there are any enquiries. Nothing to worry about.

Thanks
Marie

The following day, a letter was received from the Home Office granting parole to Maxine Croft on 19 December 1973, subject to certain conditions. Isabelle Storrow, the Chief Officer at Holloway, recalled that Cairns, as well as other officers, knew that Croft was being considered for parole.

At Caledonian Road Police Station Pat Cairns was interviewed by DS Peace and DCI McGuinness. Her fingerprints and a sample of her handwriting were taken. She denied everything that Maxine Croft had said the previous day and would not answer any question relating to Myra Hindley.

107

At 15.15 McGuinness, TDC Barr, Patricia Cairns and her solicitor Mr Hall went to Cairns' residence to conduct a search. McGuinness found one Basildon Bond airmail pad and asked Cairns if it was her handwriting on it. She replied 'It doesn't look like it.' He then found one GLC driving license in the name of Myra Spencer, 1 Parkhurst Road, N7.

> I said: 'Is this your driving license?' Cairns said: 'No, it's a friends in Manchester.' I said: 'Where is she living now?' Cairns said: 'I don't know.'
> I said: 'Myra Spencer, 1 Parkhurst Road, London, N7?' Cairns made no reply.

(At the beginning of February, Myra's solicitor, Mr Fitzpatrick, had written to the Executive Officer of GLC Driving Licenses with a deed poll, asking for the name on Hindley's driving licence to be changed Myra Spencer; 1 Parkhurst Road was the address of HMP Holloway).

McGuinness then found another Basildon Bond writing pad, and Cairns again denied the handwriting was hers. He found a stamped envelope addressed to Myra's mother – Mrs N. Moulton, 6 Clive Wood Walk, Off Bennet Street, West Gorton, Manchester 12, and asked Cairns if she knew her. She said she did but only said that the handwriting 'could' be hers. He also found two pieces of paper headed 'Patricia Cairns' and again she would only say that the handwriting on it 'could' be hers.

They found various writing books and folders which they took as evidence before leaving at 17.20 and returning to Caledonian Road Police Station where Cairns was detained.

Janet Harber recalled in her statement:

> I have an uncle, a Mr William Harber who resides at 3, Humber House, Westmoreland Close, Maidstone, Kent.
>     Not long after Pat Cairns was charged the Prison Governor asked me to find out from Pat if she was willing to move out of Collingham Gardens to accommodation near Holloway Prison. This she agreed to do but the move never came off.
>     When she was still thinking of moving Pat Cairns told me she was expecting a parcel of books from America. As she was not sure what her address would be she asked me if she could have them sent to a relative of mine. I agreed to this and gave her the name and address of my uncle, Mr. William Harber.
>     I visited my uncle on Monday 21 January 1974, but the parcel had not arrived.

Police arranged with the Post Office that if any such parcel should arrive it would be immediately intercepted.

Pat Cairns was interviewed again at 10.30 on 8 November by DS Peace and DCI McGuinness. She was asked about the drivers' license found in her flat in the name of

Myra Spencer. Laughably, she denied that she knew the address on the license was HMP Holloway and she didn't want to comment any further about it. She wouldn't say who Mrs Moulton was.

At 12.05 Cairns was formally charged and cautioned. She was also suspended from duty.

The following afternoon, DS Peace and DCI McGuinness went to HMP Holloway and interviewed Maxine Croft at 14.20.

**DCI McGuinness:** I have spoken to Miss Summers who is an ex-officer from this prison. She told me she met you on the afternoon of Monday 29 October 1973 at Speakers Corner. Is that correct?

**Croft:** Yes.

**DCI McGuinness:** Did you go with her by car to Hampstead Heath?

**Croft:** Yes.

**DCI McGuinness:** Did you tell her you were in trouble with Miss Cairns?

**Croft:** Yes.

**DCI McGuinness:** Did you tell her about the key impressions and what they were intended for?

**Croft:** No.

**DCI McGuinness:** What did you tell her about this matter?

**Croft:** I just told her I was under pressure from Miss Cairns and that Miss Cairns had met me that morning. She was up to something. Miss Summers said keep away from them. She couldn't get any more sense out of me because I was just crying my eyes out and we had to get back because it was late.

**DCI McGuinness:** Was there anything else she said?

**Croft:** Only that Miss Summers said she would tell Patricia to leave me alone and that I was to keep well away from them – meaning Miss Cairns and Myra Hindley. She had no real knowledge of what was going on.

TDC Paul Barr, with TDC Dixon and WPC Peebles went to HMP Holloway at 10.15 the following morning, collecting Maxine Croft. TDC Barr:

The four of us travelled by car to the Oxford Street area then to Paddington Railway Station where Croft pointed out the left luggage office. She then directed us to Edgware Road and pointed out a stationers. We then went to the Cumberland Hotel, Marble Arch and Croft pointed out a bar to us and we entered it and she sat in a seat which she stated she had sat in when she was there with Cairns on Monday 29 October 1973. From there we went to the Quality Inn, Oxford Street, where she again pointed out the table she had sat at with Cairns on the above date.

She was returned to HMP Holloway at 13.45 and the next day Mary McIntosh went to visit Myra to give her the latest regarding the police investigation. At the same time, Police Officer Beverly Perrin gave a statement to the police:

> At about 13.30, at the Wimpy Bar, Parkway, Camden Town, NW1, I saw Patricia Cairns with two other women. One of these women I have been able to identify as Mary McIntosh. I saw all three women leave the restaurant and approach a red saloon motor car index number LGW 51K, which was parked in Camden High Road, NW1, outside the entrance to the underground station. I saw the woman I know as McIntosh get in the vehicle and drive away. Cairns and the third woman went into the underground station.

On 16 November, Heather Longhurst gave another statement to the police and told them that: 'It was general gossip in the prison that there had been an association between Patricia Cairns and Myra Hindley. In September of 1973 it was still suspected that this affair was still going on.'

Four days later DCI McGuinness and TDC Barr went to 125 High Holborn, WC1, at 15.30, where they saw Patricia Cairns and her solicitor. Cairns finally admitted her part in the escape plot. She wrote a statement under caution.

> I have known Myra Hindley for over four years. During this period, I became convinced that she had finally freed herself from the yoke of Ian Brady's influences, sincerely amended her ways and desires only to do good in the future.
>
> She has already spent over 8 years in prison, without even a glimmer of light at the end of the long tunnel leading to freedom. We often speak of the day when she would get parole, and I promised to do all in my power to help her. We were first drawn together by the fact that we are of the same age, come from the same part of Manchester, and share a deep love of the same Catholic faith. We often discussed the faith and she told me that due to my influence, she made her confession to the prison chaplain and has regularly attended Mass and Communion since then. I have tried to be a source of consolation and encouragement to her for, just being 'Myra Hindley' is penance enough, without the added rigours of long years in prison, which this deeply sensitive person has endured. During recent months, I was distressed to observe that prison was becoming too much for her. I think that even her doctors were aware of her distress. Also, being such a political 'hot potato', it seemed that no government would wish the criticism of letting her free. The slightest incident would spark a violent outcry from the press, so what would be their reaction, when she came to be considered for parole? It seemed to be a hopeless situation and that she would never be free.
>
> Maxine Croft is a friend of Myra Hindley's. I used to see Maxine every day, because she used to make tea for the civilian staff in the kitchen where I used to take my meal breaks. On numerous occasions we had spoken of the days when Myra would be free.

She later said:

> It is only in recent days, that I have come to realise that I have been indulging in criminal activities. I was aware only of the 'end' and paid no heed to the 'means'. A case of 'our impulses are too strong for our judgement, sometimes'. I sincerely apologise for all the inconvenience, embarrassment and distress that my stupidity has caused, especially to Dr Bull, the Governor of Holloway.

It was time to hear Hindley's side of the story, but when DCI McGuinness and DS Peace went to interview her in HMP Holloway, she declined as she didn't have a solicitor present. They went back on 4 December and this time interviewed her in the presence of her solicitor, Mrs Cooper, where she denied all knowledge of the escape plot:

**DCI McGuinness:** Do you know a prison officer named Patricia Cairns?

**Hindley:** Yes.

**DCI McGuinness:** Do you know an inmate named Maxine Croft?

**Hindley:** Yes.

**DCI McGuinness:** Have you ever discussed with either of these people plans for your escape from this prison?

**Hindley:** No.

**DCI McGuinness:** Are you very friendly with Patricia Cairns?

**Hindley:** Yes.

**DCI McGuinness:** Have you ever possessed photographs of Patricia Cairns?

**Hindley:** Yes.

**DCI McGuinness:** Did you carry photographs of her in a leather pouch?

**Hindley:** Not in a leather pouch but in a piece of material pouch.

**DCI McGuinness:** Do you write to and receive letters from a person named Glenis?

**Hindley:** Yes.

**DCI McGuinness:** Were the letters you received from Glenis typewritten?

**Hindley:** Yes.

**DCI McGuinness:** Who is Glenis?

**Hindley:** Miss Cairns.

She then told the detectives that she sent the letters to her mother's address in Manchester.

**DCI McGuinness:** Has Miss Cairns supplied you with clothes?

**Hindley:** Yes.

**DCI McGuinness:** Did Miss Cairns send you letters, fruit and other gifts via Maxine Croft?

**Hindley:** She passed messages for us.

**DCI McGuinness:** What was the nature of the messages?

**Hindley:** Miss Cairns and I had been having a relationship and messages were just messages of sending my love and receiving hers.

**DCI McGuinness:** Did any of these messages from Miss Cairns mention your escape?

**Hindley:** No.

**DCI McGuinness:** I am producing an instamatic camera. Have you seen that camera before?

**Hindley:** Yes.

**DCI McGuinness:** Have you ever touched that camera before?

**Hindley:** Yes.

**DCI McGuinness:** Did Maxine Croft take photographs of you in your cell with that camera or one similar to it?

**Hindley:** Yes.

**DCI McGuinness:** Are you aware that camera belongs to Miss Cairns?

**Hindley:** Yes.

**DCI McGuinness:** Did Miss Cairns give you the divisions of officers so that you would know who was on duty in your wing?

**Hindley:** No. She gave me her division duties only and she wasn't on my wing.

**DCI McGuinness:** Did you ever converse with and pass messages to Miss Cairns through a gap in the wall between the Solicitors office and the room where you did tapestry work?

**Hindley:** Yes.

**DCI McGuinness:** Were any of these messages or conversations about the escape she planned for you?

**Hindley:** No.

**DCI McGuinness:** I understand you have piano practice in the prison chapel. Is that correct?

**Hindley:** Yes.

**DCI McGuinness:** Did Miss Cairns frequently meet you in the chapel on these occasions?

**Hindley:** Yes. Not on every occasion.

**DCI McGuinness:** Did you ever discuss your proposed escape with Maxine Croft?

**Hindley:** No.

**DCI McGuinness:** Did you tell Maxine Croft about press reports of searching on the moors?

**Hindley:** I did on an occasion when there was a press report but I discussed it with several people.

**DCI McGuinness:** Did you tell Maxine Croft that Ian Brady had a hold over you because there is more evidence on the moors which could lead to further charges against you?

**Hindley:** No

**DCI McGuinness:** Did you tell Maxine Croft that because of Ian Brady's evidence you must escape?

**Hindley:** No. That is a categoric lie.

**DCI McGuinness:** Did you tell Maxine Croft there was a lot of outside help for your escape?

**Hindley:** I have never discussed an escape with Maxine Croft or anybody.

**DCI McGuinness:** Did you tell Maxine Croft you would have to move room because it was in view of the night patrol officer?

**Hindley:** No.

**DCI McGuinness:** Did you move your room on 14 October 1973?

**Hindley:** I moved from my room but I don't remember the exact date

**DCI McGuiness:** Did you move your room at your own request?

**Hindley:** Yes.

**DCI McGuinness:** Did Miss Cairns take photographs of you in the chapel wearing wigs?

**Hindley:** No. Miss Cairns has never taken photographs of me. Maxine takes them in my cell. Certainly never with a wig and those photographs were for Miss Cairns' personal use.

**DCI McGuinness:** Can you remember the first of November this year? The events?

**Hindley:** No.

**DCI McGuinness:** On 1 November 1973 did Maxine Croft tell you the key impressions had been found by police?

**Hindley:** I have never discussed key impressions with Maxine Croft. I don't know anything about key impressions.

**DCI McGuinness:** Did Croft tell you there were notes with the impressions written by Miss Cairns?

**Hindley:** She did not. I have never discussed anything of that nature with her.

**DCI McGuinness:** Did you tell Croft she could not say anything about Miss Cairns because she, Croft, would not be believed?

**Hindley:** No.

**DCI McGuinness:** On the evening of 1 November 1973 did you destroy the letters you had received from Cairns and her photographs?

**Hindley:** No.

**DCI McGuinness:** Are you still in possession of the photographs of Miss Cairns?

**Hindley:** No.

**DCI McGuinness:** What happened to these photographs?

**Hindley:** I destroyed them.

**DCI McGuinness:** When did you destroy them?

**Hindley:** I destroyed them after a conversation that Miss Cairns and I had with Dr Bull which we requested.

**DCI McGuinness:** Why did you destroy them?

**Hindley:** I was very frightened and paranoid about everything and I just destroyed them.

**DCI McGuinness:** Why were you frightened?

**Hindley:** Because after Miss Cairns and I had seen Dr Bull together, several people had noticed that we had seen the governor together because there were rumours Myra Hindley and Miss Cairns were in Dr Bull's office and I got so frightened that people might find out about our relationship (by people I mean staff) and I was frightened that things would be found that would reveal our relationship and I destroyed them.

**DCI McGuinness:** I put it to you that you destroyed these letters and photographs on the 1 November 1973. That is some few days before your interview with Dr Bull.

**Hindley:** No it is not true

**DCI McGuinness:** Were you on 1 November 1973 sharing a cell with another person?

**Hindley:** Yes.

**DCI McGuinness:** Did Maxine Croft have the cell next door to you on that date?

**Hindley:** Yes.

**DCI McGuinness:** Did Maxine Croft have access to your cell?

**Hindley:** Yes.

**DCI McGuinness:** Did you know that on 1 November 1973 Patricia Cairns was on duty at Croydon Court?

**Hindley:** Dates mean nothing to me I'm sorry. I do not know whether she was on duty at Croydon Court or not.

**DCI McGuinness:** Did you ask Croft to get a message to Cairns at Croydon Court on 1 November about the discovery of the key impressions?

**Hindley:** No.

**DCI McGuinness:** Do you know a prison officer named Miss Longhurst?

**Hindley:** Yes.

**DCI McGuinness:** Did you give Miss Longhurst a written message to pass to Miss Cairns on the 1 November?

**Hindley:** I gave a written message to Miss Longhurst to give to a prison officer named Miss Harber to give to Miss Cairns.

**DCI McGuinness:** What was the content of that message?

**Hindley:** It was a message to Miss Cairns to say that I was very worried about Maxine because she had been acting strangely all day and I knew that she had had a day's parole and had met an ex-prison officer with whom she was very fond and had come back in a terribly upset state about having to come back to the prison and leave her, and the following night she had asked to go down to the hospital because of the way she was feeling and when she came up the next day I noticed she was acting in a very strange manner and wanted Miss Cairns to find out from Miss Summers. or rather to tell Miss Summers about this and whether she knew what was wrong.

**DCI McGuinness:** Did you tell Miss Longhurst that the message was really urgent?

**Hindley:** I asked her to give it to Miss Cairns as soon as possible.

**DCI McGuinness:** Did you later that day ask Miss Longhurst to phone Miss Cairns in case Miss Harber had not passed on the written message?

**Hindley:** No because I thought Miss Harber would pass on the written message.

**DCI McGuinness:** Did you know that Miss Cairns had met Croft outside the prison on the day of her parole?

**Hindley:** No. I knew she had met Miss Summers.

DCI McGuinness then asked Myra to confirm two exhibits that were her driving license applications and then that she had legally changed her surname to Spencer.

**DCI McGuinness:** This license was found in Miss Cairns' flat. Can you tell me how she came to have it?

**Hindley:** I handed it out on a visit with my mother and I think my sister was there I am not sure because I wanted Miss Cairns to keep it because we were going to live together when I got out of prison. That is when I was released.

**DCI McGuiness:** When do you expect to be released?

**Hindley:** I don't know.

**DCI McGuinness:** Do you expect to be released before the 8 February 1976, which is the date the license expires?

**Hindley:** I doubt it but I would have had the license renewed again as I had done three times in the past.

**DCI McGuiness:** Did you pass your previous driving licenses to Miss Cairns?

**Hindley:** No. This is my second driving license. My first one had been renewed by my solicitor at my request, and at the time it was due to be renewed this last time the original license was filled up and I had to have a new license which was renewed to coincide with the change of my surname and had to be sent in here to me for my new signature and I decided that instead of returning it to the solicitor I would like Miss Cairns to have it and renew it for me next time. This was the first time I had had a driving license sent into prison.

**DCI McGuinness:** Miss Cairns has admitted to planning your escape from prison. Can you think of any reason why she would plan your escape?

**Hindley:** I had no idea she was planning my escape.

**DCI McGuinness:** Do you think it would be possible for her to make the plans she did without you knowing about it?

**Hindley:** I didn't know anything about it.

**DCI McGuinness:** Maxine Croft also admits making plans with Miss Cairns for your escape. Can you give me any reason why she made these plans?

**Hindley:** I had no idea she had made these plans.

Fingerprints, palm prints and handwriting samples were then taken from Myra and the interview concluded at 15.40. She was put on Rule 43 on 14 December and had new mug shots taken two weeks later.

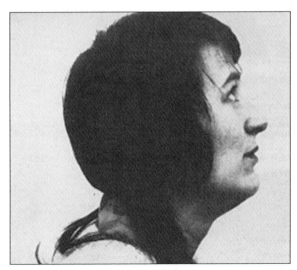

Myra Hindley mugshot.

On 17 January 1974, Myra and Maxine Croft were charged with 'conspiring with others' at Old Street Magistrates' Court and the case was remanded until 1 February.

At 10.10 on 1 February 1974 Patricia Cairns appeared at Old Street Magistrates' Court on a charge of:

> Within the Greater London area on divers date between 1 January 1973 and 5 November 1973, did conspire together and with persons unknown to affect the escape of the said, Myra Hindley, a prisoner lawfully in custody at HM Prison Holloway, Parkhurst Road, London, N7. Contrary to Common Law.

All three were committed for trial to the Central Criminal Court. Bail for Cairns was continued in her own recognisance of £1,000, with two sureties of £1,000.

Those representing Cairns and Croft were not able to indicate definitely whether or not their clients would plead guilty. Counsel for Myra had wished to make a submission that there was insufficient evidence to justify committal but was instructed to agree to a Section 1 committal.

Myra had instructed her counsel that she did not wish the jury in the upcoming case to have knowledge of her previous conviction. It was suggested that 'Counsel could consider with Defence Counsel whether the fact that Hindley was lawfully in custody could be proved in some other way.'

On 14 February, Heather Sanders, a former Prison Officer with Pat Cairns when they were both at Bulwood Hall Borstal, stated that at 13.00 she was in Oxford Street near the junction of Davies Street when she saw Cairns standing by the street barrier handing out pamphlets. She recognised Cairns and almost spoke to her but stopped herself as she was aware of the trouble that Cairns was in, but that Cairns saw her and recognised her. Cairns walked off across Oxford Street. A friend who was with Mrs Sanders went after Cairns in an effort to obtain a pamphlet but was unable to do so.

The exhibits, including the clock (top right).

Mrs Sanders stated that the pamphlets Cairns was distributing, although upside down to her, appeared to have two pictures of men on it. She said the pamphlet appeared to be identical with some shown to her several weeks ago. It is believed that the pamphlets referred to the wrongful imprisonment of members of the IRA, and as a serving member of prison staff, she should have stayed neutral in her public beliefs.

As Cairns was still a Prison Officer, although suspended, the matter was investigated because it was possible she may have committed an offence against the Prison Discipline Code.

Three days later Myra was taken off Rule 43 at HMP Holloway.

On 1 April the trial began, and Hindley appeared in the dock at The Old Bailey. The evidence was presented in court and Maxine Croft's defence was that she was in the weakest position of the three and had a fear of offending anyone in authority at the prison in case it affected her parole. The court was told how Pat Ali had previously lost remission for making a complaint against Myra Hindley and Pat Cairns.

Maxine's defence lawyer pointed out that Hindley was a woman who could persuade those about her that she was a reformed character. 'She has persuaded some of the highest in the land that she is a reformed character who merits special consideration. Such is the woman who brought Croft into her thrall.'

Mr Aubrey Myerson, Cairns' defence counsel, objected to the Judge, Mr Justice Melford Stevenson, describing the relationship as 'a close lesbian association':

> The relationship was not physical in any sense whatever. It was a bond based on mutual respect and admiration for the Roman Catholic religion they shared. It had developed because they found there was an affinity which emerged from matters of mutual interest, in that they came from the same area of Manchester, had the same kind of upbringing and both felt exceedingly strongly about their religion.

In her statement to police, Pat Cairns had said it was due to her influence that Myra had made a confession to the prison chaplain, and had regularly taken communion. She said she had become distressed at seeing how prison was becoming too much for Myra, and had promised to do all in her power to help her. She said she was only aware of 'the ends and not the means' of the escape plot. 'Our emotions are sometimes too strong for our judgement', she said.

She also said that she thought Myra's case was 'a political hot potato', and that no government would risk the criticism they would get for releasing her, adding: 'I believe suffering can be atoned for and purified in the crucible of suffering.' The 'crucible of suffering' was one of Myra Hindley's favourite themes, it cropped up repeatedly in her correspondence.

Lord Longford gave evidence on Myra's behalf, denying that he was in her thrall by pointing out that he had seen her only four times a year in the past five years, with the Governor present each time, and that her letters to him had passed through the prison censor. He said:

I offer my own strong opinion that she is not a bad woman, but a woman with much good in her, making a determined effort to make amends for her past and to do good in the future.

Only the almighty can tell us whether to try to escape when there is no hope of being let out is a sin, although it is illegal and wrong. This woman has suffered, and she is anxious to do what she can to atone.

Myra described her feelings for Cairns in a statement read to the jury:

Patricia has transformed my life completely. She has changed a barely tolerable existence into a life full of meaning and aspiration…

She awakened the beautiful things in my soul. Without Patricia I should have despaired…

I knew she had spent five years as a Carmelite nun, and it was due to her encouragement that I took my first confessions in twelve years.

I have stepped into an endless black tunnel. There was no light, just interminable darkness.

Later, I could see a tiny light called hope which sustained the remainder of me…

There are things of which I am guilty and of which I am deeply, bitterly ashamed. I have caused suffering by my sins, but I have suffered too. Both for the suffering I have caused and the suffering I have inflicted upon others I am sorry.

I believe sin can be atoned for and purified in the crucible of suffering.

Cairns' police statement of 20 November was also read out to the court.

I have known Myra Hindley for more than four years. She has already spent over eight years in prison without even a glimmer of light at the end of the long tunnel leading to freedom.

We have been speaking of the day she is released and I have promised to do all in my power to help her faith.

We were drawn together by the fact we are the same age, she comes from the same part of Manchester as I do, and we share the same deep love for the Roman Catholic faith.

I tried to be a source of consolation and encouragement for her.

Just being Myra Hindley is penance enough without the long years and rigours in prison.

Cairns' counsel Mr Aubrey Myerson QC, summed up her state of mind over Myra by saying:

She was living in a cloud-capped tower because she was unable to exercise the objectivity she should have shown.

119

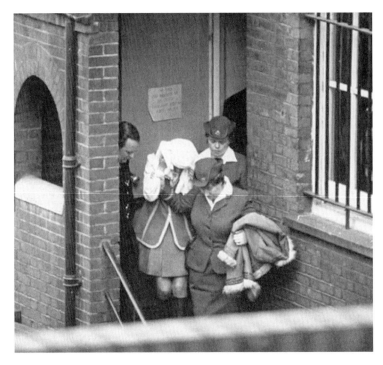

Myra leaving
prison.

Maxine Croft was sentenced to eighteen months' imprisonment, with the Judge saying:

> You were undoubtedly the victim of a very wicked woman who practiced
> upon you blackmail, and took advantage of her position to make you do
> things I do not think you would have done left on your own.
>     A little courage would have got you out of your difficulties.

She was sent not to Holloway but to another prison, and within three weeks of the trial her appeal was heard. Evidence about how Pat Ali had been treated when trying to inform about Myra and Pat Cairns was heard, and Maxine was freed immediately. She had served six months, waiting for the trial and the appeal.

However, her dealings with Myra Hindley were not over. The following New Year's Eve, in The Black Cap pub, a well known cabaret bar in Camden Town, Maxine had the misfortune to run into two of Myra's old friends from Holloway. They took her into the toilets and beat her up.

Pat Cairns was given a six-year jail sentence. The Judge said:

> The most sinister feature of this case is that you exercised pressure of
> a sinister kind on an inmate of the prison. I can find no extenuating
> circumstances to explain your conduct. You have not improved your
> position by putting forward a façade of piety which proved to be very
> brittle.

She was sent to Durham Jail, and later transferred to Styal, in Cheshire. At Styal she served much of her time in the punishment block, Bleak House, in rigorous conditions. When jobs were handed out, hers were always the worst. But she survived and found herself another close girlfriend.

When she finished her sentence – she got full remission – she moved back to the Manchester area, where her family lived. They had stood by her and remained close to her through her time in jail. She found a job as a bus driver for Manchester City Council and lived with another woman – coincidentally, just a couple of hundred yards from the cemetery where John Kilbride is buried.

The Judge sentenced Hindley to an extra twelve months, to be served consecutively to her other sentences. He said:

> You are already the subject of a life sentence and very properly so. This is a temperate sentence in regard to the gravity of the conspiracy. I pass it with the intention and hope that if in the future – and I think it should be a remote event – parole should ever be considered then the activities which led to this case will be recorded and remembered.

Hindley was sent back to HMP Holloway.

Hindley sent illicit love letters to Pat Cairns, using prisoners travelling between Holloway and Styal as carriers. Cairns recalled: 'She did send me letters, got them smuggled through. I read them then destroyed them straight away. It was dangerous though, and we used a code right from the start.' Cairns was apparently unhappy at this arrangement as she didn't want to get anyone in trouble if they were caught, so she sent a verbal message to Hindley via a prisoner on her way to Holloway saying that if Myra sent her one more letter then she would tell the Governor.

Hindley responded by sending another letter, and Cairns stuck to her promise and sent it to her Governor. Now an inmate, Cairns was greatly picked on. She had no friends or protection from anyone. The prison officers hated her for having a relationship with

Patricia Cairns.

121

Hindley and for trying to break an inmate out, and the inmates hated her for being a former Prisoner Officer. The abuse and treatment got so bad for her that she eventually went into isolation.

Prison officers in HMP Holloway were now always shouting at Hindley and she was under threat from attack from some of the other prisoners. When she didn't get her way over something, she would throw a tantrum and the officers would lock her in her cell until she had cooled off.

By now, Hindley had rediscovered her love of children, and in particular her niece, Sharon. She would go into the prison's Mother & Baby Unit and make a fuss of the babies and some of the mothers actually said that they would like her to be their baby's godmother if she ever managed to be released.

She would spend a lot of her time working on her tapestry, attending church and working on her courses. She would also read a lot, write letters and listen to music. She loved watching comedy programmes on TV, but would rarely watch it in the TV room unless she had a trusted friend with her for fear of attack. She would also blow all her prison wages on tobacco.

Her humour could also get dark at times. She was seen looking through a newspaper one day and commented: 'Can you imagine it? They're at it again. 'The Moors Murderess.' I don't remember ever murdering a moor.'

# 7

# Hindley's Prison Years 1974–1985

On 15 April 1974, Hindley wrote a petition to her Governor regarding the behaviour of a fellow prisoner who had been 'a source of harassment and provocation to me'. She told her Governor that the abuse had started since she had been moved to 'F' Wing five weeks earlier and that the woman had tried to incite others to join her cause. She told how one evening the inmates on the wing were in the TV room watching the film *Love Story* when this woman shouted abuse to her.

A prison officer on the wing then told of an occasion when she was locking the inmates in their cells for the night and got to Hindley's room, Hindley seemed upset and so the prison officer asked what was wrong. Hindley replied to her: 'If that XXXXX makes another crack to me I will kill her!'

Hindley was receiving more abuse than she had for a while from other inmates and found that some of the prison staff were also less sympathetic towards her since Pat Cairns had been sent to prison. Things were not helped when she was handed eleven photographs back from the police that they had been using for evidence.

The following month, May, she wrote to Lord Longford about her attempted escape from prison:

> I have forfeited every right to be trusted in here and I am not trusted an inch. Looking at this objectively, on the whole I agree, but with several reservations. An indisputable fact is that I have betrayed the trust which the Governor had in me and nothing I can say or do can alter this fact, nor can I ever really make amends.

She had also started to write to the former film censor, John Trevelyan, and told him how depressed she felt:

> I lie down and close my eyes, but it is worse still. The thought of the mechanical succession of day following day ad infinitum is one of the things that makes my heart palpitate, the real approach of madness. The terrible bondage of the tik-tok of time, this twitching hand of the clock, this endless repetition of hours and days and years. Oh God, it's too awful to contemplate. But there is no escape. No escape.

She told him a few months later that she was losing the will to live and was starting to feel that she would never be released, 'or if so, not until I'm quite old. I feel tortured with grief and remorse about the disaster I have caused others and I can hardly live with myself.' She also told him that she wanted to have children before she reached 40 years of age.

It was also noted in July 1974 that Hindley was writing to other people and asking them to send messages from her to Patricia Cairns. A brief note in Hindley's prison files state that, 'The governor of Styal confirms that John Trevelyan wrote to Patricia Cairns a letter which included a message from Myra Hindley. This letter was not issued.'

She was then caught, in September, trying to smuggle a letter out of prison to Kenneth Norman, who was a trustee of the Portia Trust, a charity that helped female offenders. He had written four times to Hindley and was told by the Home Office that she did not wish to reply to him, but Hindley tried to smuggle the letter out of prison with a woman who was leaving. Hindley was reprimanded but not punished.

The letter showed that she was still very much in love with Pat Cairns and that she had made a statement to the Parole Board saying that she did not wish to be considered for parole in October when she was up for automatic review. She told how she felt guilty for Cairns' imprisonment and that when they discussed her breaking out from prison, she had told Cairns: 'You would have to give up all else. I alone would need to be your sole and exclusive standard. Your motivation would even then be long and exhausting. The whole past theory of your life and all conformity to those around you would have to be abandoned.' This sounds exactly like what happened to her at the hands of Ian Brady.

It didn't take long for Hindley to get back into the swing of prison life. A new inmate called Vicky had been sentenced, along with her mother, for taking part in a conspiracy to import drugs. She was young, pretty and recently married. She was determined to have nothing to do with Hindley, but she was gradually won over.

> She made the first move, but not for a couple of weeks. That was enough to change my mind about her. We got into the habit of going back to my cell or her cell in the evenings. Then one night she bent over and kissed me. I thought it was very pleasant. We talked a lot and I gradually found I fancied her.

Vicky said she then fell in love with Hindley and they spent every available moment together, under the bed in Hindley's cell, with her bedspread draped low to the floor. A friend would keep watch on the landing and warn when any officers were approaching.

Hindley wrote poems for her and decorated them with drawings of butterflies and flowers, but after three and a half months together, the authorities got wind of the relationship between the two, and Vicky was sent to HMP Styal. She was so desperate not to go that she persuaded two friends to dislocate her shoulder, believing that she would then have to be kept in the prison hospital at Holloway, but she was moved, nonetheless.

A prison note, dated 31 October 1974, stated that Hindley was petitioning to be allowed to correspond with Patricia Cairns. She stated that her complete severance from Patricia Cairns 'is almost more than she can bear', and stated that because of the moral responsibility she felt about Cairns' involvement, 'she is forfeiting the privilege of being interviewed by either the 'Parole or Lifers Board'… She asks to be allowed to correspond with Cairns or to be transferred to Styal to serve her sentence with her.'

Hindley continued to try to contact Patricia Cairns legally and had petitioned in April and September of 1974 to be allowed to do so. She petitioned for a third time in April 1975 and stated:

> It is now almost a year since the trial and it hasn't been a good year for either of us. Even a limited correspondence would be a great consolation. The future holds very little hope of anything, even after ten years in prison. Please give me a little hope to cling on to and grant this petition. It would mean so much to both of us.

It had been noted that on the second occasion that Hindley had petitioned, in September 1974, that:

> I would say the effect on staff morale + indeed on personal morale, + also on public opinion, + perhaps that of the police too would be such that this correspondence should never be allowed. These two women have not been helpful to each other.

It was also noted that Patricia Cairns 'continued subversive and manipulative behaviour' in prison and that it should add weight to the decision not to allow them to correspond.

Hindley's manipulative behaviour was soon in evidence again as her driver's licence was coming up for renewal and she requested a meeting with the Prison Governor. They noted her behaviour:

a) She requested an interview in which she said that she had previously in 1968 been given permission to change her name twice. Since her driving licence was about to expire she wished now to change her name, asked whether she could see her solicitor for this purpose and whether I would witness the declaration as Mrs Wing had done. I immediately questioned the second change of name but she assured me with confidence that I would find the relevant papers in my safe. I accepted this and informed the Wing S/O that she could write to her solicitor. There was some urgency about the matter because of the driving licence renewal date. When I returned from leave and it had been established that no document could be found in her record and that Head Office could not confirm any former permission for a second change of name I saw her again. I believed she had deliberately misled me. She absolutely denied this and insisted that I had misunderstood. Mrs Wing had formerly obtained permission for a name change without her having to petition. She had merely asked me if she could change her name again and presumed it could be done in the same way.

b) Once she knew she would have to petition she simply had her licence renewed in the former name and no formal application was made.

125

c) I told her that there was now a document available to me that indicated she had in 1968 been given permission to change her name to a certain name which was specified. She absolutely denied that any name other than Myra Spencer had ever been part of the transaction.

d) The only document relating which we hold is that which gives permission to change her name and instructs us to notify Scotland Yard. There is no record that this was done. Her Driving Licence and, I recall, the actual declaration of the name change were in the hands of the police at the time of the 1974 trial and I assume they were also in communication with Scotland Yard, and certainly no discrepancy was mentioned at the time.

The document in question had recorded that in 1968 Hindley had changed her name to Claire Stewart, and not Myra Spencer as was on her driver's licence and subsequent paperwork. The document stated:

> It is therefore of concern that a discrepancy now exists in that the change of name recorded at Holloway (1968), as entered on the original driving licence application form, as also entered on the form for renewal of driving licence (signature undated but forwarded to solicitor Mr P. Donnelly and dated 12/2/76) and as recorded in the court proceedings (vice case of P Cairns) of 1974 was that of <u>Myra Spencer</u> and not Claire Stewart as originally notified in 1968.

In the meantime, Hindley was unhappy that her family were struggling to afford to visit her and asked for financial assistance. As her mother and Maureen did not qualify for DHSS-assisted visits, the Probation Department in Manchester were unable to resolve the problem. It was also noted that Hindley's stepfather had stated his reluctance to finance his wife's visits, but that there was provision in Standing Orders for the transfer of long-term inmates to a local prison for accumulated visits. There was no local prison for female offenders in the north of the country, but it was noted that it was feasible in principle to accommodate a prisoner, temporarily, at Risley Remand Centre.

The report noted that provided there was no extra cost involved, it could be possible to transfer her to Risley with the weekly escort en route to Styal prison, and arrange the return escort in similar manner a week or fortnight later. The arrangement would relate to an accumulation of up to twelve visits, meaning that Myra would have to wait six to nine months between visits.

The critical feature, according to the report, was 'that of notoriety and northern reaction should any publicity occur', but concluded on the point that 'from a control and security angle it is considered that a temporary change of location and environment would have practical advantages, particularly in view of recent investigations into the current practice and behaviour of this prisoner at Holloway.'

By March it was recorded again in her prison file that she caused trouble for herself and others by asking fellow inmates to carry letters for her. She looked: 'thin and haggard. On rare occasions she chooses to talk about the past, but there is absolutely nothing new to report on her revelations about her offences and there probably never will be.'

Of the letters she had asked people to carry illegally for her it was noted:

> her activities on her Wing have caused her to be constantly under suspicion of devious and untrustworthy behaviour. I had frequently warned her of the risk to which she subjected the people whom she solicited to carry letters to Patricia Cairns, but she always denied doing so. When I had to tell her that Pat Cairns requested that she stopped writing to her illegally, Myra was extremely upset, to the extent of being ill for several days.

Lord Longford was still championing Myra to anyone who would listen and on 26 May 1976, he wrote to Sir Louis Petch, Chairman of the Parole Board, about possible careers for Myra if she were released from prison. He wrote:

> When I wrote to you last, I was under the impression that when Myra was free to work outside prison, she could be sure of full time work in tapestry with a firm for whom she has already done a great deal of work in prison. It now appears that in present circumstances (or any that are likely to prevail when she obtains parole), there would be no question of full-time work, although they genuinely value her level of performances and would no doubt quite often make use of her services.
>
> This might be disappointing for her, but personally I think that she would probably be better in a secretarial job for which she is well-equipped (and where, I am sure, it will not be difficult for her to obtain work) than in some rather isolated work on tapestry.
>
> I repeat my own conviction that whether through some religious agency or otherwise, it would certainly not be difficult in these days for an efficient secretary like her to get work in that capacity.

On 26 September Hindley was violently attacked by 19-year-old inmate Josie O'Dwyer. She had been in and out of prison most of her life and had made friends with the notorious child murderer Mary Bell, but she hated Hindley. She had a violent temper and could switch her mood in an instant.

On the morning of the attack the Sunday newspapers arrived and the *News of The World* was carrying a piece regarding the Moors Murders and a short transcript of the Lesley Ann Downey tape.

At 09.00 the Deputy Governor took the precaution of interviewing Myra, informing her of the article and discussing with her the possible effect which such an article might have within the wing. Myra, according to her own written statement, although very upset by the renewed publicity, chose to regard it in the same way as previous press articles and, while recognising that it would arouse an initial hostile reaction from some of the prisoners, she hoped that it would quickly die down as had reaction following earlier, similar, publications.

O'Dwyer later claimed that she knew nothing about the Moors Murders case as she was just a child at the time, but that morning two prison officers sat her down and showed her the newspaper. She recalled how it made her 'shake and tremble with horror' and the officers took her for a walk around the prison grounds to calm down.

Josie O'Dwyer.

When she got back on the wing, Janie Jones recalled that O'Dwyer could be heard shouting: 'I'm going to fucking kill that bastard Hindley!'

Hindley was afraid for her safety following the article, so she had asked to be allowed to stay in Janie Jones' cell. She stated a fear of being on her own because, 'I'm so uptight I'm going to freak out'. She was instructed to return to her own room – this she failed to do. She asked for a decision from the duty Governor and was told that her request would be sent. Instead of going back to her own cell as instructed, she went to Jones' cell to await the decision. She grew annoyed at how long the decision was taking and so went along the recess towards the Prison Office, and that's when O'Dwyer jumped her.

O'Dwyer saw Myra and called her a 'child murdering bastard', to which Myra looked at her, kissed her teeth at her, and told her to 'Shut your bloodclart and mind your own business.' O'Dwyer: 'I said to her "You don't talk to me like that, you cunt!" She said something else to me but I don't remember what it was. It was then that I lost my temper and hit her.' She grabbed Myra's hair in one hand and punched her in the face with the other. As Myra fell to the floor, O'Dwyer kicked her repeatedly in the face with her Doc Martin boots until she was unable to offer any resistance. She continued shouting 'You bastard of a child killer', and 'Cry for mercy you bastard like those little children did.'

O'Dwyer then picked her up and tried to push her over the railings to the floor below. Janie Jones recalled:

> There was blood everywhere and I rushed to try to stop the girl. Yet there was not a sound from Myra.
>
> Myra did nothing. Absolutely nothing. Her blood was squirting all over the place, she was being kicked and punched senseless, but she simply swayed around limply as she took every blow … She didn't lift a finger to help herself.

O'Dwyer described the attack as, 'like hitting a dead animal. She didn't struggle, she didn't cry out, not until I tried to hoist her over the rail. Then she just clung on. She was afraid of dying, but not afraid of being beaten up.'

The alarm bell had been pressed and other prison officers rushed in to separate the two. O'Dwyer was taken down to the punishment cells, while Myra had suffered a broken nose (which had to be reset), a split lip and ear, two black eyes, her front teeth were loosened and the cartilage in her knee was torn and required surgery. She spent the next six weeks in the prison hospital.

She later wrote to Jones (after Jones' release) mentioning O'Dwyer:

> I have to forgive her (although I don't really, honestly believe I have, yet)
> if I want to be forgiven my sins, but I can't forget, and God forgive me, but
> I loathe her. I'd like to meet her – or I would, were I as violent and vicious
> as she is, or maybe was – and I'd give her something to be frightened of
> me for.

O'Dwyer was put into solitary confinement and lost 110 days remission, but the prison officers gave her tobacco, sugar, a radio and other 'perks'. She recalled: 'The officers treated me like a celebrity. It was: "Here's half an ounce of tobacco, Josie"; "Let me shake your hand"; "Well done, Josie, I've waited twelve years for someone to do that" etc.'

To her supporters, Myra told them that she asked the authorities for clemency for her attacker, on the grounds that it was her religious principle to turn the other cheek. To others she was swearing vengeance. But seven years after the attack, in 1983, she was asking Carole Callaghan and a friend of hers to 'find that cow and break her arms and legs'.

Following the attack, Myra had two dizzy spells and blackouts and a Consultant Neurologist was called to check her over as they were worried it may have been a delayed concussion.

She fell again, on the 1 October, but didn't suffer a dizzy spell beforehand, and as such she fell face first in her cell, breaking her nose. The officer who found her stated that: 'On opening the door I found her with a blood-stained towel around her face … She had also vomited on the mat.'

On the 20 October, *The Manchester Evening News* reported the attack on Myra. It quoted her sister, Maureen, as saying:

> The attack lasted three minutes and although Myra was screaming while
> this woman kicked her nobody came to help her. Although she has been
> treated in prison she has not been X-rayed and she has a suspected
> fractured jaw and possibly brain damage. Apparently, there are problems
> about taking her out to a hospital where she could be X-rayed.

Myra hadn't been X-rayed yet because prison staff couldn't book her into any hospitals due to the attack being made public. Any attempt to take her to a hospital would have been met by the press and her identity would have been made public.

Myra was also telling anyone who would listen that prison officers were not on the scene of her attack for at least three minutes.

One of those told was Lord Longford. He telephoned the Deputy Governor at Holloway and told him rather aggressively that he was not satisfied that Myra was receiving the appropriate medical treatment. He was advised that the Senior Medical Officer had submitted a full medical report to the Home Office and that the Home Office would be replying to any queries raised. Lord Longford repeated that he was not satisfied, that he had been visited by Myra's sister who had advised him of 'the shocking state that Myra was in', and that if he failed to receive an early and satisfactory reply then legal action against the Home Office was being considered.

Maureen even wrote to the Secretary of State at the Home Office stating Myra's version of the attack and complaining that it took longer than had been recorded for prison officers to get to her and break up the attack. She then also asked for an independent enquiry to be set up into the attack.

Meanwhile, knowing that Myra could soon be transferred, reports were drawn up regarding her behaviour in prison. On the 3 November the Governor of HMP Holloway wrote a memo:

> Myra's behaviour has for a long time been superficially very good. She is polite and cooperative and avoids involvement in any incidents which might reflect badly on any consideration for her release. There is, however, no doubt that she manipulates her fellow-inmates and at every opportunity attempts to manipulate staff into believing that she is a martyred and innocent person. The following is a report submitted by the Principal Officer in charge of the wing where she is at present located.
>
> Myra, as we all know, is a woman who has been in custody for well over ten years. She has notoriety and reputation which in a vicarious way she enjoys. Myra was recently returned to this wing in a general move around or more properly 'a relocation to streamline the transition into the New Holloway', which is to take place early next year.
>
> In the upheaval Myra has been model and cooperative as always. She settled in her new/old surroundings quite well, resuming friendships with LTIs who belong in her accepted circle.
>
> Up to date she has not had the time or opportunity to collect around herself the usual couple or so sycophants who will do the cleaning, fetching and carrying she has become accustomed to.
>
> The assault which took place on the 26 September has rather demoralised her and with some justification she has been feeling very sorry for herself.
>
> Myra Hindley is an extremely difficult woman to assess and categorise. I cannot put one definite unfavourable point to her discredit.
>
> Myra has only been employed on light duties on the wing since the recent assault. The Senior Medical Officer has advised that she is unfit for her usual work in the tapestry room until she has been seen by the optician. Arrangements have been made for this.

It wasn't until the 23 November that the Governor of HMP Holloway was told that Myra needed an operation on her broken nose and damaged knee.

> It is anticipated that she will be there four to five days or less if possible. I have been reassured by both surgeons that they will do their utmost to return her to Holloway as soon as possible and that they will continue to see her post operatively at Holloway.
>
> She will be treated at the Royal Northern Hospital in a side ward on her own and her name will be known by these two surgeons only.

It was decided that both operations could be performed simultaneously and under the one dose of anaesthetic.

Myra's injuries were so bad that even in December she was writing to her mother and telling her not to let her niece, Sharon, visit her in case she was frightened by what she saw.

She was visited by Lord Longford and his wife, Lady Elizabeth Longford, who recorded that Myra was:

> Very slim, dressed in a long skirt and white blouse, her long brown hair loosely combed – very pale complexion and dark blue eyes – black lashes and regular eyebrows… The impression she now gives is of deep sadness. Her voice is low and rather husky…She showed us her bandaged and swollen leg and knee and the marks of her two black eyes were still visible…

Myra went into the Royal Northern Hospital on the 8 December for the operation on her damaged knee cartilage and broken nose under the alias of Myra Spencer. She was put into room 69 in St David's Wing on Trevor floor, a large single room on the second floor of the building at the end of a corridor containing private rooms.

Following the operations, she wrote to her mother and told her:

> The centre of my nose wasn't just knocked right, as it appeared to have been, but the whole nose was twisted in all directions. So the first surgeon put it back in the centre, then he took out 'the hump' (my request) which we all have (our family, I mean).

She was then returned to HMP Holloway at 16.30 on the 13 December.

The next update was given on 14 January 1977, when the Senior Medical Officer wrote that Myra was 'back walking relatively easily and was coping with the staircase … She looks well and appears to be eating as well as she ever has done … We see no reason why she should not be transferred.'

Myra got wind that a move was in the offing to HMP Durham and didn't want to go. Durham was one of the hardest prisons and a letter sent from HMP Holloway to Durham just before the transfer stated that 'She has threatened suicide by fasting, has permission to draft a will … She should be under close supervision.'

At 05.00 the following morning Myra was woken and had her belongings packed for her. She was escorted through the prison yard and put into a yellow unofficial-looking van, leaving at 05.30. Because of the huge security operation to move her safely, the only people who knew about the transfer were the Governors of both prisons and a few senior officers.

She wrote to her mother, Nellie, the following day and told her all about the move. She described HMP Durham as 'pure hell', and 'like something out of a science-fiction movie'. She reacted badly to being at Durham and ended up on Valium and other tranquilisers for her depression.

She was extremely unhappy to be transferred, but soon took a new, serious, lover – Dorothy, a married woman with children. When they were later discovered together,

Dorothy was transferred to Styal Prison. After the incident, no prisoner was allowed to close the door while another prisoner was in the cell.

As Myra was now at HMP Durham, they wanted their own mugshots of her.

Due to her eyes being closed her front-on photograph was retaken five days later.

Lord Longford visited Myra in HMP Durham on the 25 February and told her that he had recently seen Ian Brady and that he still wanted to make a statement about Myra's part in the original case. He told her that: 'there is a lot to his story which has never been said and which he should have said from the beginning.'

It's believed that Brady was seeking attention from the press and was prepared to give them another version of what happened regarding the Moors Murders, still exonerating Myra, but she was highly concerned that he could say something new

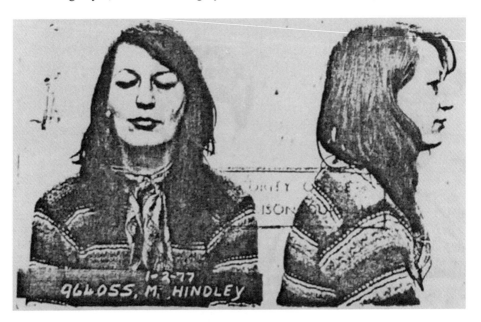

*Above*: Myra Hindley mugshot – 1st February 1977.

*Left*: Myra Hindley mugshot.

that would either implicate her accidentally, or give the police something to go on regarding more murders.

Myra wrote a couple of days later to Lord Longford and asked him:

> When you next visit Ian Brady, would you ask him if he is still prepared to make the statement he offered you last year? I would like you to ask him in exactly the same way you did then, that is, without my asking you to ask him, so to speak. Since you first mentioned the matter to me, and until fairly recently, I utterly rejected his offer, on the grounds that if he had contributed to my lingering in prison for 10 solid years before deciding to exonerate and exculpate me from the crimes for which I was convicted (I never <u>was</u> charged with what I am in fact guilty of, or should I say, in amendment, that I was correctly charged on one count), then I'd rather rot in prison for ever before I'd accept any intervention on his part. But I've reappraised the whole of my life from the time I met him and up to the present and reached a series of decisions. I don't want to talk of them yet; I'll do so eventually. So, please ask him without mentioning that I've mentioned it to you, and if he is still prepared to make a statement if you let me know, I'll instruct Peter Donnelly to visit him and take the statement. If the statement is what I suspect it may be, then it can be scrapped.

Myra was struggling to settle at Durham and felt that the other prisoners were victimising her. In May she told a Prison Officer that three inmates in particular were being 'awkward' with her. She told the officers that if she was beaten up again then she would take the matter to court. She was later found in her cell 'distressed', and Myra told the officers that an inmate had been making comments about her during the dinner patrol period. She told them that she 'cannot take much more of this sort of treatment', but stated that she wouldn't go on Rule 43 just to please others.

She needed another lover to help protect her from others in the prison and soon found a woman who was only in Durham for a short few months, but when she left she married a man, had a baby and asked Myra to be godmother.

She quickly moved on then to a Nigerian woman named Kate who was also serving a life sentence. They would hold hands around their wing, kiss and share showers.

She had other friends too, who were not lovers. They were known as 'Myra's minions' and were women who enjoyed the notoriety of being close to her. They cleaned her cell and filled her flask for her.

In April, a memo from the Home Office stated that Myra:

> is reported by two Governors (Holloway and Durham) to have the intelligence to manipulate and subvert both situations and individuals, without extending her communication into actual untruths, merely quietly and persistently pressing her case in a seductive and disarming manner, and leaving it to others to carry through the inappropriate and untoward activities.

It also stated that she was again 'pressing her attentions' upon Patricia Cairns in the form of 'illicit letters' and listed other attempts, which were continuing, as:

a)  To secure a further change of name while in prison (without making a formal application to the Governor on this matter – but arranging via her solicitor for this to be done on a driving license renewal application. The solicitor and Lord Longford maintain contact).

b)  There are numerous other 'outside' persons all with a shared concern to achieve the wish of Lord Longford, i.e. the release from prison of Myra Hindley.

c)  Related to the problems (above) is the constant uncertainty about other possible escape attempts which may be made, or may even be in process of planning, in accordance with the understandably increased level of frustration which will inevitably occur if and when the forthcoming review of this life sentence prisoner fails to produce the required decision.

d)  Myra has already been **officially warned against her mimicry of staff voices**, and discussion of the recognition of staff voices, for access to egress from the wing via the electronic unlocking system.

She was again upset by women on her wing and was found in a 'distressed' state in her room, telling prison officers that she couldn't take much more of the others' attitude towards her. Shortly afterwards she was placed on Rule 43.

When she went back on the wing she damaged her nose in her cell after a 'fall', but suspicions were that she was trying to get moved to the hospital wing and was self-harming. A report to the Governor stated that:

> I wish to inform you of my suspicions concerning possible self-inflicted injuries all sustained during the period 13–19 May ... Certainly the medical and nursing staff have been alerted and I asked Myra to demonstrate to me how she managed to bump her nose in her room on the 19 May ... Myra sat on the bed and demonstrated how this was done. I could see that if she indeed moved in the curious manner as demonstrated then she could have bumped her nose in this fashion, but I am not entirely satisfied with this explanation.

On the 6 July 1977 the TV programme *Brass Tacks* aired. It was a topical show and this week the subject was 'Should Myra Hindley Get Parole'. A phone-in formed part of the programme, together with a discussion by people directly or indirectly concerned with the issue of parole for life prisoners. The opponents of parole were Lesley Ann Downey's mother Ann West, Wyn Pilkington, who worked with the Murder Victims' Association, Joan Yonkers and Charles Oxley of the Victims of Law and Order and retired former detective DCS Arthur Benfield, who represented the police.

Those in favour of parole were Lord Longford, Sarah Trevelyan (daughter of Lord Trevelyan), Ian Fowler (a journalist from the *Manchester Evening News*), Maureen Scott, and Janie Jones, a 'vice queen' who had spent time in prison with Myra.

One of the callers to the programme was the father of John Kilbride. Lord Longford's team didn't take seriously his threat on air when he promised: 'I will kill Myra Hindley if she ever gets out!'

In the studio, Ann West asked:

> When does my parole begin? I am serving a life sentence because of that monster. I had to listen to those tapes of my daughter begging for mercy. If Myra Hindley comes out, I'll be up for murder. I've said this to Lord Longford once and I'll say it again: She will be one dead woman. I want justice.

Maureen was filmed in silhouette for the programme. She felt her own life to be in danger, not just because of the blood relationship with Myra, but because of lingering public feeling that her then husband, David Smith, was more deeply involved with Ian Brady and Myra Hindley than had emerged at the trial.

Lord Longford commented: 'No words are strong enough to denounce these appalling murders. We feel the deepest possible sympathy for Mrs West and for the families of the victims, not to mention the victims themselves.' Of Myra, he said: 'Whatever she has done she should be entitled to be considered for parole. Everyone should be considered after ten years.'

Soon after the program was aired the Home Affairs Minister, Mr Brynmor John, stated publicly that there would be no early release for Myra.

Ian Brady grew annoyed that Lord Longford was supporting Myra's bid for freedom. He had no intention of seeking freedom and felt that Myra should stay in prison too. He wrote to a prison visitor and told him that Lord Longford's visits to him were no longer welcome … 'the possibility of their serving any constructive purpose is negligible.'

Maureen Hindley (left) being interviewed. Lord Longford and Janie Jones in the background.

The following day, articles about the TV programme appeared in *The Daily Mirror* and *The Daily Express*. To protect Myra, both newspapers were withdrawn from circulation on her wing.

She wrote to her sister Maureen, upset at the diminishing prospect of parole and the effect of her notoriety on their mother Nellie:

> I often feel it would be better for her if I were dead, for although it would be terrible for her at first, eventually she would find peace of mind …
> I think Ann West, her natural grief curdled and made rancid by hatred and bitterness, perpetually robed in almost manic fanaticism, and my heart aches for her, about the state she's allowed herself to get into. But then I think of her constant harping about mothers and children, and think of my own mother, whom she never gives a thought to; my mother who is as innocent as that child was (whose innocence I was partly responsible for taking away, but whose life I was <u>not</u>) and some of her hatred and bitterness rubs off on me…

She then went on to make cruel and unsubstantiated claims about Lesley Ann's mother:

> To close the subject on her, what I told you about her was that while on remand, and after the committal, when, in court, she'd called me, among other things, a slut and a tramp, an old-time prostitute also on remand told me that it was like the kettle calling the pot black, or words to that effect, this woman had served at least a couple of sentences in Strangeways with her for prostitution. I've heard it several times before but thought it irrelevant under the circumstances.

Myra had grown tired of Lord Longford and when she was asked if she wanted to see him, she replied:

> Yes, to punch him in the face. I want a serious talk with him – he told me that he wouldn't take any more money but I read in the *Express* that he had been asked to give a talk on Radio Metro and he asked for £100 – When he was refused this amount he then asked for £75 plus his dinner. I want to know what he is doing.

She now believed that Lord Longford was doing her bid for freedom no favours by continually commenting on her plight at every given opportunity, and in conversations Myra stated: 'I'm going for a new image. I'm going to keep a low profile with no more publicity from the media and I'm going to try to do better with no more 'rewrites' or hassle. I will try to settle down here.'

A couple of days later she emerged with a much shorter hairstyle.

Myra booked for the Medical Officer to come out to see her and stated that she wanted to come off all Psychotropic drugs. She stated she did not want to become a 'hypochondriac' but would continue to need pain killers for headaches and her multivitamins.

She was seen by Lord Longford a few weeks later and he found her 'in low spirits'. He wrote to *The Times* newspaper: 'No one who knows her seriously supposes that she would be a public menace if she were released. Her state of remorse is such that she will be haunted by it all her life.'

To add to her depressed feelings, Myra was then informed that her aunt was very ill and couldn't write because she was now blind. Her aunt asked for the telephone message to be passed on to Myra because she didn't trust

Myra Hindley mugshot.

her family not to sell the information to journalist Ian McWilliam Fowler. She wasn't aware that Myra was also receiving visits from him.

On the 2 April 1978, a TV programme called *Weekend World* aired, which contained an interview with David Smith where he spoke about the time he talked with Ian Brady about possibly murdering Tony Latham. Myra's new solicitors (taken on due to her new location), Steggles Palmer, wrote to her and said:

> In my view David Smith went as far in the programme as to admit to a conspiracy to murder Latham. This being so I would expect the authorities to make a proper investigation. If this is not the case, then it is open to any other person to take proceedings against Smith by way of a private prosecution.

Two weeks later the solicitors wrote to Myra and were looking into raising a private prosecution against David Smith but were warned by Home Office officials that 'Miss Hindley would not be allowed to take a private prosecution and that if she suspected a criminal offence she should arrange for it to be reported to the police.'

Patricia Cairns was released from prison on the 17 May, having served four years and one week of her sentence. She immediately applied for permission to visit Myra but was denied by the Home Office.

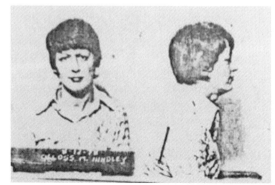

Myra Hindley mugshot – December 1978.

Myra was visited by her new solicitor, J. Morton, after Mr Donnelly left the practice, just before Christmas. It was again supervised and a report to the Governor stated:

> He made it quite clear that he thought Lord Longford did her more harm than good and asked her to ensure that the planned biography on Hindley by Lady Longford was discouraged.
>
> He told her to do everything in her power to help her prospects of parole, not to hinder them, by refusing to have review interviews as she told him she had in the past.
>
> He told her she must start getting together concrete ideas for when she was released for example offers of refuge and employment she had received from various people outside. One name mentioned in connection with this was John Trevelyan. He also informed her to deny any talk of her going to stay with Lord Longford.
>
> Throughout the visit he stressed the need for her name to stay out of the newspapers.

However, the following month, January 1979, Myra again made the news when she wrote a thirty-thousand-word document to the Home Secretary in which she protested her innocence and said she had little to do with the crimes she was convicted of. The newspapers got hold of a copy and printed it on the 26 January.

She wrote: 'To me they [the Moors] have represented nothing more than a beautiful and peaceful solitude which I cherish. Of the bodies and graves I know nothing.'

Her version of the murders was a rerun of the defence case at the trial, except that now she was acknowledging Brady's guilt: she knew nothing about John Kilbride's disappearance and death; she was present when Lesley Ann Downey was being photographed but the child left the house alive, it was only a handkerchief that she was telling the child to keep in her mouth; and when Edward Evans was killed she was in the kitchen where she claimed she had hidden because Brady and Evans were fighting. She made no reference to any other killings, and she renewed her assertions that Brady's partner in crime was David Smith, not her.

> I feel I have more than paid my debt to society and I feel that society owes me a living. Once I am released I have my own plans to begin a new life, so much so that society will not be admitting Myra Hindley into its ranks, either by name or reputation.

Her thoughts then turned to Brady:

> Although it may sound trite and dramatic, I fell hopelessly in love with Ian Brady practically from setting eyes upon him … I feel it is crucially important that the whole essence of such feelings and emotions is understood and appreciated fully for what it was, for it is this that is at the heart of the whole tragic case in which everything that transpired had its roots, and that these roots began their growth in virginal, vulnerable soil nourished,

as it were, by unassuaged grief and despair and the hopeless yearning of a young and inexperienced heart which was almost overwhelmed by the strength and fierceness of hitherto unknown emotions.

I had no sexual experience. I was still a virgin. I fell hopelessly in love with Ian Brady, practically from setting eyes on him. I now know I had confused love for infatuation – an infatuation which soon became an obsession. He became my god, my idol, my object of worship. He could have told me that the earth was flat, that the moon was made of green cheese, that the sun rose in the west and I would have believed him. Such were the powers of his persuasion, his softly convincing means of speech which fascinated me, because I could never fully comprehend, only browse at the odd sentence here and there, believing it to be gospel truth.

She also said:

I knew nothing about Ian going to homosexual clubs until it came up at the trial. I was absolutely stunned. Looking back, I think it's feasible that there was something going on between him and David [Smith]. They were always together, the pair of them, plotting and planning things.

She admitted that she knew they were talking about murders, but:

I thought it was only talk, after they'd had a few drinks. I never imagined it would actually happen … In retrospect, I think it's possible that Ian had it off with Edward Evans.

On the 24 January 1979, The Secretary of State, Mr Merlyn Rees, told the House of Commons of the decision to keep Ian Brady and Myra Hindley in prison:

Ian Brady and Myra Hindley were sentenced to life imprisonment for murder. Prisoners serving life sentences are not eligible for parole as such but may be released on license when the Home Secretary considers this to be justified. I cannot, however, order the release of such a prisoner unless I am recommended to do so by the Parole Board and after consulting the Lord Chief Justice and, if he is available, the trial judge.

There is no fixed time at which the case of a life sentence prisoner must be formally reviewed by the Parole Board. That is a matter for the Home Secretary. But the timing of the first formal review is fixed in consultation with the board, through a joint committee of representatives of the board and of the Home Office. This committee recently considered the cases of Brady and Hindley. The committee felt unable to recommend a date for a formal review, but recommended that it should consider the cases again in three years' time. I have decided to accept this recommendation.

Final decisions on all matters relating to the release of life sentence prisoners rest with the Home Secretary of the day. He is not bound to accept a recommendation by the joint committee. Nor is he bound to accept a recommendation by the Parole Board that a prisoner should be released. I cannot bind my successors, but for my part I have reached no view about the time in the future when serious consideration might be given to the release of either prisoner. My present decision means that, unless there is some unforeseen development which would justify a different course, nothing will be done to initiate the formal review machinery for at least the next three years.

In early March there was talk of Myra moving to an open prison but, because of both her notoriety and her failed escape attempt, an internal Home Office memo stated:

> Location in an open prison, where there is no perimeter security, is appropriate to those prisoners for whom the risk of absconding is considered minimal; or, if they abscond, would not by the nature of their offences present a threat or an affront to public feeling. In the case of women who are serving long term or life sentences, it is generally considered appropriate for a move to open prison to take place in the latter part of the sentence – in the case of life sentence prisoners, when the case has been favourably considered by the Home Office Life Sentence Board.
>
> Public opinion must play a great part in this; Miss Hindley is a notorious prisoner, convicted of a crime which is still in the minds of the public, and her allocation to open prison would be seen as a clear indication that she is trusted by Ministers not to run away, and that she would not be thought a danger if she did. It is difficult to accept either of these propositions – a life prisoner who has just been told she is not being considered for release is unlikely to opt to stay voluntarily in an open prison.

Just a few weeks later Myra was also informed via a telephone message from Maureen that their 18-year-old cousin had been involved in a motorcycle accident and had passed away.

On 11 September, Myra got herself a new solicitor, Mike Fisher, who she believed could finally get her released from prison. Myra graduated with a BA Humanities degree, in the Arts Faculty of the Open University on the 15 January 1980. She was back in her routine of study, pleading her innocence and taking lovers. By May it was reported that she was in a relationship with an inmate and university colleague called Shing 'May' Wong, who was serving a fourteen-year sentence for smuggling Heroin.

All was going well for Myra but then disaster struck. On the 8 July 1980, Maureen and her husband Bill were having an evening out in the Golden Tavern pub, near to where they were living on Rochdale Road, Manchester, when Maureen complained of a headache. Bill said: 'I said we would go home but she said she was all right. The next morning when I woke up she was spewing her heart out. I called the doctor and he said it was probably just 'flu. But when he came he took one look at her and had her rushed into Hospital.'

Maureen was transferred that same day to Crumpsall Hospital, where a brain haemorrhage was diagnosed. She was operated on, and started to recover well; so well that she was due to go home from hospital. Bill: 'But I got a phone call saying she'd had a relapse. So I rushed down there and stayed with her. She was in a coma and the doctors were rushing around with lots of gadgets.'

Ian McWilliam Fowler, a reporter known to Myra and her family, found David Smith and told him that Maureen was in a bad way and that it was unlikely that she would survive. John and Jody were too young to understand, so they were left with a neighbour, while 13-year-old Paul and 12-year-old David changed into their best clothes and were taken to the hospital by Fowler. The reporter told them he knew Maureen and Bill very well and that he visited Myra regularly in prison, and that it had been Bill who had asked him to tell David about Maureen (which was true).

Ian Fowler contacted the prison chaplain at HMP Holloway to say that Myra's sister had been taken to hospital with a brain haemorrhage and was on life support. Myra made a formal application to visit her.

At 09.10 the following morning confirmation was sought from Manchester police that the position regarding Maureen's condition was unchanged and that her family had spent the night at her bedside.

At 11.50 permission was given for Myra to leave the prison under a two-officer escort (in civilian clothes), and the police were notified.

She left the prison at 14.00 but Bill had telephoned the prison to say that Maureen had passed away at 16.05 – while Myra was en route. He had switched her life-support machine off because no one had told him that Myra was on her way.

Myra returned to the prison at 20.00 that night. There was no publicity and no incidents. She had been able to see her sister's body and spend time with her brother-in-law and a neighbour.

She wrote to her mother a few days later: 'It's the worst pain I've ever felt … but it must be worse for you.' She then questioned her faith but concluded: 'If we have no faith in God, how can we take comfort knowing that Maureen is in heaven with God?'

She wrote to a friend saying: 'When I gently kissed my love, my dove, my beautiful one on the forehead, a feather-light touch of my lips, she seemed to sigh, as much as to say "I've been waiting for you, you're here now and I can go now."'

Nellie and Maureen.

Maureen's funeral was held at Moston Crematorium in Blackley, Manchester, on the 15 July 1980. Rumour had it that Myra would be attending and so some members of the families affected by Ian Brady and Myra Hindley decided that it would be their best opportunity to exact revenge on her. Little did they know that Myra had already chosen not to attend. She wrote a letter to the Prison Governor saying:

> I have been asked if I wish to attend the funeral of my sister, Maureen. I wish to state that I do not want to be there. I do want to attend the funeral and share my family's sorrow, but I feel I would only add to it if the press or other media are present, which I'm sure they will be. So I have decided not to ask to go for that reason only – to protect my family and my sister's dignity.

Lesley Ann Downey's mother arrived early, shortly followed by John Kilbride's father. Security was tight and there were officers in plain clothes looking out for anyone who was likely to cause trouble. One woman arriving in one of the funeral cars had a large, blonde hairstyle; no one knew that Myra had changed her hair colour and style, and so believed this woman was Myra.

As the funeral went on, Lesley Ann's mother walked around the side of the church and found the wreaths that had been sent. One of these wreaths said: 'To my beloved sister, there are no words to express how I miss you. I love you – Myra.' She vented all her anger on the wreaths and destroyed them completely.

As the funeral service ended and the mourners began to leave, Ann was pinned up against the side of the church by the plain clothes police officers who found her destroying the wreaths, just as she was reaching in her bag for an aerosol can.

John Kilbride's father, however, had managed to break through and launched himself at the blonde woman who he had seen going into the church earlier, believing that she

was Myra. Thankfully, just before he got to her a plain clothes police officer tackled him. The blonde woman was in fact Bill Scott's daughter, Ann Wallace. 'You would have thought she could have had a decent funeral. After all, as I keep saying, it wasn't as though she did anything wrong,' said Bill.

David Smith didn't attend the funeral and nor did the three boys. They had no further communication with Bill Scott

Patrick Kilbride attacks the woman he thought was Myra.

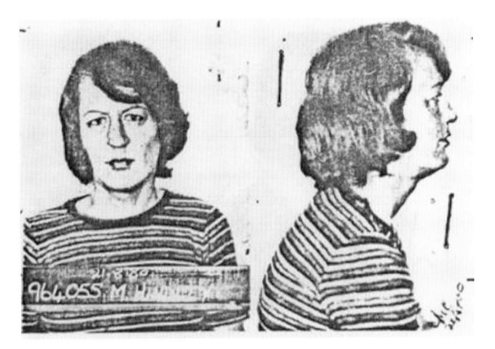

Myra Hindley mugshot - 21st August 1989.

and never met Sharon, Maureen's daughter. The pain was all too much for Lesley Ann's mother who took an overdose of the many tablets she was taking. Thankfully she survived.

On the 7 November, Myra's father, Bob Hindley, died from a heart attack. It had been Bill Scott's job to break the news of Maureen's death to Bob; the shock hit the 67-year-old hard, and his health had deteriorated rapidly. Bill hadn't been in the best of health either, suffering from a progressive spinal illness which made work impossible so he was able to spend time visiting Bob before he passed away.

> Mo and I had made promises to each other that whichever of us died first, the other would keep in touch with their family. So I still went round to see the old man, regular. I was with him the day before he died. I put him to bed that night. The next day when I went down there, I found he'd died.
>
> It was the best thing. He couldn't move about and he could hardly talk. And where he lived he was always being broken in to – the kids round about knew he couldn't do nothing to stop them. Some of them knew he was Myra's dad, so they used that as an excuse for doing it. He was better off out of it.

The cause of death was recorded as a heart attack, persistent vomiting, general debility and several previous strokes. He was cremated at Blackley Crematorium on the 11 November and again, Myra chose not to attend.

She was informed by her mother during a visit and took the news 'calmly; there has been no contact between father and daughter since shortly before her arrest some fourteen years ago when she left home following a family argument'.

On the 19 January 1981, Myra asked to be put on Rule 43. She stated that she could no longer cope with imprisonment. The Governor refused it 'as it was believed that the request was for purely "political reasons", i.e. to bring her situation into the news once more. She is not considered a threat to or under threat from other prisoners.'

Her depression had returned, and she wrote to Lord Longford to tell him that her plea to be put on Rule 43 had been rejected:

> These feelings have been building up inside me for a long time now. I can trace them back clearly to when Maureen died, because – personal grief apart – I was beginning to realise that someone whom youth and health guaranteed to be around when they finally let me out wouldn't be after all … Maureen's death … crippled me with grief.

Her Review Board notes were written on the 27 January and stated that Myra had recently asked to be put on Rule 43 and surprisingly to her, had been refused.

> However, she incurred two disciplinary reports for refusing to work and subsequently lost privileges for a period. At the time of writing this report she is again on normal routine…
>
> While employed in the work-room Myra works as an inspector in the manufacture of bib and brace overalls. She works well without any supervision and does not let the quality standards of the overalls fall or get below an acceptable level.

In September Myra was once again 'caught in a compromising position with another inmate' and lost fourteen days' privileges as a result. In protest, she went on hunger strike. She refused main meals but took liquids freely.

Upset by this, and feeling that she couldn't carry on as things were in HMP Durham for at least another nine years, she petitioned for a transfer to either HMP Holloway or HMP Cookham Wood, stating: 'I am not at this time asking for release, merely a transfer from conditions which are mentally, emotionally and psychologically destructive to an environment which can offer a relatively constructive existence, which is surely not an unreasonable request in my nineteen years of imprisonment.'

Someone else who was really struggling was Lesley Ann Downey's mother, Ann, who survived another attempt to take her own life by overdose. However, one evening when she was due to go out with her husband Alan, and ex-husband Terry Downey and his wife, she became ill with stomach pains. She sent the three of them out anyway and then took to her bed. She got worse through the evening and her son, Brett, called an ambulance. Alan returned just as they were loading her into the back.

Within thirty minutes of her arriving at hospital, she was undergoing emergency surgery and it emerged that she had ovarian cancer. Her family were told that if she had not made it to the hospital when she did, she would have been dead within half an hour.

*Above left*: Myra Hindley mugshot.

*Above right*: Myra in prison.

*Right*: Myra Hindley around the time she fractured her heel.

She was kept in hospital for three weeks to recover and was fortunate that the cancer had not spread.

Myra's Progress Report from October 1982 stated:

> She always has one close friend to pamper to her needs, I do not think this will ever change. Apart from this she keeps very much to herself but likes to be regarded as a member of the elite. ... I believe that Myra likes to be kept in the public eye, she knows that she will spend many years in prison, so she might as well be a household name rather than a non-entity.

Myra's depression was still being noted in November and, as she started a three-week hunger strike, she wrote to her friend Carol Callaghan where she mentioned Guy Fawkes Night: 'Note the date and do me a favour ... no, not parliament itself. That smaller house round the corner, inaptly named the Home Office.'

Talks to transfer Myra reached a peak in March 1983, when it was stated that if she wasn't transferred soon then 'there is a possibility that she could harm herself'.

The prison service's preference was for her to go back to HMP Holloway, but there was no Lifer Unit there since the refurbishment and Josie O'Dwyer had recently returned there while serving a two-year sentence.

The second option was HMP Cookham Wood, but it had only held lifers there for a year or two before they were either released or transferred to an open prison. The Prison Service were keen to point out that should she be moved there, that it was purely for a change of scene for Myra and not because she was soon to be released. Another reason against her moving there was, again, Josie O'Dwyer. She had recently spent time in Cookham Wood and it was feared that she might get someone to attack Myra.

There was a third option too: HMP Styal. This idea was quickly shot down, however, as it was only seven miles from Hattersley and too close to the families of her victims.

The final decision was made on the 8 March to transfer her to HMP Cookham Wood in Kent, but was dependent upon 'her clear understanding that any serious misconduct or misbehaviour will result in return to Durham'.

The Governor at Cookham Wood, however, was not so keen to have Myra there: 'We feel that Cookham Wood would not be a suitable prison to hold a lifer merely for the purpose of giving her a change of scenery but when the lifer happens to be Myra Hindley there are other more serious concerns.' The Governor later went on:

> There is no way that the wing, as a whole, could be under continuous staff supervision and I should feel uneasy about having Hindley roaming abroad in the liberal 'open-door' regime which is a crucial element of life at Cookham Wood. In such a setting I could not guarantee her safety from intimidation, abuse or actual physical violence.

There was also concern regarding youth offenders:

> A further important development is the setting-up of a Youth Custody Unit in one of the wings. Although the Unit itself will be a separate entity, the regime plan for YCT's includes integration with adults in every area of the prison and the probability that the YCT's and Hindley would not only come in to contact but actually share activities cannot be ruled out. Indeed, it is highly likely and I wonder what would be the reaction of some loving parent of a wayward YCT (short-term or otherwise) on knowing that such a notorious prisoner was rubbing shoulders with their offspring. The geography of this prison makes separation almost impossible and, in any case, would only result in a continuation of Hindley's present problems in a different setting.
>
> After considering the various factors, arguments and options I feel strongly that Hindley should not come to Cookham Wood and would summarise thus:
>
> 1. Experience has already shown the effect upon a lifer of mixing with mainly short-term prisoners
> 2. The design of Cookham Wood's cellular wings presents a severe impediment to supervision
> 3. The frequent breakdown of the gate mechanisms compromises the security of the prison making it unsuitable for a prisoner needing a high level of security

4. In the event of any medical treatment other than of a fairly routine nature, Hindley would need to be taken out of the prison
5. The inevitability that Youth Custody Trainees will have contact with Hindley might present some embarrassment to the Department and Ministers.

However, the Governor's protestations were ignored and on the 21 March Myra was told: 'The Secretary of State having fully considered your recent petition to be transferred to Holloway, and having reconsidered your earlier petition to be transferred to Holloway or Cookham Wood, has agreed to transfer you to Cookham Wood. The Governor has been asked to make the necessary arrangements.'

In April, Myra wrote to Carol Callaghan:

> I want out and you want me out. And, as you say, you usually get what you want. It's often likewise said of me that I always get what I want. There's a lot of people to win round – the press, the public, the decision makers at the Home Office. But with you and I working at it 'mentally' and others working practically, who knows? The seemingly impossible may become possible. But you'll have to wait a little longer before we can walk along the canal bank stopping at the little pubs on the way.

She was still being visited by Bill Scott, Maureen's husband and her niece, Sharon. On the odd occasion Carol Callaghan went at the same time, and after one such visit, Myra wrote to her: 'If I hadn't been holding Sharon I might have danced a circuit of the visits room with you.' They discussed whether her circumstances would be different if she were a married woman. And one with children. They even wondered whether Myra could marry Bill (he knew nothing of the plan):

> Forget the bridesmaid, maid of honour or best man or anything else. I ain't marrying no one unless it's on my terms. And I don't think they'd be acceptable to Bill... Of course I love him dearly, but only as a brother, a friend, and especially as my sister's husband and father of their child...
>
> Oh Caz. I really want to come out and be with you, or you with me, for as long as we both want. So much to do, so much to do and say. One day, please God...

That idea was quickly dismissed, as Myra had fallen in love with another of her lovers inside.

The proposed Youth Custody Centre idea was not followed through with at HMP Cookham Wood, and Myra settled in well. In fact, it didn't take long for her to become top of the pecking order, but it also made her a target for others. On the 3 August, the Assistant Regional Director from the Home Office Prison Department wrote:

> I visited HMP Cookham Wood ... and was able to see and speak with Myra Hindley. It was done in such a way that there was no indication

on my part that I knew her by sight, and so was introduced to her by the Deputy Governor as I went round the establishment.

She looked well, was not carrying any excess weight, and was dressed neatly and tidily. She spoke quietly yet positively, and her attitude towards me was good.

She said that she had settled well at Cookham Wood and was enjoying the establishment and its facilities. Her relationship with staff was good and she got on well with most of the other women. Her current employment is on the inside garden party where she is working well and gaining benefit. She joins association with the other women but chooses to eat in her cell at present. The education programme appears to meet her needs. Myra Hindley proudly displayed her sun-tan – she says her first since sentence. She added she hopes all publicity will die.

Overall, I would say she has settled in well, is coping with the demands of the regime, and is responding positively to the Governor and his staff. She is keen not to be moved; if there is any plan to move her in the immediate future I would wish to be advised, please.

For those who associated themselves with her, life became tough. A petition, which was later withdrawn, from another inmate stated:

My reason for writing to you is the hope you will have me moved to any other prison. Because staying here has made my life an absolute misery. The reason for my misery is because of extreme hostile treatment from a group of inmates. They are treating me like this because of my friendship with another inmate – Myra Hindley. The same group constantly antagonise her. As you can imagine because of this particularly hostile treatment it has caused me a lot of distress, to the point I'm terrified to come out of my cell. Furthermore, because of threats involving the cutting of my hair by this group I am absolutely terrified.

I am begging, Sir, to please have me moved to another prison.

The following month, a West Indian lady [whose name is still withheld in the records] arrived at HMP Cookham Wood and officers saw that she was an old friend of Myra's from their Holloway days.

They asked me if I would help them take the heat off Myra. They said most of the trouble was coming from black girls, and that these girls would lose their parole if they did anything rash. They were girls with children themselves – that's why they felt so strongly about Myra. But I knew how stupid they would be if they lost parole over her, just like Josie (O'Dwyer) had done in Holloway. The officers asked me to look after my own people. So after I'd been there a day or two and settled in, got my bearings, I went down to Myra's cell for a chat. Some of the other girls said, 'You talk

148

with her?' And I said, 'Sure I do. What people did outside prison I worry about when I'm outside. Inside I worry about how they goes about getting on with everybody else, and Myra never makes trouble for anyone else.' So after that, they all eased up on her a lot. And if the officers thought somebody was heading for trouble, they'd send her to me to straighten her out.

In October, Myra was visited by millionaire David Astor for the first time. He would go on to fund her legal campaign for release and believed that 'Everyone deserves the chance of redemption.' The former editor of the *Observer* newspaper later said:

I had been a friend of Frank, Lord Longford, for many years and felt that he had become the object of ridicule. He had lost his way in his high profile defence of Myra. He told me that he couldn't face St Peter at the end if he had missed an opportunity to do her good. His critics even suggested that he was in love with Myra. Auberon Waugh referred to Frank's 'crucifixion complex'.

Frank just couldn't resist speaking to journalists and insisted that anyone who claimed to be a Christian must agree with him… My support for Myra was low-key compared with Frank's. I took over from him. Frank found it difficult to accept that his tactics to champion her cause were self-defeating and doing her more harm than good.

The news that David Astor was visiting Myra was soon leaked to the press and, on top of the fact that HMP Cookham Wood was wrongly stated as an 'open prison' in the newspapers, on the 29 February 1984 Patrick Downey, Lesley Ann's uncle, wrote to Myra:

'Dear' Miss Hindley,

During the years since the atrocities perpetrated by yourself and your fellow conspirator, I have often wanted to write to you, but I have always drawn back at the last moment.

I am the uncle of one of your victims, and whenever people say how much you have changed, I always think – is she sorry for what she did, because I have never heard or seen repeated a single word of remorse or regret.

As I have said, I am a relation, in fact I am the person who had a gun, and would have killed you if the police hadn't taken the gun from me, I would still be prepared to kill you and stand trial for my crime – somehow I don't think I would get a life sentence, not with public support being what it is, bearing this in mind I ask, why do you want to come out of prison – public feeling being as it is, and why do you think you should be given back your full freedom, as being in an open prison you are part free already.

Should you receive this letter I wonder whether you would care to/or be allowed to reply, if so Miss Hindley please please answer the following for me, 'Are you sorry, is your conscience clear, do you sleep easy at night' – I can tell you one thing – you and your fellow conspirator have haunted me for the last twenty years.

Yours
P. Downey

An internal memo stated that Myra's primary concern was 'the possible influence the Downey family may exercise upon her release'. She was advised by her solicitor and the Home Office not to reply to the letter, as they were concerned that the press were involved.

In March Myra fell and fractured her heel, meaning she needed an operation and, therefore, stitches. On the 14 March she had a second hospital appointment to check whether it had healed, during which she was heavily sedated. Later that day, she walked into the prison staffroom with tea and biscuits for twenty-two firemen who had been carrying out an inspection. She went several times in and out of the room and no one had any idea who she was. Sometimes she wore her new glasses, and at other times not.

That night she wrote to Carol Callaghan:

I couldn't even see the top line of big letters with my right eye… Guess what? I had to make tea for twenty-two firemen! Good grief, I've only seen a handful of men in donkeys' years and I had to walk into a staffroom full of them.

I got someone to help me carry the urn in and told 'em to help themselves 'cos I wasn't playing mother. Just then the aggro bell went and they rushed out saying 'Hold the fort, Harry.' (I've been christened Harry because it goes with Hindley). She told me later that one of the firemen said, 'You've got Myra Hindley in here, haven't you?' She said yes and the guy asked if they'd seen me this afternoon. She didn't say where, but she said they had. Ha! Chief said it would help to break me in, seeing all those men. Well, I don't wanna be that broken in! Twenty-two is a whole heap!

Soon though, the depression came back and she was sent to the sick-bay. Her next letter to Carol Callaghan stated:

Too much prison and too many hassles, too much publicity and too many brainwashed prisoners. Too much noise. Too many pressures … it all became just too much to handle any longer. I know I'm perilously close to falling off the tightrope I've been balancing on since I can't remember when.

I swear if suicide wasn't a mortal sin I'd top myself. Too many reasons why I can't – mum and Sharon, etc. And I ain't gonna give the goddamed rags the scoop of the century or any of the death wishers their thrill of a lifetime. And I can't be a bigger pain in the Home Office's proverbial alive than dead.

She said that part of her depression was because another prisoner had shown her photographs of her baby daughter. 'That's what I've missed because of this. I'll never be able to have a baby now and I would have liked one so much. I'd have loved to have been a mother but I've no chance now. IF I got out tomorrow I'd still be too old.'

At Cookham Wood she was now a 'trusty', working in the kitchen, looking after the prison library and the chapel, spending so much time in the latter that other prisoners had nicknamed her 'The Church Warden'.

She was still having fleeting lesbian affairs with other inmates too. One was called Sandra and she and Myra had a passionate affair which lasted for many months after Sandra left Cookham Wood. Myra often referred to her in her letters, and said that when she was released Sandra would be a part of her life. She even arranged for Sandra to visit her mother, although she said she would not tell her family they were anything more than friends.

In another letter to Carol Callaghan, Myra told her how different life was at HMP Cookham Wood, compared to HMP Durham:

Too much like real living. It's one helluva place. I hadn't realised how institutionalised I had become … although I clung to my individuality, dignity and self-respect. Now I'm here I feel almost as free as a bird … I've just looked at the calendar to see what the date it is … the 19 [April]. A shattering alarm bell reverberated around my whole head. Seventeen years ago today I was climbing up the steps to the dock in Chester Castle. And the judge and jury are still sitting in condemnation. Oh well, it takes all sorts to make a world but I'm damned if I'm going to be a coat hanger for all their hang ups for much longer…

She was finding a way to cope however – Cannabis. She had first tried it in HMP Holloway and a fellow inmate recalled: 'Myra told me the only time she got a good night's sleep was if she had a smoke. Then she would sleep for six, maybe seven hours: for her that's a long time.'

On the 16 May Myra received another letter from Patrick Downey:

Miss Hindley,

I would like to thank you for answering the questions in my recent letter to you! Perhaps you are thinking:- 'But I did not write a letter of reply,' exactly Miss Hindley! Your lack of response leads me to draw the conclusion, that you cannot answer the questions asked because you are not sorry.

I have given considerable thought to 'your answer' and I have come up with the following solution:- I have always believed that kindness should be rewarded, and as you have so 'kindly and eloquently' answered my questions, your reward for same is a copy of my last letter to you, forwarded to the Home Secretary, along with a letter asking him to present them to the Parole Board, as how can any Parole Board ever consider the release of a person who is so obviously not sorry for what they have done.

Perhaps on receipt of this letter you might feel inclined to reply and answer the questions asked, but it will be too late, as I would never know if your letter was the truth or written in fear of any Parole being denied.

Yours
P. Downey 'UNCLE'

Four days later the press ran a story that had obviously been given to them by Patrick Downey, regarding the non-replies to his letters. Myra saw this and wrote to the Governor of HMP Cookham Wood:

To the Governor,

I have seen an article in today's *Sunday Mirror* about a letter sent to me by Mr Patrick Downey, and I would ask you to consider the following, and place it on record.

When I received the letter, I suspected, at first, that it may in fact have come from a journalist, since the letter was a photocopy and the contents of it were written in a different handwriting to the signature. (I had already received a letter from a *Sun* reporter, purporting to have come from someone who was interested in befriending and helping me). However, I thought about it and decided it probably was from Mr Downey and that I would reply, not just to his questions, but to try to offer him and his family some kind of comfort and sympathy, and to express my deep remorse and regret that certain actions of mine, in the past, had caused them so much pain and suffering. I consulted my solicitor about this when he visited me in connection with the court action against the *Sun*, and also Mr Rumball, the Asst. Regional Director, who was paying a visit to the prison. Both their reactions to the letter and my decision to reply were similar. If I replied, my letter would undoubtedly appear in the press. And as with many letters of mine which had come into the hands of the press, would be printed out of context, its context distorted, and be detrimental to me, and counter-productive. Alternatively, the lack of a reply, would ensure that I was callous and devoid of any feelings of sympathy and remorse, etc; It would yet again be a 'no win' situation; that I couldn't do right for doing wrong, whichever course I tried to steer.

So I reluctantly decided not to reply, and this has resulted in today's article, preceded by a phone call to the prison, a letter to myself from the reporter who wrote the article, plus another letter from Mr Downey, which I haven't seen. I would ask you to consider the dilemma that such a situation has placed me in, not just a present dilemma but one that has always existed and which will continue to exist. I feel that I cannot now write to Mr Downey or any member of his family because I'm afraid that it will be thought that I'm being coerced into doing so because of certain threats made, not just to my life, but the implied threats of writing to the Home Secretary for a Government pledge that I will never be paroled, and to the Parole Board.

In fact, I've always felt 'threatened' by this family, fearing to contact them in any way in case ulterior motives were construed for doing so – i.e. that I was only concerned to create a favourable impression for when the question of parole arose. I expected this to happen when I decided to reply to Mr Downey's first letter, but I was prepared to accept this and write regardless of it. This isn't the first time I've wanted to write such a letter. Many years ago, in Holloway Prison, I discussed doing so with both Mrs Wing and Dr Bull, but prison rules then prevented me, and the feelings of both Governors were that such an action would rebound with detrimental results. I even discussed with Dr Bull the possibility of asking Mrs West to visit me so that I could talk to her. This, too, was not allowed by prison rules, and Dr Bull also felt that it was a risky and potentially dangerous suggestion.

And now I feel totally trapped by this Catch-22 situation. I cannot see a way out of it by any efforts of my own, and I am asking if there is any way the Home Office can help, for I really do feel very threatened. I am not for a moment detracting from the tragedy of the Downey family, or from their sufferings resulting from it, but I know of no other prisoner who has been the object of such a prolonged, concerted and implacable campaign as that undertaken by them against me. I am not mitigating the extent of my own misdeeds which have caused their suffering, but I am forced, on occasion, to wonder whether there isn't something else sadly wrong at the root of the matter, for which I am an additional target. Mr Downey said that I and my co-defendant have haunted him and his family for twenty years. I feel equally as haunted, and hunted, not just by my own past actions but by their increasingly threatening campaign.

Yours Sincerely
Myra Hindley

She was attacked again on the 2 June and sustained various injuries, including having hair pulled out from the crown of her head, bruising to the nasal and mastoid areas, a bruised shoulder, bruised thumb, and a cut lip. She was taken to Rochester for X-rays, but her injuries were not as bad as first feared.

A report on the attack states:

A civilian workman was in the area of an office door and from that position was able to see the assailant leaving Hindley's cell (with something in her hand which could have been a shoe). He then saw Hindley stagger out in some distress and he then called staff to assist her. What appears to have happened is that Myra Hindley was in her cell sitting on her bed when XXXXX came in, dragged her to the floor, sat on top of her and thumped her. It appears likely that she took off her shoe and used it to hit Myra Hindley on the head. There was no evidence prior to the incident of any hostility between the two women. XXXXX has recently been on home leave and has found it difficult to settle back since her return. She was on report on Friday 1 June for using abusive language to the staff. However, since the incident XXXXX claims that another prisoner had told her that Myra Hindley had said she would chop her legs off. Also since the incident Myra Hindley claims that XXXXX is one of the women in Cookham Wood of whom she has felt wary.

Myra's former prison mate Janie Jones visited her several times, despite not seeing her for several years. They had stayed in touch via letter and Myra told her about the attack:

I was assaulted by a sewer-rat who took me from the back in my room – it was so unexpected and such a shock I couldn't do a thing – just as well; there's nineteen years of pent-up everything inside me, and I dread to think what would've happened had I seen her coming.

I don't like violence of any kind, not even verbal violence, and I stopped fighting after I left primary school – except to beat up great bullies who terrorised my sister – and I'd hate to soil a nineteen-year record of non-violence but – it was as well for both she and I that she did it the way she did.

No bones or anything broken, but she slapped me around the face and head with her shoe (she pinned me in a corner on the floor with her ton of weight kneeling on me, so I was helpless, my right arm and leg pinned underneath me) and tore out a chunk of hair. Head ached for a while, and a stiff shoulder and neck, and a very tender scalp, but I'm a fast healer and what bruises and scratches did show soon faded.

On her 40th birthday Myra was transferred to the prison hospital, where she remained for the next two months.

Another report, an assessment for the Local Review Committee written by the Assistant Governor at Cookham Wood, stated that Myra was: 'Hard working and reliable. Needs minimum supervision. Always willing to undertake extra tasks for staff.' It noted her gardening and work as a Library/Chapel Orderly and that her general behaviour was 'Excellent'. She had 'A strong, pleasant personality with a self-deprecating sense of humour' and that she was 'Intelligent, self-sufficient and caring.' It also noted that:

Myra's offences were committed under the influence of Ian Brady. She certainly shows no signs now of being of being influenced by others

Myra Hindley in
Cookham Wood.

to offend. [She has the] ability to assess her own moods and behaviour past
and present and has developed amazing self control.

[She has] no current welfare problems but if released would need help
and support in adjusting to the changes which have taken place in society
during the period of her imprisonment and with the pressures created by
her release. Myra has received a number of offers of accommodation and
work from people of good reputation who are in a position to offer either
or both; which she accepts will depend on the time scale to release and
circumstances prevailing at the time.'

Of Myra's attitude towards her offences, he said:

Myra says that to her 'eternal shame' and against her better judgement
she participated in the photographic session with the victim Lesley Ann
Downey and she did so because she was afraid that by thwarting Brady
she would lose him. She is adamant that the child left the house with
Smith alive and unhurt although distressed. She admits that she was
in the house when Edward Evans was killed but denies taking part in
his murder. She claims that Brady and Smith planned to dispose of his
body and she knew they wanted her help. She did not argue nor contact
the police and says that in this she was wrong. She claims to have
known nothing of the victim John Kilbride until asked about him by
the police. She says she pleaded guilty to being an accessary after the
fact re: Kilbride as a 'compensatory plea' for her knowledge regarding
Evans on the advice of her lawyer. She has been absolutely consistent
in this story.

155

The Assistant Governor then stated that 'Since coming to Cookham Wood she has worked and behaved in an exemplary manner even under pressure and provocation. She has used her time constructively to further her education and personal development.'

Myra's bouts of depression were again noted and that:

> There is nothing more she can achieve in prison which would be constructive. She already shows signs of institutionalisation although there is no accompanying personality deterioration.
>
> During the time Myra has been at Cookham Wood she has shown no propensity towards violence and when children have been around, e.g. Carol Service, visits, etc. she has shown a proper attitude towards them. Family loyalties are very strong and she has a number of good friends, who are in a position to help her. Some members of the public no doubt would be against her release but correspondence received at the prison about her is generally in her favour. Those letters against her usually appear to have been written by 'cranks'. I have no doubt she would cooperate fully with the terms of licence.
>
> If this woman is ever to be released she must know now that there is a 'light at the end of the tunnel' if her resilience is to last until she gets there. I believe that the time is right to give her some indication of release and to start to prepare her; a process which cannot be undertaken quickly with one who has already been in prison twenty years.

On the 11 March 1985, Myra Hindley made representations to be considered for early release. Her statement read:

> I feel there is little or no point in making this representation for two reasons. One is that the sheer repetition of being interviewed for F75's required by the then Joint Committee, by professional people who have known me for years, has wearied and demoralised me to the point of exhaustion. Even worse is the knowledge that the people referred to – those who interviewed me and with whom I discussed the salient factors at great length were, sadly, wasting their time.
>
> For the second reason is that I know, when my case reaches its final stage, I will have already been prejudged. I had a trial by newspaper; I've had Joint Committee considerations by newspaper, and I know I will have 'no parole' by newspaper. The media – the 'popular' press in particular, have created a myth which has virtually obscured the facts; the public believe this myth, the public are the electorate; no politician will be prepared to risk his place in the cabinet, let alone his seat in the House, by releasing me on parole. I am a pawn on a political chess board, and am painfully aware of this fact. Even were the Local Review Committee and the Parole Board to recommend my release, a Home Secretary may feel unable for political reasons to accept that recommendation. Therefore, I feel that the LRC and the Parole Board are, like those who have written reports on me, wasting their time.

However, I do wish to be released on parole. After almost twenty years of an existence, a half-life, of course I wish to be free. With respect, I feel that 'how I think parole would help should I be selected', is obvious. I could give you dozens of reasons, but two paramount ones are my mother, aged 65, looking and feeling twice her age through <u>her</u> life-sentence outside, and my late sister's child, my niece, aged almost 10, whose father is 60 and partially disabled. I want, in time, to be able to look after them, once I've sorted out my own life. They would come to wherever I am – I have no intention of ever returning to Manchester or anywhere near the place. I cannot plan a route until a road has been built, thus I can't at this stage say to which area I intend to go. But I have numerous offers of accommodation from friends who are all respectable, many of them professional people.

I also have offers of moral and financial support from them until I find employment. This latter will be no problem since I can type and can work from wherever I am based. I have actually had two manuscript typing jobs waiting for me to do for a number of years. I can also do tapestry work (I taught many inmates how to do this in the tapestry workroom at Holloway) which could be done from where I am based.

I have an Honours Degree, and intend to do a Masters degree, and have three languages – Spanish, German and French. A refresher course in each would enable me to do 'at base' translation work.

Ideally I would like to leave the country for a period of time, were I to be released. I have friends abroad. The same offers of accommodation and employment exist in this respect. I would, of course, change my name and identity – probably more than once. I have a current driving licence, renewed for life – I just need the other life licence to use it. Finally, I am prepared and willing to accept any conditions of release on licence, and will cooperate fully with the Probation and Aftercare teams.

The decision was made on the 23 May 1985 that neither Ian Brady nor Myra Hindley would be released. The Home Secretary, Leon Brittan, announced, following parole board recommendations:

> The board have recommended to me that neither Ian Brady nor Myra Hindley should be released. The case of Ian Brady should be considered again by the local review committee where he is then held in ten years' time. Myra Hindley should be similarly considered in five years' time.

Lord Longford called the decision 'brutal', 'revolting', 'astounding' and 'disgusting'. This was despite the Local Review Committee unanimously recommending release.

Shortly before the decision, a pair of scissors had gone missing from an office in the prison canteen at Cookham Wood. Myra had heard unofficially of the decision before it was announced publicly, and according to 52-year-old Dorothy Moore, a former inmate: 'She just went to pieces. She knew there was going to be a recommendation that her application shouldn't be heard again for some time, but she didn't know how long it would be.' Myra had told her. 'I won't be able to bear it if it's too long.' She had access to the office in which the scissors had disappeared in her role as a 'trustee' and kitchen orderly. Prisoners were stripped and searched, every cell, to which the inmates were confined for two days, was combed inch by inch until the scissors were found – in another room in which, also, she was the only one allowed.

'An officer told me they were sure Myra had taken the scissors to kill herself if the parole news was too bad,' Dorothy Moore recalled.

But by the time of the official announcement, Myra was heavily sedated in the hospital wing of the prison. She had collapsed with nervous exhaustion.

A week later she went on hunger strike, which lasted for ten days until the threat of being returned to HMP Holloway and maximum security called it off.

She then started a new job as a hospital orderly, despite her Valium medication making her seem 'rather dazed'.

By June, Myra decided to take the Government to the European Court of Human Rights over their 'inhuman and degrading treatment'.

Ian Brady decided that enough was enough. He was fed up with Myra constantly being in the news and stating that she should be released. He felt otherwise.

Myra in Cookham Wood.

# 8

# Brady's Prison Years 1974–1985

A report was written in March 1974 – just before Myra Hindley went on trial for trying to abscond from prison – which showed that Brady was still in HMP Parkhurst and that he had virtually isolated himself from the other prisoners as he had not left his landing to take exercise since January 1973. The report further pointed out that he would be in danger from the other prisoners on the landing if he were to leave his cell to mix with them. The report further concluded that Brady wanted to be transferred to HMP Gartree in Leicestershire so that he could be put on Rule 43.

He got his wish on the 11 June 1974, but instead of going to HMP Gartree, he was transferred to HMP Wormwood Scrubs in London where he was placed in the Segregation Unit. His Probation Officer wrote in his Transfer Summary that: 'Never at any time has he showed any remorse for his acts, or even given a thought to the next-of-kin of the children involved. I am of the opinion that this man should never be released.' Indeed, the Principal Medical Officer reviewed Brady's time at HMP Parkhurst:

> Brady spent a long time in the hospital at Parkhurst, and was eventually transferred to Wormwood Scrubs on 11 June 1974. While he was here, he never emerged from his cell except to go to the recess or to have a bath; he resolutely refused exercise and association. When he first came under our charge, Brady was very polite and indeed affable, and would converse with me on such topics as literature and poetry. With the passage of time, he became increasingly taciturn, until he would only answer in monosyllables. He continued to stand up when one entered his room, but plainly showed his irritation at being interrupted in whatever he was doing – generally transcribing Braille. This withdrawal may have been due to a mild degree of depression, brought about by his prolonged voluntary segregation; but he did not seem to lose his powers of concentrating, and on occasion showed that he could still think very quickly and cogently if the situation demanded it. At first he seemed to welcome his occasional visits from Lord Longford, but I am not in a position to say what his attitude became latterly.
>
> I never tested him, but I formed the opinion that Brady had a high-average intelligence. We never detected any evidence of mental illness in him, apart from the probable mild depression to which I have already

referred. On the other hand, sadism was obviously one of the great – perhaps the greatest – interests in his life. Repeatedly he tried to get hold of books dealing with sadism, or sadistic subjects, and I had to ban a number of these from reaching him. He never spoke to me about his offences, but it would appear from his demeanour that he regretted nothing. I think he will continue to be a sadist, and would return to practising this perversion if given the opportunity. I do not think that Brady should be released from prison for a long, long time – if ever.

In conclusion, I should say that his general health was good, in spite of his lack of exercise and fresh air.

The Assistant Governor at HMP Parkhurst also stated his thoughts on Brady:

I formed the impression that Brady was an arrogant, perverse and dangerous man. He was obviously intelligent, but there are occasions when his discussion of literature, and books he had read, was patently superficial. He was also, obviously, in no way filled with remorse or guilt about his offences…

I am of the opinion that Brady was amoral. I never knew him to express real concern for any issue or for anybody save himself. Increasingly Brady became so self-centred as to verge on the obsessional…

When Brady left Parkhurst I was in no doubt that he was still an extremely dangerous man, and in no way ready for release.

Once Brady had settled in he requested to be allowed visits from his mother, but felt that it was something he *should* do rather than something he wanted to do.

He was seen by his new Probation Officer on the 24 September and they discussed Brady's prison life and how he felt that the conditions he had been kept in were 'uncivilised'. Brady then said that HMP Wormwood Scrubs had nothing to offer him in terms of work or recreation, and so he was looking to move on to somewhere like HMP Gartree. He was continuing his Braille work and that was all he seemed to be interested in doing. He then talked about his interest in the German language and Hitler's use of oratory; referring to his tape-recordings of these. It was noted by the Probation Officer that Brady was 'giving a bleak, cracked grin on his reference to tape-recordings'.

He was seen by the Medical Officer, Dr Hines, on the 13 December and he ascertained that Ian Brady 'Does not suffer from any mental illness.'

Things were fairly quiet for a while, with Brady's only misdemeanour coming when he was barred from using his radio for fourteen days in April 1795 because he kept playing it at an excessive volume.

That summer his deviousness found new depths when he began another hunger strike in order that he be heard louder as he wanted to be transferred to a different prison. He was moved to the prison hospital as he rapidly lost weight, but allowed himself to be 'artificially fed' when he discovered that boys as young as 15 were sent to the hospital from Feltham Borstal if they were suffering from mental health issues.

By September, Brady had been constantly interviewed by various psychiatrists and doctors and they had concluded that his mental state remained unchanged. A report was written by a Dr Lotinga where he gave his opinion that there was no evidence whatever that Brady was suffering from any form of mental illness and that his refusal of food was purely a manipulative measure.

Brady stated to his Senior Welfare Officer that the purpose of his refusal to take food was to either obtain better conditions in the Segregation Unit or a transfer from the prison.

He continued to lose weight through October, despite taking liquid food and was visited by his mother, who begged him to give up the hunger strike. Staff reported that for a while Brady became more pleasant to deal with and he began to look forward to letters and visits from her and Lord Longford. He had also managed to arrange a visit from an old blind lady called Mrs Mottram, who also visited Myra. He was able to pass on to her some of his braille work, including poems that he had transcribed from a book by William Blake.

He continued the hunger strike through November and, although he was losing weight and holding out for a move to a prison where Rule 43 was 'more liberally interpreted', he was found to be 'mentally ... very rational and is in control of his own destiny as regards his prison sentence'.

He was again visited by his mother on 11 December, but Brady was not in a good mood. She had become shocked at his physical condition and believed him when he told her he was being mistreated by the authorities. Upset and agitated, she later telephoned Brady's Welfare Officer and told him that she was going to go to the press regarding her son's condition if things didn't change rapidly. Later that day Lord Longford telephoned Brady's Probation Officer after meeting with the Home Secretary to tell him it had been agreed that if Brady ended his hunger strike, he would be allowed to remain in the hospital for the time being and possibly have association.

Despite being made aware of the decision, Brady continued his hunger strike until the 31 December, when he began to eat well again and it was noted by his Probation Officer that 'this is typical of Brady's orderly and tidy mind'. He also began to put weight on rapidly and by the end of January 1976 he appeared bloated around the face. He was also allowed a record player and proceeded to order records of bird songs and then moved on to pop music.

On the 12 April, Brady was visited by Lord Longford and the meeting was supervised by Assistant Governor Peter Meakings. Lord Longford apologised 'for forgetting to bring cigarettes'. Meakings recalled: 'I remember Brady was really angry about that.' Brady preferred the French brand, Gauloises, which could be hard to get hold of. In a note written at the time, Meakings said that Brady made 'frequent acrimonious comments about the Home Office', and 'various offensive remarks concerning individual prison staff'. He remembered that Brady seemed very much in charge – telling Lord Longford what to do, and being very curt and abrupt with him. At the end of the month Brady was assessed by a Dr Hines who found that:

> there are no signs whatever of any mental illness and he is quite frank in discussing how in the past he tried to get into Broadmoor as a patient

and later decided that he would avoid this at all costs. Mr Brady was keen to have the benefit of an opinion from Dr Scott and following an interview, Dr Scott wrote: 'In summary, he remains as I found him in 1971, not mentally ill, but with no great change in his personality disorder. If anything, he is less trusting and more hardened in his defences than formerly.'

At long last here was Brady admitting to fake symptoms in order to get what he wanted.

Brady was still on the hospital ward in August 1976, on Home Office instructions. He was still refusing to associate with the other inmates and refused all attempts to get him to exercise. Instead, he stayed in his room where he continued his braille work. From there he could see out onto the landing and paid particular attention when there were boys from Feltham Borstal around. However, the attention he was giving these boys was being noticed by staff and the Principal Medical Officer noted on the 2 September that: 'He takes an unusual interest in any adolescent inmate who may be located on the landing and his influence in such a situation is certainly not a wholesome one.' He added that the staff had had to move boys off the landing to get them away from him.

Despite this report and numerous other objections made by staff, arguing that Brady should be moved, he was kept in the hospital wing and had his privileges steadily increased. As his health and weight had been improving he was given duties to perform, such as cleaning the toilets and showers.

Brady was given a new Probation Officer in 1977 and took an instant disliking to him. A new Acting Principal Medical Officer then wrote to the Prison Governor saying

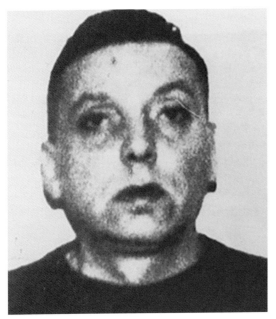

that Brady should be returned to segregation. Brady complained and wrote to Lord Longford, saying how grateful he had been for the chance to show his 'progress', and how much he valued being given 'a modest opportunity to integrate in a constructive community of staff I have the highest respect for'. This worked and Brady stayed on the wing.

Like Myra, he had also become annoyed with Lord Longford for constantly bringing their names up in public and speaking to

Ian Brady.

newspapers about them. In fact, Brady grew so annoyed that in January 1978 he released a public statement to the *Daily Mirror*, via an intermediary:

> Noting the alacrity with which the quality and popular Press publish L.L.'s lamentably frequent utterances re the question of parole for Myra Hindley and myself, it is not widely known that he does not and never has represented my opinion on this subject.
>
> Over the years I have repeatedly made strong requests, verbal and written, that he desists from publicly using my name in connection with parole. He has ignored all such requests and prisoners cannot write to the press, nor can they take legal action of any sort without Home Office permission. Last summer when I heard he and Janie Jones intended to take part in a BBC television programme devoted to the possible parole of Myra I finally stopped receiving visits from him. Eventually I saw him again last October and forcefully put my objections to him. I thought he at last understood – but no. Lord Longford is well aware, as is the Home Office, that I have never applied for parole and have no intention of applying and that I have always accepted that the weight of the crimes both Myra and I were convicted of justifies permanent imprisonment, regardless of expressed personal remorse and verifiable change…
>
> I have done all I personally can to impress on L.L. the insensitivity of his repeatedly raising the question of parole, not only from my point of view but also from that of the general public. But he is receiving encouragement from Myra. I can't do anything about that, for I let her go her own way seven years ago…
>
> I wish to emphasise that the public need feel no apprehension re the possibility of parole in my case, for the situation shall never arise.

Brady's attention to the young Borstal boys was still being noted in March 1978 but there was very little done about it. The Senior Medical Officer expressed his concerns about Brady's presence in the prison hospital and his contact with the vulnerable prisoners: 'I deplore his association with young Borstal trainees and adult mentally ill patients. There is little change in his hard, remorseless, egotistical attitude. He is one of the few men to whom I would attach the label "evil".'

Unfortunately, he concluded that there was no way of segregating them, given the 'therapeutic milieu'. This alone is probably the reason that Brady changed his mind and was now adamant that he wanted to stay at HMP Wormwood Scrubs.

In mid-1978 members of the prison's Board of Visitors objected to Brady's 'privileged' treatment but were told by medical officers that it was the 'best solution to an impossible problem'.

The board was unimpressed and wanted to make a formal complaint. This led to an exchange between the prison's Principal Medical Officer and the Deputy Director of the Prison Services Department. 'If he is sent back to the segregation unit he will go on hunger strike and we shall be back to where we were several years ago,' the Principal Medical Officer wrote in a letter dated the 5 June 1978.

He said he was not too worried about Brady's position 'except for one aspect of it and that is his having access to young inmates'. He went on: 'A malicious newspaper could make great play of it.'

His penchant for young boys was again picked up in September when one of the hospital officers was asked to write a report about Brady:

> At no time has he appeared to have struck up a deep friendship with another patient. However, he has managed to get on quite well with most of the other patients. There has been, at times, an apparent attraction to younger patients and Brady has been advised regarding the suitability of such friendships.

Brady was continually assessed while on the hospital wing, and in November Professor Gunn wrote:

> I can find no evidence that he [Brady] has ever required or received formal psychiatric treatment for a mental illness. On examination I find him willing and eager to talk about his predicament. There was no evidence of affective disturbance or psychosis… The diagnosis in this case is not in doubt. Ian Brady suffers from a severe personality disorder.

He went on to state that he agreed with his fellow colleagues (who had assessed Brady previously) that he would be better off in a Special Hospital such as Broadmoor, but was also aware that Brady was against such a move.

Brady being in the same location as young boys was again brought up in reports in August 1979, with the Senior Medical Officer at Wormwood Scrubs recommending that Brady be discharged from the hospital wing. 'Into Ward G2 are admitted both boys and men who are mentally ill. Is it proper to have Brady in with them?' He admitted that Brady might try 'blackmail' as a way of staying on the wing by going on hunger strike again, 'But then I would deal with him as I would any other inmate – in the proper ethical medical manner.'

When nothing was done to remove Brady, he again wrote in January 1980 that boys in Feltham Borstal had been talking about Brady and he wanted to know why Brady was given access to 'those of tender years'.

Two weeks later the Prison's Medical Officer wrote that the case:

> is an odd one. We have been over it many times. Under the present circumstances it would be impossible to prevent Borstal trainees who are admitted to G2 from coming into contact with Brady. For what it is worth, I doubt if Brady has any effect whatsoever on 'those of tender years'.

On the 5 June, Brady's Probation Officer wrote that not much had changed in his relationship with Brady and that Brady was annoyed at the restrictions placed upon him as a Category 'A' prisoner; the main one being that his movements were confined to the wing.

He still expresses the opinion that he should continue serving his sentence for the rest of his life. He cannot conceive of any circumstances under which he should be released into open society. He has expressed these feelings to me also concerning Myra Hindley, his co-defendant. And there are certainly occasions when he finds the ministrations of Lord Longford distasteful and wishes that they would come to an end.

Lord Longford visited Brady on the 27 February 1981, and commented:

> He was in a thoroughly bad temper and indeed he had something to be in a bad temper about. I have been long of the opinion, which on the whole has been shared by him, that Broadmoor would be the best place for him. Not long ago I discussed the question with the psychiatrist who visits him in the prison hospital. The latter seemed to concur. When, however, I wrote to Lord Belstead, the Minister at the Home Office, I eventually received a negative reply. I had requested that the psychiatrist's opinion should be obtained. John Belstead replied that the principal medical officer at Wormwood Scrubs did not consider this necessary. I sent the Belstead answer to Ian Brady as permitted. Ian tells me that the principal medical officer has no objection to the views of the psychiatrist being obtained, so who is fooling whom?
>
> I will take up the matter through Birnberg, Ian's solicitor, with renewed irritation. Ian, as I say, was in a thoroughly bad temper and indicated not obscurely that I had not exerted myself sufficiently. We were soon for the moment more angry with each other than with the authorities. I must write and apologise to him. Considering that he has been in prison fifteen years, I really ought to make more allowances.

Back at HMP Wormwood Scrubs, the Prison's Medical Officer was visited by a young prisoner from the landing where Brady was located. The officer wrote a letter to the Governor, saying: 'He was in a very agitated state.' Another prisoner 'wanted to have homosexual relations with him', and knew that Brady had had sex with him 'some months ago'. The young man was terrified of what this prisoner might do if he refused and asked to be moved, which he was.

His letter continued: 'I am most concerned about Brady. I never have been happy about locating disturbed boys or young men on the landing. Brady has shown rather too much interest in them in the past.' As it seemed easier to move the victim rather than the perpetrator, Brady was again left on the wing.

Lord Longford visited him again on the 29 May and it became clear that Brady now wanted a transfer to Broadmoor Hospital (possibly because he was being restricted in his interactions with the young offenders and he had lost his jobs cleaning the showers and toilets). Lord Longford commented on this visit:

> Ten years ago, Reggie Maudling, the Home Secretary, tried to get him into Broadmoor but was thwarted by Keith Joseph, then Minister of Health.

The Home Office psychiatrist who visits Ian regularly and whom I have met appears to be favourable, but the Home Office at the moment are preventing us from drawing on his evidence. I admit to a feeling of guilt at not having pushed things along faster. I wish that Ian and I could get back to our old discussions of Tolstoy and Dostoevsky, but I cannot blame him for trying to make the fullest use of me for business purposes. His true gifts are wasted.

Three weeks later, Lord Longford visited John Belstead, the Under-Secretary of State in the House of Commons concerning Ian Brady and his demand that he be sent to Broadmoor:

I was accompanied by Sir Roger Falk, who has visited him in the Scrubs for the last seven years, also by the well-known criminal lawyer Ben Birnberg, Ian's solicitor.

I opened by stressing the efforts of Reggie Maudling, when Home Secretary, to get Ian sent to Broadmoor in 1971, efforts defeated by Keith Joseph, the Health Minister, and our strong impression that the Home Office psychiatrist seeing Ian regularly now favours this course. Roger Falk threw in a dramatic warning that if the hospital wing where Ian is housed is closed down there is no saying what steps he would resort to. He was already talking about killing a prison officer or, alternatively, himself. John Belstead had with him one of the top officials and the head of the Prison Medical Service. There was some discussion as to whether a prisoner could be sent to Broadmoor if he was not thought to be treatable, but there appeared to be no doubt that such a transfer could and should take place if two psychiatrists were ready to describe him as mentally ill. We believe that 'mentally ill' is just what Dr Marjot the Prison Medical Officer says he is.

Somewhat to my surprise, it was agreed that if Ian himself had no objection we could see a report which Dr Marjot would be asked to prepare about him. The head of the Prison Medical Service warned us that it might not assist our argument as much as we suppose. I shot him a rather cynical look. We would be enormously unimpressed if Marjot's known opinions were known to have been modified under guidance from his superiors. However, we came away pleased for the time being. At the very least we can demonstrate to Ian that we are fighting his battle energetically. Not that we shall convince him of this at all easily.

It was agreed that Brady could be moved to Broadmoor if two psychiatrists described him as 'mentally ill'. So far, none had. When this was shared throughout the prison system, he was (as will be seen) suddenly found to be 'mentally ill'. On the 9 September his Probation Officer started to tell how Brady had:

expressed to me grave dissatisfaction at the outcome of his trial and has said that he feels he was unfairly dealt with. He has insinuated that were he free he would try to get back at those Officers of the Court who were involved in his trial. He did not say specifically what he meant by this statement.

In the four years he had known Ian Brady previous to this report, he had written constantly of how Brady hardly spoke to him and never spoke of his crimes. Now, suddenly, Brady was seeking revenge on those he believed had done him wrong.

In the same report, the Probation Officer also wrote:

> In my opinion Ian Brady demonstrates many of the characteristics usually associated with a psychopathic personality. He is, I believe, emotionally immature, marked egocentric, and is unable to form stable relationships. These factors tend to make him basically unstable and I sincerely believe that if this man were to escape he would be highly dangerous to the public and in particular to those officers of the law who had taken part in his trial … I have not seen in him any reason to make me think that the basic personality disorder which originally led to the murders which he committed has been corrected or even favourably modified. Hence it seems to me reasonably conceivable to believe that were he to escape he might indulge again in the same practices which brought him to Court before. In short, I do see him as a man whose escape would be highly dangerous and I therefore recommend that he continue to be Category 'A' prisoner.

The following day, the Probation Officer noted:

> During period under review Brady has been moved from the cell he has occupied for several years. This angered him and he plainly showed it. He has been heard to say he will kill a prison officer as soon as the opportunity presents itself. Officers take this threat seriously.

Brady underwent a period of regular consultations with Dr Marjot, a Consultant Psychiatrist, and in a report dated 14 October he expressed the strong suspicion of a well organised and systematised delusional ideation and feeling underlying his past and present behaviour. It had not been confirmed by subsequent interviews with him but that there was an account of an apparently profound affective change about the age of 16 to 18 reminiscent of that seen in psychoses such as schizophrenia. Therefore, while Brady was not formally psychotic he considered him to be seriously mentally disordered and that if the category of disorder was psychopathic, he did not consider him incurable in the sense that very considerable change could occur under the influence of the process called maturing, aided and abetted by an appropriate environment and suitable therapy. He concluded a Special Hospital would seem to be an appropriate place.

Five days after this report, Brady made it 'abundantly clear that he [had] no intention of returning to Rule 43 conditions in any prison and that he will do everything and anything in his power to get into Broadmoor – not for treatment but because the regime would be more agreeable there.'

On the 2 November, Lord Longford commented:

> A few days ago I received the report of his psychiatrist, for which I had pressed so hard. It is a very-well considered document based on two years' interviewing of Ian and showing itself favourable to his going to a special hospital, presumably Broadmoor. This, of course, is what the Home Office favoured ten years ago but were tripped up by Keith Joseph, then Minister of Health. But this time I have a document in my hands, as has Ian's solicitor, which gives us much better ammunition. Ian showed no special excitement over the news. But that is his way. He leaves me in no doubt that he does like me to visit him, which is all the encouragement I need.

Brady was transferred on the 31 March 1982, following structural changes in HMP Wormwood Scrubs which necessitated inmates being transferred from the hospital wing. Instead of being sent to Broadmoor as he wanted however, he was sent back to HMP Parkhurst. He was angered by this and wanted to get his own back on those he felt had done him wrong, so he started to make noises regarding the murders, hinting that he may have information that could be useful.

Having heard that Brady wanted to speak to them, detectives soon arrived from Manchester. DCS Geoff Rimmer spent seven hours questioning him, but Brady didn't actually have anything of use to say. He spent most of the time staring straight ahead. His devious mind knew that the visit would be reported in the press and that people would think that he had wanted to talk about the missing children Pauline Reade and Keith Bennett. He also knew that Myra would think that too. His Probation Officer commented in July that:

> He has stated on more than one occasion that he has no wish to leave prison but he is desperate to move from Parkhurst and the influence of our hospital which he is almost paranoid about. He says this is to do with events which he witnessed there in the early seventies and he is endeavouring to stir things up in this regard.
>
> He has remained in the Seg Unit since arrival and has isolated himself so far as he is able. He spends all day, every day, in his cell (without exercise) translating braille for a blind school on Merseyside.

Everything was quiet for a while, up until February 1983, when Brady's condition started to worsen. It was noted that he 'is going downhill. He eats meals regularly but sparingly, taking prodigious amounts of salt therewith.'

Brady got his wish on the 22 April 1983 when he was transferred to HMP Gartree in Leicestershire. His prison notes state that he 'appeared very retarded and expressed answers only after long pauses and stares into a corner of the room'. The switch in prisons fuelled rumours that it had happened because he was talking to the police – and Myra had heard those rumours too. She decided to write to her friend Carol Callaghan:

I couldn't make statements regarding something I know nothing of and whatever he had to say, regardless of any allegations he might make, I could only do as I've always done: deny and disassociate myself from them. If he was believed, there was nothing I could do. My conscience is clear whether I'm believed or not.

Brady's condition was said to have steadily worsened and on the 27 May it was recorded that he was having admitted difficulty in concentrating and that his thoughts were being controlled by someone else. He said that at times he could hear thoughts repeated in his head.

Thinking that he was showing signs of paranoid schizophrenia he was seen by Dr Smith, who had known him for some time, and the doctor confirmed that his mental and physical conditions had deteriorated markedly and that he was now extremely paranoid. He was then seen by Dr McKay, who noted:

There can be little doubt that this man's personality is basically schizoid, that is to say pathologically detached, cold and unfeeling. In addition to his psychopathic personality, there can be little doubt that he now has a slowly developing paranoid schizophrenic illness with feelings of thought control, hallucinations of hearing and paranoid delusions, all accompanied by considerable tensions and resultant weight loss.

He was seen by Dr Reid, a visiting Consultant Psychiatrist, a few days later, who also came to the conclusion that: 'Mr Brady must be regarded as a schizoid personality, cold, distant, unemotional and with an air of perverted arrogance, very probably enmeshed in a basis of paranoid thinking.'

As he continued to shed weight, possibly because he was still adding copious amounts of salt to his food, he was seen by a specialist. He would grow angry at the slightest thing and became extremely paranoid regarding the Home Office, whom he blamed for still keeping him as a Category 'A' prisoner, meaning he was given very little freedom within the prison. He grew so angry that he would punch and head-butt the walls, and he actually managed to fracture one of his fingers when he hit a wall in sheer frustration. He would also be awake for a lot of the night when he could be heard swearing to himself and talking to himself about the injustice of the Home Office.

A journalist by the name of Fred Harrison wrote an article regarding Brady's weight loss, suggesting that he was suffering from a serious psychosomatic condition. After reading this article, Lord Longford phoned Harrison to congratulate him on the piece and suggested he send it to Brady. Harrison and Brady exchanged a few letters and Harrison began visiting Brady on 29 November 1984 in order to write a further series of articles. By December he was moved to the hospital wing of the prison, where he was to spend many months.

In March 1985, Brady was seen by Dr MacCulloch and Dr Hunter, both psychiatrists, and they concluded that Brady suffered from a personality disorder which could be characterised as psychopathic disorder within the Mental Health Act 1983. He said that he suffered from a psychotic illness which did not have the features of process schizophrenia, but was relatively covert and, from what Brady told him, had been present but concealed for some years. He recommended that Brady be transferred to a hospital. Both Dr Hunter and Dr MacCulloch completed Section 47 transfer forms dated 17 July 1985 and 9 August 1985 respectively.

Dr Hunter:

> Brady has developed during the course of his long imprisonment, a psychotic mental illness of a schizophreniform nature, characterised by persistent auditory hallucinations, olfactory and somatic hallucinations, passivity feelings and a complex paranoid delusional system. His mental illness is severe and chronic in nature. His paranoid delusional system, which is at the core of his illness, concerns the Home Office and prison authorities and entirely militates against any hope of improvement in his present environment.

Dr MacCulloch:

> [Brady suffers from] a personality disorder of the psychopathic type characterised by emotional coldness, obsessionality, sadistic fantasy and practice. He has now developed a mental illness of a psychotic nature, characterised by persistent auditory hallucinations, olfactory and somatic hallucinations and a paranoid delusional system. His paranoid delusional system prevents him from accepting the advice of the prison authorities and militates against improvement in his present environment.

The following month, knowing that Myra's parole hearing was coming up, Brady sent a recorded delivery letter to BBC television news, in which his paranoia regarding the Home Office came to the fore:

> In early March a prison official entered my cell and offered me a parole application form to fill in. I refused. He then asked if I would sign a blank form. I again refused. Two weeks ago the same prison official – the principal officer of this landing in which I am the sole patient – again entered my cell and informed me that the parole review committee had arrived at the prison to see me. I refused to see them.
>
> I wish to make it clear that I am taking no part in a political farce on parole consideration that the Home Secretary, Leon Brittan, is pretending to take place. That is all.

At this time Brady had dropped from thirteen-stone in weight to just eight. He would not fall asleep in his bed, instead sleeping while in his chair, holding a hot water bottle. He continually complained that he was cold and was often found sitting against the radiator in his room with a grey prison blanket wrapped around his shoulders.

He would tell his solicitor, Benedict Birnberg, that:

> The Home Office has been, and still is, piping garbage at me through the air ventilation system, i.e. a continuous series of questions designed to extract information from me about past cases not yet cleared from their books. This has been, and is, keeping me awake till three, four or five in the morning. I haven't been to bed for over a year, but fall asleep from exhaustion in my chair by the window.

He could still be heard at night swearing about the Home Office and he even spoke of Myra, saying:

'You've turned against me. I'll crush you with the other scum bastards … you'll never get out while I'm in here you two-faced bastard … Silly bastard her … thinks she's going to get out … no fucking chance.'

He was desperate to be transferred back to Broadmoor, but they refused to take him. He was still refusing to leave his cell as he feared an attack from a fellow inmate and started to horde food in his room, convinced that someone was trying to poison him. He may have had a point, as he had been having difficulty in breathing and had a problem with his bladder. A prisoner who was in at the same time as Brady later claimed that inmates in charge of the food had been slipping crushed powdered glass from lightbulbs into his food.

He again refused visits from his mother, telling her that he did not wish for her to see him in such an emaciated state. He told her that the weight loss was: 'caused by a programme of systematic harassment, goading and baiting conducted by the Home Office in combination with the withholding of adequate medication'.

He was still losing weight and was in a state of psychological deterioration in June and, during one of his interviews with Fred Harrison, he told him that he was going to court because he felt that he was being maltreated. He told the journalist that he expected to lose, but that he would then get some satisfaction by killing a prison officer.

When he was asked what the point of going to court was if he expected to lose, Brady replied:

> I want people to see an example of what twenty years of an enlightened, modern penal system produced – fuck all. They don't neglect me, as far as harassment and goading me is concerned. They treat me like a monkey in a cage – they keep poking me with a stick. The monkey might not react for days, but when it does react, they say 'Ah, I told you so.' That's the position I'm in. No matter how much positive effort I make, they want that label [the Moors Murderer] stuck, because it's a question of 'isolate, store, destroy'.

# 9

# 'Places of Interest to Ian Brady'

In the summer of 1985, a series of newspaper articles appeared in which Fred Harrison claimed that Brady had confessed to the murders of Pauline Reade and Keith Bennett, as well as other 'happenings'. The Home Office and the Director of Public Prosecutions contacted Greater Manchester Police to ask what they were going to do about it.

The first article appeared in the *Sunday People* newspaper on 23 June, 1985.

The following week the second part of the story was printed and it was implied that Ian Brady was claiming that Pauline Reade had been killed in David Smith's house, but that it couldn't be proven because the house had been demolished.

By that evening, Myra had read the newspaper and told a fellow inmate that she knew Pauline Reade and her mother Joan, but didn't know anything about her disappearance:

'I wouldn't leave that poor woman not knowing whether she was dead or alive, for twenty years. I was doing life already, so I had nothing to lose. If I knew anything, I would have told them.'

Myra was also annoyed that Lesley Ann Downey's mother was again in the press, trying to keep the story alive. She wrote to her mother and expressed her feelings: 'Mrs pain in the neck West got back on her bandwagon and threatened to dig up the moor herself if the police didn't. She seems to feed on such publicity with a somewhat masochistic compulsion.'

She again wrote to her mother about the press coverage:

*Sunday People.*

What on earth is amiss when they have to start scraping the bottom of a twenty-year-old barrel for news when there is so much happening out there? Anyway, my precious one, for your sake more than mine, I hope they don't print any garbage. I hate them. God forgive me, but I do.

Myra's mother then gave an interview to the *Sun* newspaper:

Myra should die in prison. It's better she dies there than comes out of prison and gets killed out here. Myra's been in prison all these years now, so what difference does it make if she stays there forever? If Myra came out she couldn't come here. I don't know where she would go. People wouldn't let her alone. She might as well die in prison.

Poor Myra. Life means life for Myra. For others it means just a few years. When they call her a beast or a devil, they don't know what they are talking about. They don't know her. She is still my daughter. I love her just like I always have done. Something like that does not change.

Greater Manchester Police's DCS Topping contacted Cheshire Police, who held the files on the Moors Murders, because the murder of Edward Evans had happened on their patch. On 3 July Topping went to see Ian Brady at HMP Gartree, Leicestershire, along with Neville Jones, Deputy Head of Cheshire CID, and DSI Jim Grant. Brady was not happy to see them and Topping recalled:

I had heard reports that his mental and physical condition had deteriorated in prison, but I was not prepared for what I saw. He was emaciated, his face drawn and gaunt, his eyes bulging, and he looked extremely ill. He was up and dressed, in a sweater and trousers, but he was in a shocking physical condition. He was clearly very agitated and excited. He was also hyper-active, constantly walking about the cell, unable to sit still.

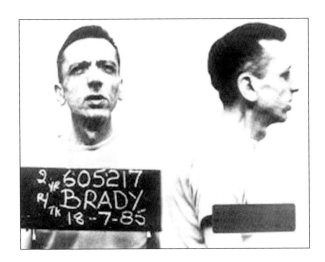

Ian Brady mugshot July 1985.

173

Brady was angry and abusive throughout. He refused to confirm or deny anything that was in the newspaper reports and told the detectives that he had written to his solicitor regarding the matter and didn't wish to discuss it any further. He then told Topping that he didn't want to see him again.

At this point Topping had nothing new to go on and thought about closing the case, but felt it was up to him to do more. He set up a small enquiry team which consisted of DI Geoffrey Knupfer and DS Gordon Mutch and tasked them with going back through the previous files on the case. They then went on to interview as many of the policemen who worked on the original investigation as possible and as many of the witnesses who had given evidence at the trial, too.

The original police files didn't contain much regarding Pauline Reade and Keith Bennett as they had been put together around the prosecution's case of the murders of John Kilbride, Lesley Ann Downey and Edward Evans, but there were hundreds of photographs taken by Ian Brady of the moors.

They believed that all of the victims had been killed elsewhere and that their bodies had been driven up to the moors to be buried. This belief, matched with the fact that the terrain on the moors was rough and uneven, meant that they worked on the premise that any other victims were likely to be buried within 100 yards of the main road. The more they studied the files and photographs, the more they believed they would be able to find any further burial sites.

The detectives looked into any techniques which may have been developed since the original case and thought that the best hope lay in the use of police search dogs. Greater Manchester Police didn't have police dogs at the time, so borrowed dog handler Neville Sharp and his dog from West Yorkshire Police, which was allowed as some of the area's that they wanted to search were in their jurisdiction.

During that summer, Neville Sharp and his dog discreetly searched around Hollin Brown Knoll and Shiny Brook but found nothing of any significance. They also searched areas where Ian Brady and Myra Hindley had visited regularly, such as Whaley Bridge in Cheshire, but again found nothing.

The investigative team was then increased from three to eight, with DI Martin Flaherty, DS Stephen Southward, DS Ronald Peel, DC Patrick Kelly, DC Gerard McGlynn and DC Alan Kibble joining the team.

On the 21 November, as the investigation was happening and the searches drew to a close, Ian Brady was assaulted. Brady was making a complaint to the HSO while his assailant was waiting in line to see the dentist when his assailant suddenly punched him on the ear; it was recorded in his prison notes that 'There was no reason for the assault except that it was Brady.'

Just eight days later, Ian Brady was transferred to Ashworth Psychiatric Hospital in Merseyside. At the time of his admission the doctors described his condition as follows:

> Brady has both an anti-social and narcissistic personality disorder. There is no evidence to support or refute any paranoia as a child or adolescent. There were no indications at the time of his conviction that he was suffering from schizophrenia. Shortly thereafter there were some factors which led to the suspicion that he might be suffering from such. By February 1971

they appeared to have developed so that Dr Duggan-Keen concluded that he was in the early stages of paranoid schizophrenia though Dr Scott disagreed with that diagnosis. During the 1970s views similar to those of Dr Scott were expressed. They were alive to the possibility of Mr Brady trying to manipulate and achieve a transfer from prison to hospital. Any transfer seems to have been contemplated on the basis of personality disorder rather than paranoid schizophrenia. This may have affected the opinions of some who examined him both before and after this period.

Then, in the 1980s, opinions started to change in favour of there being a mental illness. His behaviour included muttering to himself and paranoid ideation, especially in relation to the Home Office. His condition appeared to deteriorate with auditory hallucinations and paranoid thoughts being noted. This led to his admission to Hospital under Dr MacCulloch and Dr Hunter.

After hearing the news, Myra wrote to her former cellmate, Janie Jones, and said:

So he's got what he's been after for the past sixteen years at least. This is why I'm reserving judgement about things. I don't think he's as mad as he's made the doctors believe he is, and that although he's obviously got problems, he's as shrewd and intelligent as he always was.

In early 1986, now that he had got his way and was in a hospital, Brady allowed his mother to visit him again. After visiting him she recalled: 'It was lovely to be with him and actually talk face to face again after so long. It was a visit I had been longing for and one I shall remember for a long time.'

Lesley Ann Downey's mother, Ann West, decided that she would start to correspond with Brady, to see if she could get him to admit to her where the other bodies were on the moor and knew that anything he may admit to would help to keep Myra in prison. She later said: 'I used to think it would kill me to see him, but he has said that he could keep her in jail for a hundred years if he really spilled the beans. I must see him, and try to get him to talk.' Her first letter began:

I am the mother of the little girl you murdered. Seeing as you never want parole and want to die in prison, please tell me where Pauline and Keith are so we can give them a proper burial.

You destroyed my life when you killed Lesley, so at least bring a little happiness back for me and help find the other children. Can we meet and talk?

It was six weeks before she got a reply:

Dear Mrs West,

You had no need to assure me you meant no harm in wanting to visit. It pained me that you felt the need for such an assurance, as you have every right to wish me harm.

He told her that she would not be allowed to visit him because the prison authorities thought that the press would invent stories. The letter continued:

> You know beyond doubt that I have stated I have never applied for parole and never shall. I can assure you personally of the remorse I feel, but I prefer actions to words.
>
> I've spent the last eighteen years doing braille work, transcribing books into braille for schools. I know I can't balance the past, of course, but at least I can do something positive and useful. The satisfaction I get from doing this is beyond measure.
>
> I kept your letter on top of my table as a constant reminder. It has taken me weeks to reply because I couldn't find the words that cover pain and further distress. I only knew I had to answer.

Between May and August 1986, Ian Brady wrote to Ann West three times as they began their correspondence which was to last for five years. In those letters between May and August, Brady complained bitterly about the way David Smith had been treated with such leniency by the police and was insistent that there was a cover-up to repay him for having turned on him. Ann West remained convinced that the events of her daughter's murder took place with the help of others.

Ian Brady lied and told her that David Smith was writing to him in prison and then at the Park Lane Hospital in Liverpool, but that he wasn't reading them and returned them unopened.

On the 30 June 1986, the Internal Lifer Review Board met to consider Myra Hindley. Myra was present at the meeting. The minutes of the meeting showed that:

> Myra avoids discussing her offences … complains about a number of ailments. She is presently taking some hypnotic medication … she complains about publicity but obviously misses it when it is not around! A clever and manipulative woman … Myra is not an easy woman to know. A clever, controlled and articulate person. Her 'weak spot' is her mother…

By November 1986, the preparations for a search of Saddleworth Moor were well advanced. DCS Topping and his team had decided that they were going to search an area of two-and-a-half miles around the A635, going in from the road a hundred yards. The search was divided into one hundred-yard sections which would be searched by a dog, and then by a second dog. The team wanted to search Hollin Brown Knoll, as that was where the other bodies had been found, and Hoe Grain, an area two miles away.

As part of the investigation, DCS Peter Topping visited Doreen Wright who worked as a nurse at HMP Holloway when Myra was there. According to Doreen, during the first year of Myra's imprisonment she had shouted about the murder of Pauline Reade. She told Topping that on the day in question she received a telephone call telling her that an inmate was suffering with indigestion pains.

The following account of what happened next is based on a Statutory Declaration sworn by Doreen Wright before a Commissioner of Oaths:

A woman stopped me and asked me if I wanted to look at her drawings, which had been hung on the walls in the common room. She said: 'Would you like to look at my drawings?' They were quite good pencil sketches. I said: 'I'm sorry, I haven't got time.' I had got time, in fact, but I felt a sudden feeling of not wanting to bother.

Instead, I went through a door and into the glass cubicle used by the prison officers who keep a watch on the inmates in this block. The cubicle had partition walls that were about 8 ft high. I put down the medicine and started talking to a Prison Officer. I asked the officer who the person was who had spoken to me, and she said 'Myra Hindley'. At first, I had thought she was a member of the staff dressed in civvies – she was so smart. Her hair was dark, and Myra's was blonde in the photographs that were published at the time.

Suddenly, I heard shouting and I looked up. I saw Myra Hindley doing her nut. She had lost her rag. She was so angry she didn't know what she was saying. She was looking at me, and calling me a snotty bugger, or something like that. Then she started ranting about someone called David Smith. I was familiar with the name, because of the Moors Murder trial, but it didn't mean anything to me.

Myra said: 'I'll get that fucking David Smith. He helped us kill a 16-year-old girl that he was going with, and she's still on the moors. Her mother thinks that she might have gone off to Australia; she doesn't know she's dead. She's on the moors with the others. David Smith used to go out with her, and he got tired of her. We did her in Smith's house. We helped him get rid of her in his house, and they'll never find her. But when I get out, I'm going to tell the police where she is.'

I thought to myself: 'Blimey, it sounds like she thinks she's going out tomorrow.' The other officer said: 'We are going to have trouble with her tonight.' I also distinctly remember certain other phrases that Myra used. One was 'There are other bodies up there.' Another was her description of the police as 'pigs and fucking idiots'.

Somebody – I think it was Ethel Gee, with whom she was speaking – said something like 'What age was she?' Myra said: 'Bloody 16 and he knows it.' By this, I presumed that she meant that Smith knew more about the death than other people were aware of. Myra said: 'He had a girlfriend and he was tired of her. He wanted to get rid of her.'

She said very distinctly that it happened in Smith's house. She repeated: 'And I know where she is, and when I get out, I'm going to get Smith for it.' She also said: 'He killed a fucking 16-year-old girl in his house, and he's got away with it. There's worse people outside than in.' Also: 'We did her in Smith's house because Smith had been going out with her.' She started to laugh, and I thought at the time that she was a bit nuts.

She was angry because I had ignored her, so she blew her top. I did not know, at the time, that there was a 16-year-old girl who had gone missing.

I did not know the name Pauline Reade, and she did not mention Pauline Reade's name.

I asked a Prison Officer if what Myra was saying was true, and she said: 'She's been ranting about that every time she loses her temper.' I asked her if she had told anybody, and she said she had not, because the Official Secrets Act was strictly enforced in Holloway. And anyway, the Governor was friendly towards Myra Hindley. Myra was saying it, and nobody in Holloway would believe her!

I was asked to wait for five minutes, while another officer went across to Myra to quieten her down. I then left, with two officers accompanying me through the common room. Myra Hindley tried to be friendly, as I passed, but I ignored her.

Although I was told by some officers that there were no other bodies on the moors, I was still worried about it. It was getting to me that there was a mother looking for a daughter, who thought that she had gone abroad. I did not go to the Governor; she would not have believed me. It was this Governor who took Myra out of Holloway for a ride in a taxi and a walk around a park.

Doreen Wright claimed that the outburst was also witnessed by two other prisoners, but the police were unable to check this as one had since passed away and the other was in Russia as part of a spy exchange. Topping recalled: 'I felt that Mrs Wright was a truthful person, not someone who was merely seeking publicity. She had been genuinely troubled by what she believed she had heard…'

This interview gave Topping hope that Myra Hindley would not be as immune to telling what she knew as Ian Brady was. Myra denied that she had ever spoken about Pauline Reade to anyone, as she maintained that she hadn't killed her. It should be remembered that at the time of Pauline Reade's disappearance David Smith was just 14 years old, had never met Ian Brady and only knew Myra to nod to in the street.

At around this time Myra Hindley received a letter from Winnie Johnson, the mother of Keith Bennett:

Dear Miss Hindley,

I am sure I am one of the last people you would have expected to receive a letter from. I am the mother of Keith Bennett, who went missing no one knows where on 16 June 1964. As a woman I am sure you can envisage the nightmare I have lived with, day and night, twenty-four hours a day, since then.

Not knowing whether my son is alive or dead, whether he ran away or was taken is literally a living hell, something which you no doubt have experienced in your many, many years locked in prison. My letter to you is written out of desperation and faint hope, desperation because I know that for so many years you nor Ian Brady has ever admitted knowing anything about my son's disappearance, and hope that Christianity has softened your soul so much that you would never any longer knowingly condemn someone to permanent purgatory.

Please, I beg you, tell me what happened to Keith. My heart tells me you know and I am on bended knees begging you to end this torture and finally put my mind at rest. Besides asking for your pity the only other thing I can say is that by helping me you will doubtless help yourself because all those people who have harboured so much hate against you and prevented you from being released a long time ago would have no reason left to harbour their hate. By telling me what happened to Keith you would be announcing loudly to the world that you really have turned into the caring warm person that Lord Longford speaks of.

I am a simple woman, I work in the kitchens of Christie's Hospital. It has taken me five weeks labour to write this letter because it is so important to me that it is understood by you for what it is, a plea for help. Please, Miss Hindley, help me.

A staff memo from Cookham Wood recorded Myra's response:

She became extremely upset and tearful while reading it and it took a very long time for her to compose herself sufficiently to talk (this is most unusual as Myra is normally very controlled). She is adamant that she knows nothing about this child and that Brady never mentioned his name. She claims that she knows she will never be released and that therefore she has nothing to lose by telling the truth. Her exact words were: 'I wish I did know something – I could at least then put the poor woman out of her misery.'

On 3 November Myra wrote to Reverend Peter Timms (a former prison governor turned Methodist minister who had been giving her private counsel) about the letter, telling him that she had nothing to hide, nor harboured 'any guilty secrets'. She then asked him not to visit:

for the sake of this poor, demented woman. The awful tragedy is that I cannot help her in any way – if I could, I would, I swear this as God is my judge. I'd even be willing to contact the police and ask them to take me to those awful moors [but] those moors are so vast, I wouldn't know where to start or even what I was looking for.

Two weeks later, at 14.00 on the 17 November, Topping and Knupfer visited Myra at HMP Cookham Wood. They were followed on their journey down from Manchester by Fred Harrison, the man who broke the news claiming that Ian Brady had confessed to him that he and Myra had killed more people. The Deputy Governor was told by the detectives to keep an eye on the journalist.

When they saw Myra, they took a different approach to the way detectives had interviewed her before, noting that from the transcripts the questioning previously had

179

been quite confrontational. They didn't caution her, nor did they demand that she told them all she knew about Pauline Reade or Keith Bennett. Instead, they told her that they believed Ian Brady was responsible for their disappearances, that they knew he took her up to the moors and photographed certain locations, and that therefore they would be grateful if she could look at some maps and photographs to try and locate places that were special to Brady.

Knupfer recalled: 'To everybody's astonishment – certainly ours – she more or less said: "What do you want to know?" and intimated she would point out "areas of interest to Ian Brady".'

At around 15.00, Myra asked to pause the interview and phoned her solicitor, Mike Fisher, who then headed for the prison; the interview resumed at 17.00. Topping told Myra's solicitor that he was not going to caution her, and that anything said during the interview would not be admissible as evidence in court. They then went over what had been discussed before her solicitor arrived and Myra began to tell the detectives of the places she had visited with Brady. She agreed that on the following day she would look over old photographs and maps of the moors and point out places that she and Brady had visited. The interview finished at 19.30.

At 09.30 the following morning, Topping telephoned HMP Cookham Wood and enquired for the first time about the possibility of taking Myra Hindley up to Saddleworth Moor to help identify certain locations. Just half an hour later the press office were informed that Myra would be interviewed during the day. There were already plenty of cars containing reporters situated outside the gates of the prison, hoping to get a picture or a word from either the detectives or Myra's solicitor.

The interview with Myra resumed at 15.00 and she showed particular interest in photographs of Hollin Brown Knoll and Shiny Brook, the two areas already highlighted by the detectives as top priorities in any potential search. The detectives were certain that some of the photographs of Hollin Brown Knoll in their possession were taken before Lesley Ann Downey was abducted, killed and buried there, so it was a good contender as a site for further burials.

Shiny Brook, the other area the detectives were interested in, was a stream that ran across part of the moor but was around three quarters of a mile inland from the road. Because of the distance from the road it didn't seem like an ideal place to bury a body, working on the detective's hunch that the children were killed elsewhere and their bodies carried on to the moor. However, from the large volume of photographs taken by Brady of that area, it must have been one of his favourite places. Some of the photographs had been taken in the streambed and others were taken by a small waterfall; many featured Myra. There were also the photographs taken on the day David and Carol Waterhouse were taken there by Ian and Myra.

That area became of enormous significance to the police and that was confirmed by Myra. She told the detectives that she could not be sure of the locations favoured by Ian Brady without going back to the moor – something she said she was willing to do. The interview drew to a close at 19.30.

Michael Fisher, read out a statement to the waiting press on her behalf, in which she claimed that it was the letter from Winnie Johnson that had made her realise that she needed to talk to the police. The truth was that she realised Ian Brady could tell the police what had really happened and where the bodies were at any moment. After discussions with her legal team and others, she had decided to embark on a case of damage limitation:

> I received a letter, the first ever, from the mother of one of the missing children and this has caused me enormous distress. I have agreed to help the police in any way possible and have today identified, from photographs and maps, places that I know were of particular interest to Ian Brady, some of which I visited with him. In spite of a twenty-two-year passage of time, I have searched my heart and memory and given whatever help I can give to the police. I'm glad at long last to have been given this opportunity and I will continue to do all that I can.
>
> I hope that one day people will be able to forgive the wrong I have done and know the truth of what I have and have not done. But for now I want the police to be able to conclude their inquiries, so ending public speculation and the private anguish of those directly involved.

Michael Fisher then told the gathered press:

> I saw it happening when I was with her. She was in a state about that letter. She had got to do something about it. I genuinely believe that she was greatly moved by the letter and that she wanted to assist the police for genuine reasons and wasn't thinking in the back of her mind that this would help her to be released one day.

He was then asked about the possibility of Myra being taken to Saddleworth Moor. He replied: 'I would have thought that that was completely out of the question. I think in view of the information she has been able to give to the police today that it won't be necessary – and neither do I think it would be permitted by the Home Office.'

Lord Longford took advantage of these developments to say:

> I think this is a breakthrough in the sense that the public will now realise that she is a good woman. If she was a character in a Dostoyevsky novel she would be the heroine. I think Myra will be released from prison. It would be a terrible thing if she was not. She is still in her forties and if she was not released it would show cowardice on the part of the Government and keep alive the hatred towards her.
>
> I think the Home Secretary [Mr Douglas Hurd] is a good man and will do the right thing. Myra had a change of heart two years ago. What people will not believe is that she feels remorse and has done for many years. People cannot get it into their heads.

The following day Topping and Knupfer travelled back to Manchester and held a press conference alongside Deputy Chief Constable John Stalker and Assistant Chief Constable Ralph Lees.

Topping told the gathered press: 'At the moment I am looking for the bodies of Keith Bennett and Pauline Reade. I am keeping an open mind so far as any other bodies being found.'

Deputy Chief Constable John Stalker said:

> Many policemen have had their opinions on these two missing children, and it was always felt that there was a certain amount of unfinished business to attend to. This has become far more than a local issue – it has become part of international murder folklore. People of this region want the matter brought to a proper and compassionate end and if that is the discovery of children's bodies, it will satisfy a lot of people.

He then said it was difficult to believe that both Pauline Reade and Keith Bennett would now be in their thirties had they lived. 'They are frozen in time to the people of this region and it is important for us to try to do everything humanly possible to put the minds of their parents at rest.'

Topping finished by saying that he had spoken to the parents of the two missing children and added:

> Their lives have been affected as would be lives of the parents of any murder victim. But they have the anguish – and they feel it very deeply – that the children have not been properly buried and they feel deeply they can never put it behind them until that has happened.

Winnie Johnson, mother of the missing Keith Bennett, again wrote to Myra:

Dear Miss Hindley,

> Suddenly the world which stopped for me so many years ago is beginning to spin faster and faster. First I read of your confession to Mr Topping about your part in the disappearances of Keith and Pauline and then I woke up the next morning to find your letter to me waiting on the doormat. It is so difficult to know what to say. To say I am grateful to you is like saying a cursory thank you to someone who has saved your life. Because that's what you have done by opening your heart to Mr Topping and telling him everything you know about what happened to Keith and Pauline all those long nightmare years ago, you have brought me and my family back to life. The torture was not knowing what had happened. Now I do know and it is because of your compassion that situation has been brought about.
>
> I know what hell the years must have been for you when you finally found the courage to face up to the monstrous crime you committed with Ian Brady. It is a hell we shared, me because I did not know what happened and you because you did know. From your statement issued through Mr Fisher I began to realise how you tried for so many years

to block from your mind the enormity of what you have done. To find the courage to face the awful truth and the possible consequences took enormous courage.

It would be a lie to say I can now forgive and forget. My emotions are so jumbled, the way I feel at the moment I have to admit that I cannot forgive you for your part in the death of my son, an innocent little boy who never did anyone any harm. He had the same right as every other child to grow up and live life with whatever that might hold. But you helped Brady rob him of that right. It will take time, maybe the rest of my life to find it in my heart to begin to forgive you for that.

But do not think that I do not feel for you at this time. I do because you are now going through the pain that I have lived with for so long. You helped bring unimaginable pain to me and now you are finding great courage to transfer the agony from my heart to yours and begin to pay penance for the horrific things you did so many years ago. I cannot find it in my heart to like you, that would be asking too much, but I can begin to understand the nightmare you have lived through and I respect the feeling and the sheer guts it must have taken to bare your soul.

My heart goes out to your family because I know the sort of emotions they are now going to have to learn to live with. They too are innocent victims of this nightmare. It is not easy to live with the finger-pointing and some of the mindless things people say, but it can be done if they accept you are now an entirely different person to the one who fell under Ian Brady's evil spell. Like me they have to face reality, that is never easy – but it is not impossible and the one thing I have learnt, and I hope your family can say this too, is that there are always special people you can lean on for help and guidance through the darkest hours.

It is about one of my special friends that I would like to tell you about now. His name is Ian who is known to Mr Fisher. Ian and I have become close over the last few years and I have every reason to trust him implicitly. If proof were ever needed of his honesty and integrity he has demonstrated it over and over again. Without Ian's help I do not think we would be where we are today.

Please talk to Mr Fisher about him, find out everything you want to know about him and [indecipherable] there is just one thing left I need to know … what happened to Keith. I know you have told Mr Topping everything but what I am frightened of is that the only way I am going to find out anything near the truth is through rumour, gossip, and half-truths. Can you understand how unbearable that would be? I would not be able to avoid fastening on the most awful things and live them over and over, never knowing whether they were fact or fiction. Mr Topping has been wonderful to me, he is a man who obviously cares deeply and I know he will tell me what he thinks I can bear to hear. But I know in my heart that he will not tell me everything in an attempt to spare my feelings. What I do not think he understands is that I <u>need</u> to know everything no matter how hard it is going to be to face because only then can I start coming to terms with it. I have got to learn to live with the truth, no matter how hard it is.

So from my heart I beg you a second time to help me, this time by seeing Ian and telling him everything so he can tell it to me. I would ask you to see me but I do not think I could face sitting in a prison visiting room and being told what happened. It would be impossible for both you and me. I want to be in my own home with my own family so Ian can tell us all together in a way that because I know him so well will be the kindest and the gentlest.

Once I have faced that and the police find Keith as I know they will thanks entirely to you, I will be able to put my son to rest in a proper cemetery which I can visit, be alone with him and put flowers on his grave.

I need that final act of courage from you, I need to know everything. Then we will both be able to live again with some peace of mind. I know in my soul that Mr Topping is going to find Keith very soon and that moment will be more bearable if I am forearmed with knowing the facts.

Please discuss my request with My Fisher then try and see Ian. I have asked and he has agreed on my behalf to accept any conditions you impose.

I want to thank you for everything you have done and I mean it from the bottom of my heart. Your facing the truth means we share something now and who knows, maybe one day we will be able to look each other in the eye and you will not see any hate in mine.

Mrs W. Johnson

Myra's former prison mate, Carole Callaghan, told the press how she couldn't believe that Myra had lied to her for years and had killed more children:

I persuaded myself to believe her when she said she didn't kill those children. I paid a heavy price for my foolishness. My two children, Richard and Jane, turned their backs on me because I defended her. I felt I had to stick by Myra. I had lived with her for three years – as long as Ian Brady had – and I refused to acknowledge that the young woman who lived in the next cell had been guilty of those terrible crimes.

I know that she said things which contradicted her claim to be innocent, and I goaded her about it. But in the end, I was still a young woman who had to live with her. I didn't want to believe she was guilty.

But after I read Ian Brady's confession that they had killed Pauline Reade I knew it was not possible to continue deceiving myself. I haven't spoken out before now, because I couldn't see any reason for raking up the past.

But I've read in the newspapers that there is talk of sending Myra to an open prison. I know Myra better than most people, and I am sure that she would do a runner from an open prison … there is no way that she should be allowed to walk free again.

Early in the morning of 20 November, the search of a misty Saddleworth Moor began, with thirty men and dogs provided by Lancashire and West Yorkshire Police. Topping had chosen three further teams, each consisting of a detective sergeant and a detective constable. Detective Sergeant Steve Southward was teamed with DC Alan Kibble and Detective Sergeant Martin Flaherty with DC Pat Kelly. The third team consisted of Detective Sergeant Ron Peel and DC Gerald McGlynn.

The press were bussed up from Stalybridge and when they arrived they could see that an area around Hollin Brown Knoll had been cordoned off. Four areas, each 150 by 100 yards had been marked out and the police dogs were asked to search it. Any spot which the dogs found of interest would be searched further by policemen.

Topping faced the press and TV cameras and said: 'If we don't have success in the next few weeks we won't be disappointed. We won't give up.' He said that the search area had already been decided before he had spoken to Myra, 'but as a result of seeing her we are much more optimistic that we are in the right area.'

The search continued the following day, but was slowed down by snowy conditions. Meanwhile, Topping travelled down to London for a meeting with the Home Office. They discussed the public interest in Myra's proposed visit to the moors, as well as the seriousness of the investigation and the likelihood of any visit producing a positive result. The Home Office were concerned with the public's safety and the safety of those who would accompany Myra as it was well known that people had threatened to kill Myra given just half a chance. The press were also discussed, and it later became apparent that newspapers were offering up to £20,000 for a clear picture of her on the moors.

Police search Saddleworth Moor.

185

Police dogs search Saddleworth Moor.

Police dogs search Saddleworth Moor.

Back in Ashworth Hospital, Ian Brady was upset that Myra was indicating 'places of interest' and not taking any responsibility for her roles. He was annoyed that she seemed to be getting the upper hand and got his solicitor, Benedict Birnberg, to issue a short statement:

> He is very concerned about things that have been said by Myra Hindley implicating him. That has stung him. He wants Myra Hindley and her

186

advisers to know that letters she wrote to him over a period of years when they were first in prison and before their relationship broke up are still in existence.

This threat was a clear warning to Myra to be careful with the path she was choosing, otherwise he would release these letters and show the world her true thoughts and feelings at the time of their incarceration.

On 23 November, David Astor made arrangements for Reverend Peter Timms to become Myra's media spokesperson, rather than her solicitor Michael Fisher. He was given a once-only special social visit to her that afternoon but would not be afforded the regular daily facilities of her legal advisor.

After a two-hour meeting between Myra and her solicitor on the 25 November, he told the gathered reporters:

> I discussed with her reports that Ian Brady will publish letters that she wrote to him and she told me she will not be deterred by anything he might say or do. She is determined to continue to give the police every help in resolving these mysteries.
>
> We don't know if she will be going up to the moors. There has been a lot of speculation, but it's a matter for the police.
>
> Myra has told me she is not frightened by anything Brady may say or do. This has been a great strain for her and she is feeling rather frail and tired.

By 28 November there was great concern that the delay in getting Myra to the moors was causing her harm. An internal prison report stated that she was 'under considerable stress and may change her mind'. It also stated:

> the media aspect of the production is so out of hand and so unable to be controlled that to take Hindley to the moors now would be to expose her to a situation that could only be described as disgraceful. For the Prison Department to be a party to this I felt was unprofessional. There was no doubt Hindley should go to the moors, but as things were so out of hand with the police operation efforts should be made to postpone the visit until the media attention was diverted. Possibly delaying until next spring even, using weather conditions as the cause for the delay.

At 18.30 Winnie Johnson, the mother of murdered Keith Bennett, was taken to the gates of HMP Cookham Wood by a reporter from *The Sun* newspaper. They were told that they would not be given entry unless they had received a visiting order directly from Myra, which they hadn't. The Deputy Governor of the prison spoke to Myra who said that she would like to see Mrs Johnson, but only on the condition that she signed a form stating that she had no photographic or hidden recording equipment on her. She was also advised that the reporter would have an obvious interest in what was said if such a meeting were to take place and advised her to have her solicitor present at the meeting as what she would say would 'undoubtedly be misconstrued' by the reporter.

On the 30 November, Ann and Alan West visited Ian Brady's mother. The meeting had been arranged by Maggie Enfield, reporter with the *Daily Mail* newspaper, and the three of them went to Mrs Brady's house in Chorlton-on-Medlock.

That evening, an interview appeared in *The People* newspaper between journalist Val McDermid and Mrs Brady. She broke her twenty-year silence:

> He wasn't a bad lad till he met Myra Hindley. I never thought there was anything strange about my Ian. He was moody sometimes, but I don't believe these terrible things would have happened if he hadn't met Myra Hindley. His real trouble started when he got mixed up with her.

She told of the times she used to go and visit Myra in jail: 'Ian asked me to go and see her, to make sure she was all right. For a while she wrote to me. She always tried to play the innocent with me, all charm. But I felt she was a manipulator.'

In a meeting with her solicitor on 1 December, Myra said she was now not so keen to see Mrs Johnson, as she was involved with a reporter. The Reverend Peter Timms was also present at the meeting, despite having been clearly told by the prison authorities that he was only to visit on receipt of a visiting order from Myra. He and Mike Fisher advised her against seeing Winnie Johnson and the Rev. Timms volunteered to see her on Myra's behalf.

Outside the prison, the press gathered as Michael Fisher gave a statement. He told them that Myra would find meeting relatives of the victims 'enormously distressing' and added:

> I have been discussing with Myra today reports that relatives would like to see her. With regard to visits to Myra by relatives, I have advised her that as this investigation is being conducted by Mr Topping of Greater Manchester Police, everything she has to say about this should be said to him. She has accepted this advice and feels that a meeting between herself and relatives would be enormously distressing for her and for them. She will continue to offer all the help she can to Mr Topping and Greater Manchester Police.

The press, however, did manage to get hold of a prison officer who was willing to talk. Anonymously, she said that these days Myra was a 'wizened old lady' who 'saw her chances of freedom slipping away. She sees herself as some kind of heroine, but she takes a lot of stick from the staff and other inmates. They tease her about Christmas being so close and that there are only a few more shopping days left.

> You wouldn't recognise her now. She has changed so much since the last pictures were taken of her. She has all but given up on any hopes of parole. She feels the recent publicity about the new search has killed off all possibility and this has hit her hard.

Arrangements were also put in place for Topping and Knupfer to visit Myra again at HMP Cookham Wood on the afternoon of the 4 December.

Myra asked for permission for a special letter to be written and handed to Lord Longford by her solicitor, Mike Fisher. Lord Longford was due to appear on the TV show *Wogan* and Myra asked him not to appear and not to visit her until she told him to, as she wanted her name kept out of the press as much as possible.

Myra's stepfather, Bill Moulton, gave an interview to the *Daily Mirror*:

> When she got life, so did we. We shall suffer forever. Our lives are in tatters. Hetty [Nellie] can't go to the shops without being pointed out as Myra Hindley's mother. We just want to be left alone and try to forget the past.
>
> There will never be a place for her here. Myra is on her own. She's killing her mother. I don't want to see or talk to her again. Hetty's health is going down fast. How do you think she feels when she reads dreadful stories about her daughter? She is a broken woman. Stories about Myra being a beast and evil obviously upset her.
>
> In her heart Hetty still loves Myra, but she has severed all contact. She used to visit prison and write but the letters stopped years ago.

The investigation got a boost when, on the 5 December, Home Secretary Douglas Hurd gave his permission for Myra to be taken up to Saddleworth Moor.

A week later Topping called upon the expertise of DCI's Ivan Montgomery and Chris Baythorpe of the CID Operational Support Group. As the details of the operation were being sorted out, Myra's solicitor called Topping saying that she needed to see him urgently. Topping was not happy but felt he had to comply in case of any hiccup when the day to take her up to the moors came.

The following day he drove down to Cookham Wood where Myra asked him to speed up the process to get her up to Saddleworth Moor as she was finding all of the publicity difficult to cope with. Topping, however, described her reaction to the publicity as 'schizophrenic', adding: 'she says she hates it, yet she revels in feeling important.'

Myra told him that she was getting herself ready to divulge everything that she knew and Topping thought that she may have been close to confessing. She told him that she was going to need a lot of support before, during and after any formal statement that she may give. She told him that she was unable to talk to the Roman Catholic priest at the prison, and that she wanted to be counselled by the Methodist minister who had visited her, Reverend Peter Timms. Effectively, Myra was trying to manipulate Topping into getting her visits with Rev. Timms again.

Topping realised that he had to have everything in place to persuade Myra to confess after just over twenty years of denial and that she needed to come to terms with the fact that she had lied to her mother, her brother-in-law, her niece, Lord Longford, David Astor, Janie Jones and Sarah Trevelyan. All of these relationships, the only ones she really had left in her life, were on the line.

Topping then made a visit to Ian Brady at Park Lane Hospital.

I think if I had not known who it was I would have found it hard to recognise him. The emaciated, bulging-eyed, ranting skeleton of a man I had met at Gartree Prison had been replaced by a calm, polite, normal-looking person. He was not fat: he has a naturally rangy build. But he had put on some weight, so that he looked healthy; his manner was quiet, he talked sensibly.

His solicitor, Benedict Birnberg, was present at the meeting but Ian Brady said that he did not feel he was able to help at all, although he did say that Topping could go back to see him at a later date.

In early December, an anonymous letter, purporting to come from a Prison Officer at Cookham Wood, was received by The Home Secretary:

I am writing to express deep concern that the establishment and the public do not be taken in by Hindley's sudden desire to be of so-called assistance with regard to the finding of the bodies on the Saddleworth Moors. She is looking upon it all as a macabre joke … never has she shown any remorse for her evil deeds. She is totally without conscience or guilt. The only thing she feels is the desire to be released – in other words she is stir crazy. She has only spoken out now to get her word in before Brady – she has told me so – as she is scared he will reveal even more atrocities she was responsible jointly with him for.

Hindley is a menace to society and should suffer the ultimate penalty for her unmitigated evil. There is no redeeming feature in the creature

that she is. It is an insult to womankind to call her a woman. Brady may be called mad, but at least he does know better than to want to be free. Please God do not let Hindley be free – there is enough evil in the world already.

Myra was now having to watch her back in Cookham Wood and a note was written to the Governor on the 12 December stating that:

She saw me today in order to express her anxiety that another inmate XXXXX has

Ian Brady.

been threatening to attack her before her release in January and that she has been putting psychological pressure on her by following her around whenever she can.

She intends to inform you herself in writing about this fear but asked me to tell you that she had seen me about it.

At 05.30 on the 16 December, Myra was woken and told she was be taken to Saddleworth Moor. She and all accompanying staff were dressed in identical clothing and bulletproof vests provided by the police. A small convoy of unmarked police cars arrived inside HMP Cookham Wood and other police vehicles pulled up outside in order to intercept any cars that may attempt to follow the convoy.

Twenty-two minutes after being woken, Myra left the prison and the convoy headed to Maidstone, the headquarters of Kent Police, where the Metropolitan Police helicopter was waiting. Myra boarded and was accompanied by two prison officers with whom she got on well. Also boarding the helicopter were DI Roy Rainford from the firearms branch, who acted as Myra's Personal Protection Officer.

The police had managed to keep her visit quiet, but at 07.30, about an hour before she was due to arrive at Saddleworth Moor, David Mellor, then a junior minister at the Home Office, was interviewed on Radio Four's *Today* programme and told everyone who was listening that Myra was on her way to the moors.

Myra's solicitor, Mike Fisher, arrived at the scene at 07.30 in order to prepare for his client's arrival.

The plan had been for the helicopter to land at the junction of the A635 and the B road to Meltham, but because of poor weather and cloud cover, it had to land two miles further down the A635 at 08.40. They were picked up and taken down to the mobile headquarters.

Myra Hindley landing on Saddleworth Moor.

Myra Hindley landing on Saddleworth Moor.

Myra told Topping and his team that she was most interested in finding a site on Shiny Brook, near the waterfall seen in the photographs, so it was decided that they would go there first. The convoy consisted of Topping, Commander John Metcalfe from the Home Office, Myra's solicitor Michael Fisher, the two prison officers from Cookham Wood, Roy Rainford and DI Geoff Knupfer. They were surrounded by other officers from the Moors inquiry team, some of whom were armed. Everybody was dressed in black anoraks, black trousers, rubber boots and navy-blue balaclavas in order to confuse any photographers or anyone wishing to seek revenge on Myra.

They were informed that because of radio interview the press knew what was happening and there would soon be helicopters flying overhead (at one point there were four); Topping took the decision to send three decoy parties out over the moor too.

One of the conditions the Home Office made in allowing Myra out of prison was that she was to be handcuffed at all times, but as the already difficult terrain was covered in snow, Commander Metcalfe took the decision to remove them as he could see that there was no possibility of her running off. Topping then had to hold Myra's arm most of the way to the site; she was not able to get her bearing properly so they carried on walking.

Commander Metcalfe recalled that Myra was 'noticeably unnerved and distracted by the high security operation which accompanied her visit'. At approximately 12.00, as they got near the waterfall, Myra asked for a private conversation with her solicitor and then informed Commander Metcalfe and Topping that she wished to make it clear to the Home Secretary that she had not asked for immunity from prosecution and that furthermore, she would not wish to be considered for parole in 1990. This led them to believe that they must have been very close to one of the graves.

When they reached the A635 again, Myra showed the group where she and Brady used to park. By now there were three press helicopters overhead, as well as the police helicopter that was trying to chase them away.

At 13.15 they broke for lunch and sheltered from the snow back at headquarters. Myra stated that she was concerned that, because of the snow, it was taking longer than she had anticipated to identify the sites that she had visited with Brady. She then asked if it would be possible to remain at the site for a further day, but Commander Metcalfe told her it wasn't. When the party then went back out, Myra told them she wanted to return to an area called Hoe Grain, where the vehicles had parked.

Hoe Grain was the valley that led from the car park down to Shiny Brook, and as they walked there Myra told Topping that it was the way she and Brady had come on to the moor. She then pointed out a couple of areas that she thought might be significant, but couldn't narrow them down.

At that point Topping decided that they should leave the Shiny Brook area and head to Hollin Brown Knoll, where the body of Lesley Ann Downey had been found previously.

As they looked around the area, Topping could not discuss with her the site of Lesley Ann Downey's grave because she and her solicitor were sticking to the story that she knew nothing about the murder; she also made it clear that she did not want to know the grave sites. She mentioned one or two small areas that she thought the police should look at closely.

A helicopter then dropped off a couple of journalists close to the group, but they ran off across the moor when they were challenged by police officers. Journalists were desperate to land that £20,000 shot of Myra and two of them from the *Daily Mirror*, who had walked five miles to get a photograph of her, were quickly surrounded by armed

Myra Hindley on the moor.

193

officers and told to lay face down in the frozen, snow-covered peat while they were searched and handcuffed before being driven to Greenfield where they were released with a warning.

At this point Patrick Kilbride, father of John Kilbride, turned up at a roadblock armed with a knife, hoping to see Myra Hindley. He said: 'I would cut her to ribbons if I got my hands on her. I tried my best to deal with her. I just want her dead. I will kill her.'

Temperatures soon dropped below zero and visibility began to fade, so the search-party made their way back to their headquarters at 16.30. Due to the conditions on the moor, the police helicopter had to land at Woodford, Stockport, so a police convoy escorted Myra back to the helicopter and she was flown back to HMP Cookham Wood. Myra made another strong plea to be allowed to continue her search the following day because she was sure that with more time, having now orientated herself with the surroundings, she would be able to further locate particular areas that the police would be interested in, but she was again told that the Home Office order for her release covered one day only.

Topping gave a brief press conference to inform the press that he thought the search had been useful as it confirmed the two areas they should be searching.

On Friday 19 December, the last day of the search, David Smith was taken up to the site again to see if he could show Topping and his team the areas that Brady was interested in.

Myra Hindley (third from left) on the moor.

Smith was now living on a farm in Lincoln with his family when detectives contacted him to ask whether he would be willing to look at Brady's 'scenic' photographs again: 'They offered to send two detectives to pick me up and bring me to their headquarters in Manchester. It was very hush-hush because they didn't want the press to get wind of anything – that suited me. I agreed immediately.'

He was collected in an unmarked police car and was expecting to see Topping in his office, but discovered that he was in fact being taken to Saddleworth Moor. He was angry at this and felt that he had been misled:

> We approached the moor and all I could see apart from the snow was the press. They were there in vast numbers and came running forward with their microphones and cameras as we pulled up. I hadn't a clue where we were because the moor looked identical in every direction, blanketed in snow beneath a heavy sky… It was freezing up there and I was in very bad humour, let me tell you. We had to make our way to a mobile police unit about 40 yards away, where Topping was waiting with about half a dozen detectives.
>
> I didn't get so much as a 'good morning' out of Topping. He was very, very abrupt and told me to sit down. Then he said: 'We've brought you here to look at a few areas where we think you've been before.' His attitude really got my back up and I gave him an earful. He interrupted me: 'Shut your mouth or you'll be walking back to Lincoln.' That was it – I hated him then. When we left the van, I was in a filthy mood, and Topping paraded me through the press with all the cameras going off in my face. We climbed into another car, but I can't tell you whether we drove left, right, or straight on because the snow made everything look the same, and besides, my temper was ready to erupt. After ten minutes, we stopped. A long convoy of press vehicles had followed us. Topping told me to get out. When we were stood on the roadside, he asked, 'Do you recognise this?' I honestly didn't – he could have turned me round twice and I wouldn't have known which direction I was facing in because the left-hand side of the road was identical to the right, just thick, thick snow. Topping knitted his brow at me and said: 'You've been here before and we know that you've been here.' I insisted: 'But I don't recognise it. So how can I tell you if I've been here or not?' My reply really pissed him off. We went on to another spot, which looked just like the last. It was obvious to both of us by then that our meeting was a dismal failure.

Topping recalled of the meeting: 'He was obviously deeply affected by the moor, and it distressed him to remember that time in his life.'

The weather deteriorated further, and it was decided that there was no point in continuing the search. The police managed to remove the last piece of their equipment just hours before the road became completely blocked by a snowdrift.

Topping told the waiting press:

> The digging has stopped and will not be restarted until the spring when it gets warmer. Temperature is vital for us to be able to use the search dogs.

Meantime we will be evaluating information we have gathered so that we will be able to pinpoint specific areas to search when we return. Myra Hindley's visit was very useful and I am hoping to see Ian Brady again. We are temporarily leaving the operation with our tails high and in a more optimistic frame of mind than before.

On the 29 December Topping, Knupfer, Myra's solicitor Mike Fisher and Rev. Peter Timms met for lunch a few miles away from HMP Cookham Wood, where both Mike Fisher and Rev. Timms felt that it was in Myra's best interests to offer a full confession. Reverend Timms also felt that it would help her mental well-being.

The two detectives then went to visit Myra to tell them what had been discussed and Topping agreed that Rev. Timms should counsel her; he further said that after a couple of visits he would expect her to tell him whether or not she would confess.

In the meantime, the RAF provided help in the investigation by agreeing to fly over the Moors as part of their training exercises and take aerial photographs, just as had been done in the original investigation. The investigators were able, with the help of RAF experts in photographic interpretation, to pinpoint the same rocks and even tufts of grass that were there in the original photographs.

The police were also advised by other experts, including an archaeologist from Manchester University. He showed the officers how to search the ground thoroughly and how to look for signs of disturbed vegetation.

On the 27 January 1987, Topping, DI Geoff Knupfer and Michael Fisher went to visit Myra. She told them that none of the murders had taken place in the house at Bannock Street where she had lived with her grandmother before they moved to Wardle Brook Avenue. Then, for the first time, she confirmed that David Smith had not been involved in the murder of Pauline Reade.

However, she made it clear that she detested Smith with a passion. She told them about the time that she had been alone in her parked car, Brady was out of sight on the moor and a police motorcyclist pulled up. Whereas Smith had told the police that Brady was burying a body, Myra was adamant that he was actually practicing with the guns and some new ammunition that they had picked up from one of Brady's contacts in Bradford. She used the opportunity to try and prove that Smith either lied or misunderstood what was told to him and she disputed the evidence he had given to the police against both herself and Brady.

Myra then spoke of the tape recordings that had been made of Lesley Ann Downey; the tape had been made while photographs were being taken and not while she was being tortured as had been reported in some quarters and she completely denied that Lesley Ann had been subjected to any physical torture.

Myra then confirmed that the police should be searching Shiny Brook and Hoe Grain for the body of Keith Bennett and Hollin Brown Knoll for the remains of Pauline Reade.

Following the meeting, Myra's advisors held an emergency meeting to discuss whether she should make a full and frank confession to the police. Together with solicitor Lord Goodman, they decided that it was in her best interests to do so.

Remarkably, Myra's solicitor then told the press: 'The heroine in this story is my client. She has been very, very brave.' There was an unsubstantiated rumour that he leaked the news of the meeting with Lord Goodman to the press, giving David Astor and Rev. Timms the incentive they needed to convince her to ditch him, although she later did so reluctantly.

On 19 February, Mike Fisher called Topping to arrange an urgent meeting with Myra. Topping, Knupfer and DS Southward travelled down to Cookham Wood, and when they arrived Myra and Mike made it clear that she was going to make a full confession for the first time, but Myra wanted to tell Topping about her involvement in the murders informally, which meant without caution, without note-taking, and with no tape recorder running.

The detectives agreed to this and Myra talked almost non-stop, pausing only to drink. At times she was emotionally distressed and medical staff had to bring her medication. When she was giving details about the actual killings, she became almost hysterical.

She agreed that the detectives could return the following day and that the conversation could then be tape recorded for a formal confession.

The following day the detectives returned to interview Myra on tape and under caution. She talked in greater detail than she had done the previous day but again she required medication at times to help to calm her. On this first day of her confession she spoke of her early life before she met Ian Brady and of the first three murders.

Her eventual confession was over seventeen hours long, but even then Topping could tell that she wasn't being completely truthful regarding her actual role in the murders. He described it as:

> A very well worked out performance in which, I believe, she told me just as much as she wanted me to know, and no more.… [I] was struck by the fact that she was never there when the killings took place. She was in the car, over the brow of the hill, in the bathroom and even, in the case of the Evans murder, in the kitchen.

He added that he felt he: 'had witnessed a great performance rather than a genuine confession.'

Myra's 'confession' began when she told the detectives about how she had become infatuated with Brady at work and how he had forced his beliefs on to her. She told the detectives about Brady drugging both her and her grandmother, and at that point she realised that he needed professional help but was too afraid to say anything in case he followed through on his threat to kill her grandmother.

She then lied to the detectives and told them that Brady only told her he wanted to commit the 'perfect murder' on the day Pauline Reade went missing, and that he blackmailed her into it by saying he would show her family the pornographic photographs he had taken of her when he had drugged her if she didn't agree to help. (Topping had seen these photographs, some of which also included Brady, in the original police file but he could not tell whether she had been drugged or not).

Then, for the first time, Myra gave her version of how Pauline Reade was abducted, murdered and buried on Saddleworth Moor.

According to Myra, Brady drove her home to Bannock Street on the back of his motorbike after work on 12 July 1963. She had already agreed to help recover her friend Ben Boyce's broken-down vehicle that evening, but as usual Brady took priority.

Brady told her to drive the old van (which she had borrowed from Ben Boyce) and he would follow on his motorbike. When he spotted someone he wanted her to pick up he would flash his headlights. She was to tell whomever she picked up that she had lost a glove while out picnicking and that if they would help her to go and look for it then they would be paid with records.

She told how they drove along Gorton Lane and a small girl walked towards them from Peacock Street. Brady flashed his headlights for her to stop, but she just slowed down and finally stopped when they were both past the girl. Brady then pulled up beside her and asked why she had not picked the girl up. She told him that she recognised the girl as Marie Ruck who lived just two doors down from her mother. Brady accepted that as a good enough reason and told Myra to drive on, which she did, and turned left into Froxmer Street.

Halfway down the street they both spotted a girl walking away from them who was wearing a pale blue coat and white high heels. She told the detectives that she did not recognise the girl at this point. Brady then flashed his headlights, so she drove just past the girl and pulled over. It was then that she turned and recognised the girl as Pauline Reade. Myra told the detectives that she hadn't really spoken to her before but she knew her family. She said that they would acknowledge each other in passing.

Myra was then asked what the difference was between her and Marie Ruck, to which she replied that Pauline lived a little further away and was older. She said that she knew there would be less fuss made if a teenager went missing compared to a 7 or 8-year-old, but said that it wasn't something that she and Brady had discussed.

Myra offered Pauline Reade a lift and she readily got into the van. Myra then asked her if she would help to look for an expensive pair of gloves, offered Pauline the records as a reward and that she was keen to have them. She told Myra that she was on her way to a dance but wasn't in any great hurry.

Myra then pointed out that they had come across her purely by chance and that it could have been anyone – male or female – and that was the case in all five murders.

She said that they drove up to Saddleworth Moor and she parked in a lay-by as previously instructed by Brady. She discussed this lay-by at length with the detectives as it was important in the search for the location of Pauline Reade's body. She told them that it was a rocky area on the Manchester side of Hollin Brown Knoll.

Brady then arrived a short time later on his motorbike and Myra introduced him to Pauline as her boyfriend and told her that he had also come to help look for the glove. She said that Pauline accepted this, said 'hello' to him and had no reason to be suspicious of him.

Brady then suggested that he would take Pauline to look for the glove, while Myra was to drive along the road to the next parking place, which was just the other side of the knoll. She said she did as he suggested and then sat waiting in the van. She said that she knew before she picked up Pauline Reade that Brady planned to kill her, therefore she considered herself as guilty as him – and perhaps more so.

She said that around half an hour later Brady came over the hill and asked her to go with him. They went up behind some rocks and it was dark, but she could see Pauline lying on the ground. She thought that there had been a struggle because Pauline's shoes had come off and there was blood on her neck. She said that she could hear a gurgling noise coming from Pauline and that the amount of blood made her feel sick. She said that she wanted to leave, but Brady threatened her and told her that if she didn't do what he told her then she would end up in the same grave as Pauline.

According to Myra, Brady then told her to stay with the body while he went and got a spade that he had hidden (without her knowledge) in a trench nearby. While she was alone with the body she could see that Pauline's coat was undone and that her clothes were in disarray. She had guessed that Brady had sexually assaulted her from the time he had taken.

Brady then returned with the spade and he told Myra to go and wait in the van. By this time the gurgling noise had stopped and she assumed that Pauline was dead. When she reached the van she realised that Brady had taken the ignition key. She said that she had considered driving off and going to either the police or her mother when Brady first took Pauline onto the moor, but was afraid of what he would do to her family if she accused him of murder and he hadn't gone through with it. She said she regretted not going to the police then as there would have been no further killings.

Topping asked her if she knew beforehand that Brady had a sexual motivation but she didn't answer. Instead, she just repeated that she guessed he was sexually assaulting her because of the time he took and that she didn't think Pauline's coat had been undone when she went off with him. Later, when they were both in the van, Brady told her that he nearly had to call for her to help him hold her hands down, as she was struggling so much.

Myra said the spade was the same one used for the first three murders, but they had then lost it and had to buy another. She admitted that she knew Brady would bury the body because he had told her that to commit the perfect murder the body must never be found. She said that Brady wiped the knife that was used to cut Pauline's throat on the grass and put it on the dashboard of the van, wrapped in newspaper. He put the spade in the back of the van and together they lifted his motorbike into the back before driving back home; on the way they passed Pauline's mother and brother walking along Gorton Lane. She remembered telling Brady who they were.

Myra had then parked the van on some waste ground at the back of the house and they took Brady's motorbike out. Brady insisted that they went to Ben Boyce's house, as he didn't want anything to draw suspicion upon them. Boyce was in bed when they arrived; Myra apologised for bringing his van back late but Ben said it was OK and he still wanted her help to collect his broken-down vehicle. Ben drove Myra and Ian to the Abbey Hey area and then Myra steered the broken-down vehicle while Ben towed it back. She said that she was so upset by the events of that evening that she twice drove into the back of the van.

When they got home Brady burned his shoes and his trousers but she couldn't remember if he burned his jacket. She said he cut the clothes up, wrapped them in newspaper and threw them onto the fire. He washed the spade and burned the handle of the knife, a kitchen knife. He then tried to snap the blade but it wouldn't break, so he put it on the fire and blackened it. When everything had finished burning he removed the contents of the grate, wrapped them up and put them in the dustbin.

It wasn't until the following morning that they cleaned the van. They took his overcoat to a dry cleaners in Manchester, and then drove through Stockport towards Macclesfield, where Brady threw the remains of the knife into a stream near the road.

She told the detectives that while they were cleaning the van, Brady told her that he had found four half-crowns in Pauline Reade's jacket, and on the journey to dispose of the knife he had spent them on cigarettes and a chocolate bar for her. She said that she was terrified because at that time the death penalty was still in force for certain murders and a murder involving robbery was one. She said that the following day they drove up to Hollin Brown Knoll and Brady scattered four half-crowns where he believed Pauline's body was buried.

It was her 21st birthday eleven days after Pauline's murder and Ben Boyce gave her the van as a present. It wasn't taxed and it had no MOT or insurance, but she drove it around using the tax disc from another vehicle until she was reported to the police. Technically the van still belonged to Ben and he was charged and pleaded guilty to permitting the offence.

She said that in the weeks after Pauline Reade's murder she was aware of the rumours circulating that Pauline may have run off with a fairground worker and she had read a notice in a newspaper from her parents asking her to come home. Myra had cried and when Brady asked her what was wrong she told him; he was angered by this and began to strangle her. She said that she didn't believe that he tried to kill her, but he did bruise her neck and she had to wear a polo neck jumper for a few days. He then told her that if she displayed any more emotion of this type then he would kill her sister Maureen.

At this stage of the interview Myra was very distressed and barely able to talk. Topping asked her if there was anything else she wished to tell about the death of Pauline Reade and she denied what Doreen Wright had said about her shouting about Pauline Reade's death while in HMP Holloway.

After she had gathered her composure, Myra told of the murder of John Kilbride. According to her, Brady arrived at her house at around 16.00 on the day John Kilbride disappeared, put a spade and a .22 rifle into the car, and they drove to Ashton-under-Lyne Market. The boot of the car had been lined with sheets of polythene, obtained from Millwards, their place of work, to prevent muddy marks being left by the spade.

Myra was wearing a black wig and headscarf – she said the wig was Brady's suggestion because her blonde hair was conspicuous. She insisted this was the only planning they had done that day, and that they had not gone to the market previously to scout for potential victims.

She said they had been at the market for five or ten minutes, when: 'we spotted a small boy, standing by the biscuit stall'. She stated that John Kilbride was buying broken biscuits and Ian went to speak to him. The three of them went back to the car and Brady said to her: 'Do you remember that bottle of sherry we won in the raffle – I've promised it to Jack.'

She said John had obviously lied to Brady about his name and that he sat in the front passenger seat of the car – next to her – and Brady sat in the back. They drove up to Saddleworth Moor and stopped at a lay-by, as per earlier instructions from Brady (contradicting herself when she had just said that this hadn't been pre-planned). This lay-by was on the opposite side of the road to where she had stopped with Pauline Reade. She said that it was about 17.30 when they had picked him up and it was now dark.

According to Myra, John Kilbride had agreed to go back to their house for the Sherry, but at no point did they tell him where they lived. On the journey up to the moors, Brady had mentioned Myra's lost glove and said they would look for it. She again contradicted herself and said that she had been told beforehand that when she dropped them off, she was to drive down to Greenfield and wait there for about half an hour, and then return and flash her headlights three times. Brady would flash his torch three times. He had also apparently told her that while she was in Greenfield she should take the gun out of the boot and put it next to her on the passenger seat.

She said that when she stopped the car to let John Kilbride and Brady out to look for the glove, Brady went to the boot for a torch and he may also have taken the spade, but she didn't recall seeing it. John Kilbride stood in the car doorway and the two of them then walked off together down a slight slope. She said that the boy went willingly and she knew that Brady was going to kill and bury him.

She said that she drove off and parked opposite the Clarence pub in Greenfield, stopping en route to take the gun out of the boot and put it on the front seat. She said she didn't know what Brady wanted her to do with it, but he had described it as 'insurance'. She said she didn't have a watch but waited for what she thought was half an hour before driving back to where she had dropped Brady and John Kilbride off and flashed her headlights. The torch then flashed back at her from a little down the hill. She turned the car around so it was easier for Brady to get in, but when he came up to the car he unlocked the boot and put the spade and one shoe in. He told her that he had found the shoe after burying the body.

Brady told her that he had killed the boy and that he had taken out a small knife, about six inches in length and with a serrated blade, but that it was too blunt to cut the boy's neck so he had strangled him with a thin piece of string. The string was white and Brady put it in the back of the car with the knife. Myra said it could have been nylon or it could have been the lace from a plimsoll.

She said Brady told her that he had pulled the boy's trousers and underpants down and slapped his bottom before covering him over in the grave. She asked him what else he had done and was told: 'It doesn't matter.' She believed that he had sexually assaulted John Kilbride. When they got home the spade was washed in the sink and the shoe was burned, along with Brady's shoes and trousers, the string and possibly his jacket.

Myra then told the detectives that the following morning they cleaned the car, taking care to wipe the surfaces to remove any of John Kilbride's fingerprints – but they made sure that it didn't look too clean.

She said that two or three weeks later they collected a suitcase from the left luggage office at one of Manchester's train stations, that it was the first time it had happened and she did not know it had been deposited. This time Brady had drawn up a disposal plan and had burned the knife after he snapped the blade off, but she could not remember how he disposed of it.

Myra then moved onto the abduction and murder of Keith Bennett. She could not remember whether Brady was already at her house, or whether she drove over to his home on Westmoreland Street to pick him up. She told the detectives that she remembered driving into a side street and, when no one was around, she put on the black wig again. On this occasion Brady had taken the suitcase on his own to the left luggage office again, giving her no details of any plan he might have, but she knew that she would be driving up to the moors again.

When they went out that evening, Brady decided to sit in the back of the car and he told Myra he would tap on the window that separated them when he saw someone he wanted her to pick up. She drove along a road leading off Hyde Road – it could have been Morton Street or Grey Street – when they saw a boy walking on his own. Brady tapped on the window and she pulled over. She wasn't sure of the time but thought it could have been about 19.00.

She said that it was her who spoke to him first, and she asked him if he would carry boxes from an off-licence – a story she had rehearsed with Brady. She said she wouldn't have been able to think of anything to say if it wasn't for Brady. She then told Keith that she would drive him home. He accepted and jumped into the front seat and they drove off. After a short distance Brady tapped on the glass and asked Keith to get into the back with him. She told Keith that her boyfriend was helping with the boxes, too.

Myra told how none of the children ever queried anything or objected to anything they were asked to do. She admitted: 'It was probably because of me being a woman – they never had any fear.'

She then said that she drove to the lay-by at Hoe Grain at Brady's request. It's approximately two miles further east than the lay-by they had used previously.

Brady and Keith Bennett got out of the back of the car, using the story about looking for a lost glove again. They walked on to the moor together, Brady with a camera round his neck. She described the boy as going 'like a lamb to the slaughter'.

This time, however, Myra said that she locked up the car and followed them, from quite a distance, carrying a pair of binoculars. They walked down the stream until they were quite some distance from the road, crossing the water from side to side but mostly sticking to the right-hand bank. They reached a point where Brady signalled to her to stop and scan the horizon with her binoculars, in case there were any hikers or shepherds in the area. Myra said that Brady didn't have a spade with him and must have hidden one on his own at the spot he had chosen on a previous occasion. She again made the point that no child would have gone with him had Brady been carrying a spade.

Myra then said that she stayed at that spot, scanning the horizon while sat down. Brady and Keith then went into a dip about twenty-five or thirty yards away. She said: 'I don't know how long I was there. It seemed like ages. It could have been thirty or forty minutes.'

Brady then came back alone, carrying a spade. She asked him how he had killed the boy, and Brady said he had strangled him with a piece of string. She said that Brady never volunteered any information and never bragged about what he had done. He then told her that he had taken a photograph and that he had sexually assaulted the boy.

Myra said that she looked at the photograph two or three days later after Brady had developed it and could see that there was blood on the boy's body, but because of that she didn't look too closely. She said that Keith was lying on his back with his trousers down but she was unable to tell whether he was dead or alive. Brady then told her that he was going to destroy the photograph as it was blurred.

Myra said she and Brady then walked back together along the streambed and he buried the spade in a bank of shale or peat.

When they got home, Myra said that they burned their shoes. She said that hers had to be burned this time too as she had been on the shale and had been close to where Brady and Keith were.

Brady counted all of the buttons on his clothes and tore and cut up his trousers while Myra burned them on the fire. He then ticked off all the items on his disposal plan. She told the detectives that this was the first time she had seen the disposal plan and had no idea where it had been kept. Brady then threw the piece of string he had used to strangle Keith onto the fire. He told Myra that the murder had been the same as John Kilbride's, but without the knife. When he was happy that everything had been accounted for Brady then burned the plan.

They tidied the car up that night but did not clean it properly – they both had work the following day. After work Brady cleaned it thoroughly. Two or three weeks later he collected the suitcases on his own. She told the detectives that she had no idea what was kept in them, but one day got them out from under her bed and wanted to open them, but realised that a hair had been put across the lock – she didn't want to open it as Brady would have realised.

She then told Topping that she had only later found out where the grave of Keith Bennett was when one day they went up to Hoe Grain with the dog. They had taken wine and sandwiches with them and Brady put the drink in the stream to cool. The dog disappeared into a dip and was found sniffing around a dead lamb. 'Brady kicked the dog away and picked up the lamb and threw it as far as he could away from the spot.' She then knew that this was the place where he had buried Keith Bennett.

Myra was given the weekend to compose herself and the detectives went back on Monday 23 February to hear the rest of her confession. She told them just how exhausted yet relieved she had felt following the previous interviews and that she had needed medication all weekend. She also told the detectives that she knew that when the news of her confession broke, she could be attacked by other inmates and could lose the friendship of those who had believed her and supported her.

Myra then gave her account of events when Lesley Ann Downey was abducted and murdered. She told the detectives that they drove to the fair and parked nearby. She was again wearing the black wig and headscarf – she had to wear the headscarf to keep the wig in place as it didn't fit properly. They were both carrying boxes, pretending that they had been shopping. They looked around for a victim, and again she insisted that Brady didn't care if they were male or female. They just needed to be alone and approachable.

She recalled that it was between 17.00–18.00 and said that as they looked around for someone the music that was blaring from the loudspeakers was *Little Red Rooster* by the Rolling Stones. It was then that they spotted a girl on her own by the dodgems. Myra said that the fair was busy, but not packed, and that Brady had always told her that the most obvious approach was also the least likely to be suspicious.

Myra said they walked over to her and when they got near they dropped some of the shopping. They asked Lesley Ann if she would help them carry the boxes back to the car and then on to their house, and Myra said that she would give her some money for doing so.

She said that they put Lesley Ann in the passenger seat and piled the boxes of shopping around her, so that if anyone happened to look into the car they wouldn't see much of her.

They drove to Wardle Brook Avenue, where Myra knew that Brady had already set up his camera, tripod and lighting equipment; although she claimed not to know that he had set up the tape recorder. She told the girl to take the boxes up to the bedroom, where Brady had already gone; she was going to follow Lesley Ann up the stairs, but the dogs had run into the hallway and she didn't want them going up the stairs. She said that it took her a couple of minutes to lock them in the kitchen, and by then she could hear the girl screaming loudly. Brady was either trying to take her coat off or had told her to take it off.

Myra said that she went upstairs into the bedroom but did not notice the tape recorder as it was hidden beneath the divan bed.

She said that Lesley Ann was crying as Brady was trying to take her coat off. She said: 'I know I should have tried to protect the child and comfort her but I didn't. I was cruel, I was brusque and I told her to shut up because I was frightened people would hear. I just panicked.'

Myra then described how Brady tried to put a handkerchief in the girl's mouth, and how she was pleading for her mother. When Brady held the back of her neck and tried to push the handkerchief into her mouth Lesley Ann said that it hurt. Brady then got a bigger handkerchief and tied her up, but the girl was still crying and making noises.

She said that the window in the bedroom was open and she was frightened of anyone hearing her and it was because of this fear that she kept telling Lesley Ann to shut up. She put the handkerchief in her mouth and told her to bite on it hard or she would pack it in more tightly. Myra then said that she would swear 'on her mother's life' that it was just a handkerchief being put into Lesley Ann's mouth and not Brady's penis.

Myra said that she then went downstairs – she didn't know why. She went back up to the bedroom and said the girl seemed to calm down and so she put the radio on to try to relieve the tension. She said she tuned the radio to Radio Luxembourg, where a recording of *The Little Drummer Boy* was playing. Lesley Ann was now sitting on the bed.

She assured Topping that up until this point – when the tape recorder finished recording – Lesley Ann had not been physically harmed or hurt, apart from when Brady had grabbed the back of her neck. She did, however, acknowledge that Lesley Ann was 'mentally terrified out of her life, hysterical and frightened to death', and again said she had no defence.

Myra then said that when Lesley Ann became calmer Brady plugged in a very bright light. The tripod was in the bedroom, and the three loud cracks on the tape were the opening of the tripod's legs. She then corrected herself and said that the tripod legs were pulled out *before* the light was switched on and there was only one plug in the bedroom, so when the light went on the tape recorder went off.

It was then that Brady told Lesley Ann to get undressed, which she did, and he tied a scarf round the bottom half of her face in an attempt to conceal her identity. She said that photographs were then taken in 'various unpleasant poses, not only for a child but for anybody else'.

Ian then told Myra to go and run a bath for Lesley Ann, to get rid of any dog hairs or fibres. He told Myra to wait in the bathroom. She said that she didn't hear any noise (the bathroom was less than 2 metres from the bedroom) but after she waited twenty to thirty minutes the bath water had gone cold, so she drained it away and refilled the bath. Eventually Brady came into the bathroom and she went into the bedroom.

Myra then said that Lesley Ann was lying half on and half off the end of the bed, facing down on the bed. There was blood on her legs, from which Myra realised that the girl had been sexually assaulted. The scarf was still around her face. Brady picked her body up and lowered her into the bath to wash the blood off her legs.

Myra noticed that there was also blood on the bedsheet. He told her to wash out the bath, while he carried the body into the bedroom and took the scarf off. There was a deep red mark around her neck where he had obviously strangled her, and the piece of string that he had used to do it. Brady then wrapped the body in a sheet, putting her clothes in with her. Once Myra had finished cleaning out the bath Brady told her to bring the car nearer to the house.

As she brought the car around she realised it was snowing and guessed that it must have been around 20.00. She said that it was extremely quiet outside and Brady had no problems as he carried Lesley Ann Downey's body and clothing down to the boot of the car. They then set off for Saddleworth Moor.

She told the detectives how it was very cold and that the roads were very slippery, which made driving difficult. She said that they got halfway up a hill near her uncle's in Dukinfield but couldn't go any further and they would have to take the body back. Brady told her to ring the AA and ask about road conditions over Saddleworth Moor. They advised her not to travel unless it was essential, so they decided to wait until the following day.

Myra said she needed to collect her grandmother, but Brady told her it was impossible, so they drove to an area of level ground nearby and she left Brady in the car while she walked to her uncle's. She told him that she had tried to drive there but it was impossible since the gritting lorries had not been out.

Her uncle was angered by this and Myra explained to the detectives that he had had a son who died aged 21 after a blow to his skull. Her aunt and uncle had turned his bedroom into a shrine and would not let her grandmother sleep in there. (She subsequently spent the night sleeping on the floor on a bed made up of cushions and blankets).

Myra and Brady returned to Wardle Brook Avenue and Brady carried the body of Lesley Ann back up to Myra's bedroom. She said that she never slept in the bedroom again; after that night she hated going into it, even to clean it. (This is disputed by the testimony of both David and Maureen, who said that she often slept up there with Maureen).

Ian Brady developed the photographs straightaway and showed them to her, and she heard the tape recording. She said she begged him to destroy them all and he told her that he would. She believed this had been done until she was shown the photographs and heard the tape following her arrest.

She then said that the following morning the gritting lorries had been out and conditions were better. In the late afternoon, while it was still light, they took the body back down to the car and put in a new spade that Brady had bought. She drove up to Saddleworth Moor and parked in the same spot she had when Pauline Reade was taken up there. She recalled seeing few vehicles on the road and from where she had parked she could see any approaching traffic from either direction.

Brady then got out of the car and ran up Hollin Brown Knoll with the body of Lesley Ann wrapped in the bedsheet in his arms. He came back a minute or two later for the spade. She said that he had practiced carrying bodies on the moor by putting her over his shoulder and walking with her while she was as limp as possible.

Myra said that she stayed in the car, acting as a look-out. She had no idea of the time but said that it was getting dark and too cold to get out; there were several inches of snow on the ground. Brady then returned with the bedsheet and told her that the girl's clothes were in the grave. She said she did not know what he eventually did with the sheet because he couldn't burn it in the house as they lived in a smokeless zone (despite having burned clothes there previously).

Myra went to collect her grandmother while Brady washed the spade at home, and then made a start on dinner. He then went to pay his mother a late Christmas visit, and did not return to Wardle Brook Avenue that night. She assumed he disposed of everything while he was away.

This was in stark contrast to the proof that Myra actually collected her grandmother at around 10.30 am so it couldn't have been 'getting dark' while Brady was burying the body.

Finally, Myra gave her version of what happened on the night Edward Evans was murdered.

She told the detectives that David Smith was having financial troubles and that Brady had said they could 'roll a queer'. They were in the living room and Brady told Smith that he and Myra would go into Manchester to try to pick someone up.

They drove to Central Station and Brady went to buy a couple of bottles of wine or beer to take back, Myra parked on a double yellow line to wait for him. A policeman told her to move and that he would book her if she was still there when he came back.

Brady and Edward Evans appeared shortly after and Brady introduced him to Myra as 'Eddie', telling him that Myra was his sister. As with previous abductions, Brady sat in the back seat, directly behind the front passenger. They drove back to Wardle Brook Avenue and when she was locking the car up Brady told her to go and get David Smith. She walked to Underwood Court and it was Smith who answered the telecom and invited her up to the flat. He was fully dressed apart from his shoes as he knew that Brady was going to pick someone up. Maureen appeared in her nightie and asked why she was there, so Myra gave her a message to pass on to their mother that she would be round on the Friday to do her hair.

Smith walked Myra home and Brady opened the front door to them both; he and David went straight into the living room, while she went into the kitchen to feed the dogs, closing the door behind her so they couldn't get out. While she was opening a tin of dog food, she heard a chair crash across the living room and scraping on the floor. She looked through the serving hatch and saw Brady and Edward Evans struggling, each holding the other's lapels.

She then ran into the hallway and saw Smith standing in the doorway. She shouted at him to help Brady, then ran back into the kitchen and shut the door behind her. She said that then 'all hell let loose'. She could hear very loud screaming, which she assumed was coming from Evans. She said she couldn't see what was happening, but that all three men were in the room.

Again, she had no idea how long it lasted, but when the house fell silent she went into the living room. She said that everywhere 'was one complete pool of blood'. Evans was sinking face down on to the floor. Her dog Puppet then ran into the room followed by the other.

She couldn't go into the room as she could not stand the sight of blood; anyone who knew her well would vouch that she had never been able to stand it. She ran into the kitchen and was 'horribly sick'. Brady came through and went to a drawer where tools were kept. He pulled out a piece of electric wire from an old iron.

'He told me to pull myself together because he said I had to clean the place up', Myra said. Brady went back into the living room to finish Evans off.

Her gran had shouted downstairs to ask what all the noise was about, and she was scared that her grandmother would come down and have a heart attack if she saw what had happened. She told her gran that she had dropped the tape recorder on her foot and that the dogs had started barking.

Brady again told her that the place needed to be cleaned up, but she said she couldn't face it. She said she managed to refill two bowls and buckets with clean water and throw out the dirty water, which was red with blood. After they had finished cleaning Brady told her to go and get some of the polythene sheeting from upstairs. She again said that she was unable to see anything through the restricted vision of the serving hatch. Brady had told her that he had hit Evans with the axe, and the boy kept on shouting so he kept on hitting – the more they tried to quieten him, the more noise he made.

The detectives asked Myra if she knew why Brady had hit him in the first place, because if someone was planning a robbery, they wouldn't bring the victim back to their house. She replied: 'I think they wanted to kill him.' She was asked whether the intention all along was to kill him rather than rob him, to which she replied it was to do both. She thought Brady and Smith had been discussing killings, although she said that they had not talked about it with her. As Topping said:

> The whole explanation of this killing does not ring true to me, and I do not believe a lot of thought had been given to it. No criminal, however stupid, would take someone they intended to rob back to their home. If Smith and Brady had been planning to do a robbery together they would have gone out together.

According to Brady, Evans had resisted when he had asked him for money and a fight had started. Brady had weak ankles after being kicked by Evans and was limping quite badly, and said that he could not dispose of the body that night.

Smith and Brady then carried the body upstairs and Myra said she held her grandmother's door closed in case she came out to use the bathroom. They put the body under the window in Myra's bedroom before going back downstairs to finish cleaning up. Myra said she went into the kitchen to make a cup of tea and then all three of them sat in the living room. She denied that she had her feet up on the mantelpiece.

She said Brady was sitting on two chairs at the end of the room, with some notepaper on the coffee table. He was writing his 'disposal plan'. Myra remembered that Brady had previously opened Evans' jacket and removed his wallet. Although he knew Evans' first name was Edward, and later said in court that he knew Evans visited homosexual bars in Manchester, it was from the wallet they discovered that his surname was Evans and that he was an apprentice of some sort. She did not know whether there was any money in the wallet. She thought it was possible Brady might have known Edward previously.

Myra was then asked about the electric flex and she said she saw Brady use it on Evans, who had been lying face down with a cushion cover over his head. Brady leaned forward, put the flex around his neck and pulled it from behind. She said the string from Smith's stick was used to tie up the body, but she didn't know that until the trial.

She then told the detectives that there was almost as much blood on Smith's clothes and stick as there was on Brady's clothes, whereas she had only a few spots on her shoes, which happened when she went into the living room to get the dogs out.

Myra then told the detectives more about Brady's 'disposal plan'. She said his first idea was that they should hide the body in some bushes on a very dark road nearby to make it look like a hit-and-run accident. She claimed that it was Smith's idea to bury the body. She thought he didn't know anything about it, so commented sarcastically: 'Where, in the garden?' Smith then said: 'No, Penistone.' She said that she thought that 'PB' on the disposal plan produced in court stood for Penistone Burn, she did not know about the ticket in the prayer book until the court case.

She was then asked by the detectives if she knew what the 'WH' stood for in the disposal plan; she lied and said she thought it meant Woodhead, which is on the way to Penistone. Topping then asked her if, in the light of developments, she now thought it stood for Wessendon Head on Saddleworth Moor. She did not think so, since she and Brady did not know the names of specific areas up there; they just knew the whole area as the moor.

Myra said Brady's ankle was very painful so they had to leave the disposal of Evans' body until the following day. She said Smith showed no fear or any other signs that he was appalled, frightened or sickened by the events that had taken place. She was sure she would have noticed if he had.

By the time they had finished making the disposal plan, Myra said it was around 03.00. Brady told her she would have to go to work the next day, as it would look suspicious if they both took the day off – he couldn't go because he couldn't walk.

According to Myra it was agreed that she would pick Smith up in the car on Hyde Road at 17.30 the following day and they would drive to his grandfather's house where a pram was kept. They were to use this to move the body.

It was at this point that Smith left. Brady then insisted that Myra went outside to lock the car up properly and put the anti-theft device on, but because she did not want to go out he did it himself (this doesn't make sense as Brady would have had to climb over the fence and walk down a small, steep incline to get to the car and then do the return journey – all on a leg that Myra said Brady couldn't put any weight on).

When the police took her car away the following day they found Ian's wallet on the dashboard; in it was the disposal plan. She thought his wallet must have fallen out of his pocket when he was putting the padlock on the wheel and he put it on the dashboard then forgot about it.

Myra couldn't sleep and spent what was left of the night in an armchair in the living room. As she was getting ready for work, she took a cup of tea up to her grandmother as she always did. Brady was in the living room writing a letter to their manager, excusing himself from work because of his injured ankle. Then there was a knock at the back door.

Myra was asked if there were any other possible victims and if they ever had any failures. She said no to both questions and said that was why she wanted to write a book – so that she could give a warning to children never to go with strangers. She said Brady had never mentioned any other murders to her and that she had not been involved in more herself.

She was asked if she thought that Brady could have been involved in homosexual activities and she replied that she did wonder what he and Smith did downstairs all night, but thought that when he wasn't with her and went off into Manchester on his own, he was probably off with other women. (She later stated to other people that she thought he was off with other men.)

Myra was asked what her relationship with Brady was like and she said that at first he didn't show a lot of interest in her sexually, but for the first few times they had normal sexual intercourse. There were times when he had just wanted her to relieve him, and on a couple of occasions he had forced her to have anal sex with him, which she described as 'dreadfully painful'. On other occasions he liked her to insert a candle into his anus while he relieved himself.

He never showed overt affection towards her, she said. The most they would ever do was sit in the car kissing. Kissing was as much as she had ever done with other boyfriends. Brady, she said, didn't even know how to kiss properly – it seemed to her that he had never had any experience of it. She told the police that if she was ever out with Brady and she linked her arm through his he would take his hands out of his pockets and say: 'Don't do that. Walk normally.' But there were times when he was loving and affectionate. He would call her 'Kiddo' as a term of endearment. Despite everything he had done, she told the officers she could not think of him as wholly evil at all times. Sometimes he was kind, and he would surprise her by bringing home unexpected presents.

She said they went up to Scotland as many as eight times while they were together. She was given no reason to think that he had killed while they were there, and even on one occasion she saw a child walking alone past them and she asked him: 'Don't you want to do another one?' He told her that he could not kill one of his own – meaning anyone Scottish.

Myra then admitted that Smith had not been involved in any of the murders apart from Edward Evans. She admitted she had done him irreparable harm in court by accusing him of bringing Lesley Ann Downey to the house and taking her away again, unharmed, after Brady had taken photographs of her. This explanation had grown out of a statement by Brady that there was another man involved; it was he, she said, who had started the lies about Smith, and she had carried on with them. She said she would one day like to write to Smith and ask for forgiveness for the damage she had done to him. But the statements he had made to the police and in court about the Evans murder, she pointed out, had accused her of a deeper involvement than she in fact had in that killing, and she believed he made things as bad as possible for her.

When asked about the grave sites on Saddleworth Moor, Myra said that as far as she knew Brady didn't use markers to locate the graves. She then told the detectives that she thought she would have been able to offer more help to them on the moor if the weather had been better and had they not had the media flying above. She told them that she was 99.9 per cent certain that on a clear day she could locate the remaining graves.

Then came one of her most ridiculous claims. She said that she wished Winnie Johnson had written to her fifteen years earlier, when she broke off contact with Brady, and that the police had visited her then but because they hadn't the parents of the remaining unfound victims had endured twenty-two years of agony.

She said that she was asking God for the bodies of Keith Bennett and Pauline Reade to be found, to ease the minds of their mothers. She said that she knew she was twenty-two years too late, but at least she was trying to redeem herself and make her peace with God.

'I did not gain any sexual gratification from the murders. The prime motivation for the murders, for Ian Brady, was the feeling of power and control. In my case, it was rather compensation in the sense of being different from other people and being set apart from the world.'

The detectives returned on the 24 February to conclude Myra's confession. She apologised for being hesitant at times over the previous few days and said that it was due to her reading from her notes. She then said that she wanted to add a few details to the statement that she had already given.

She said that on the days of the murders, Brady bought her records as a present for the 'anniversaries' they were sharing. On the day of Pauline Reade's murder, he bought her the theme music from *The Hill*, a film about an army prison. On the day of John Kilbride's murder he bought her *Twenty-four Hours from Tulsa* by Gene Pitney, for Keith Bennett's murder it was *It's Over* by Roy Orbison, for Lesley Ann Downey's murder it was *Girl Don't Come* by Sandie Shaw and for Edward Evans' murder it was *It's All Over Now, Baby Blue* by Joan Baez. She told the officers that when he gave her a new record, she knew that a murder would take place that evening.

Winnie Johnson wrote another letter to Myra Hindley around this time. She was sympathetic towards the criticism surrounding her first visit to the moors. This time Myra replied, thanking her for both of her letters, explaining that she had not replied to the first letter as a result of the negative publicity surrounding it.

On the 11 March detectives visited Ian Brady again and told him of Myra's confession, but he refused to believe it. He told the detectives that he had been ill and was suffering from amnesia, and as such, he couldn't remember their previous visit in November. He was presented with some of the evidence that Myra had provided of Pauline Reade's abduction and he then decided that he too wanted to confess, but on one condition only: that immediately afterwards he be given the means to commit suicide, a request that was impossible for the authorities to comply with.

He asked DSC Topping if Myra had told him about the evidence he had asked her to destroy while he was in custody, to which Topping told him that he knew about the envelope destroyed at Millwards. Brady then said that Myra had failed to get back in to the house at Wardle Brook Avenue because the police were there, and had therefore not been able to get the ticket for the suitcases at the left luggage office.

He told how he and Myra had agreed to kill David Smith because he knew too much; he had also wanted to get rid of Maureen, but Myra had been against murdering her sister. Later, when they were both in custody, she had agreed to Maureen being killed; he said this was contained in code in letters between them.

In a surprise move, Myra returned to Saddleworth Moor on the 23 March in a covert operation. She was taken from HMP Cookham Wood at 22.00 in an unmarked police car and stayed overnight at the flat of the Chief of Police in charge of Greater Manchester Police training at Sedgley Park, Prestwich, arriving at around 03.00. The flats there had previously been used to hold notorious prisoners while they helped the police with their enquiries.

At 06.30, in heavy mist, the party containing Myra was dropped off at Hoe Grain. The mist was so bad that vision was down to just a few yards. At 09.30 they stopped searching and had tea and sandwiches. They then went back out and Myra said she wanted to concentrate on the Hoe Grain area – stating that it was the most important place to look for Keith Bennett. She was trying to find the spot where she had kept look-out but couldn't find it. The search continued until they broke for lunch at 12.30.

Following lunch they moved to Hollin Brown Knoll to see if anything jogged Myra's memory regarding the burial spot of Pauline Reade. Topping recalled that Myra was: 'very enthusiastic, very keen to help. And therefore very frustrated that she could not give us an exact location.'

At 14.45 the search was called off as both Myra, and the police and prison officers with her, had hardly slept the previous night. She was then taken back to Sedgley Park.

Before leaving there on the 25 March, Myra asked to see Topping and confirmed that Hoe Grain and Hollin Brown Knoll were the correct areas to be searched for the missing bodies. She also told him that Brady had buried a metal box of some significance on the moor. She wouldn't say what it contained and the police were unable to find it. She was then taken back to Cookham Wood at 11.00 and arrived at 15.45. The detectives continued to search.

On the 4 April Myra's solicitor persuaded her to release a public statement regarding the reasons for her confession to the police. The statement in full read:

> When I was arrested, tried and convicted I was still obsessed and infatuated with Ian Brady. I could not bring myself to admit the truth about our crimes.
>
> Between 1966 and 1977 I served my sentence at Holloway Prison. There I did what I could to hide the truth from myself and from others believing this was the only way I could survive the ordeal of a very long prison sentence.
>
> From 1977 to 1983 I served my sentence in Durham, where I became completely ostracised from the outside world, living a totally unreal life with thirty or so life and long-term women prisoners. I was aware that public hostility towards me was, if anything, increasing and I reacted by withdrawing more and more into myself.
>
> In 1983 I was transferred to Cookham Wood prison. This move was interpreted by some as a first step towards my eventual release but I knew this was simply an alternative prison for me.
>
> Since I have been here, I have received considerable help and encouragement which has strengthened my resolve and I began to become more confident that I could be open and frank about my case.

Throughout my sentence I have been haunted by the continued suffering of the relatives of the two children that were missing at the time of my arrest and until recently I have been utterly overwhelmed by the difficulties of revealing the truth.

I have had to consider the consequences for my family who have suffered far more than I have and I have been fearful of the effect that facing up to the truth would have on me and my existence in prison, which has always been a tremendous ordeal.

In 1985, under the personal direction of a Jesuit from Farm Street, I continued the Ignatian Spiritual exercises which I began in Durham prison with the Jesuit chaplain. These spiritual exercises lasted over a year and gave me great strength and brought me closer to God than I have ever been before. It was then that I realised I could no longer live a lie.

The former prison governor, Peter Timms, now a Methodist minister, agreed to help with the task ahead. His experience of dealing with life sentence prisoners and their cases has been invaluable.

On the 31 October, 1986, I received a letter from Mrs Johnson, begging for help. This was the first such letter I had received and on 18 November, I resolved to assist the Greater Manchester Police who had reopened the case of the two missing children.

I felt able to cooperate with the officer leading that inquiry, Det Chief Supt Topping whose approach to me was professional, but kind and sympathetic.

I was taken to the moors a few weeks later and did what I could to identify the places where I believed the two children were buried. However, this visit was frustrated by the enormous press interest and by the weather.

It was Peter Timms that I first was able to make a full admission of guilt and immediately afterwards, I instructed my solicitor to contact Det Chief Supt Topping who attended at the prison with his assistant, Det Insp Knupfer, to hear my voluntary statement on the 19, 20, 23 and 24 February. In this statement, I admitted my role in these awful events and said that I considered myself to be as guilty as my former lover, Ian Brady, although our roles were different.

Later, I was taken to the moors secretly and out of the glare of publicity I was able to be far more specific about the location of graves and I now believe I have done all that I can in helping the police in this respect.

I know that the parents of the missing children may never to be able to forgive me and that words of mine can NEVER express the remorse I now feel for what I did and my refusal for so long to admit to the crimes. I hope that my actions now in making my confession to the police will speak louder than any words. I want nothing more than to help the police find the bodies so that their poor relatives can at last have the comfort of giving them a Christian burial.

To those who believe that I am seeking some narrow advantage I would stress that I am in my twenty-four years of imprisonment, that my next parole review is not due until 1990 by which time I shall have served twenty-six years.

I have informed the Home Office that I do not wish to be considered for release on parole in 1990 and for as far ahead as I can see I know I will be kept in prison.

M. Hindley

Myra's solicitor, Michael Fisher, then commented:

After sitting in on all of the prison interviews conducted by Mr Topping I have not the slightest doubt that the bodies of Keith Bennett and Pauline Reade will be found very quickly. I warned her she could be walking into a murder charge. She accepted the risk. Her message is that she wants to put an end to the case and at the same time do her public duty.

Ian Brady gave his view on Myra's confession:

Hindley has crafted a Victorian melodrama in which she portrays herself as being forced to murder serially. We both habitually carried revolvers and went for target practice on the moors. If I were mistreating her, she could have shot me dead at any time. For thirty years she said she was acting out of love for me; now she maintains she killed because she hated me – a completely irrational hypothesis. In character, she is essentially a chameleon, adopting whatever camouflage will suit and voicing whatever she believes the individual wishes to hear. She can kill, both in cold blood or in a rage.

News of her 'confession' upset her family and almost everyone who had supported her throughout her imprisonment. Many of them stopped visiting her, including Maureen's widower Bill and Myra's niece Sharon. Bill Scott commented:

We've stopped going ever since she confessed to the other two killings. Maur had asked Myra outright twice about those two kids. She was especially worried about Pauline Reade, because she and Myra knew the family when they were kids.

Myra denied knowing anything. She said she would never have left that poor woman Mrs Reade suffering all these years. Maur believed her. Now she's admitted she was lying, so I reckon that lets me out of my promise to Maur that I would carry on visiting her. Also, I think it's wrong for Sharon now. She doesn't want to go, she doesn't want anything to do with Myra.

Myra's mother, Nellie, refused to leave her home for a time and sat with the curtains drawn. Bill again:

> [Nellie] sits in there in darkness, rocking backwards and forwards in a chair. She has the telly on but she doesn't watch it. Sharon normally goes there for the weekend, but she can't since it has all been in the news again. We wouldn't risk it. People always turn on the old woman for what Myra did. So when Sharon sees anything in the papers or on telly, she knows it means she won't see her Nan for a while. She hasn't got much family – all my lot live down south – so her Nan means a lot to her. They sit and talk together, watch telly, or they go out and do a bit of shopping.
>
> Normally at Christmas her Nan takes her down to town to see the lights and do some Christmas shopping, but not when Myra is in the news. So Sharon misses out. At Christmas in 1986, when they'd just started digging on the moors again just before Myra's confession, she didn't see her Nan at all.
>
> Funny how it all seems to blow up over the papers around Bank Holiday times. Me and Sharon have had a lot of holidays spoiled by it, because we've had to stay indoors.
>
> I'm happy-go-lucky normally, but I can't afford to be careless for Sharon's sake. There are always people after her, trying to find out about her.
> …
> [Nellie] got through all those years by never believing her Myra did anything. She hates Ian Brady and thinks it's all down to him. But she feels a shame from it all, and that's why she locks herself away.
>
> When Myra confessed to being involved in the other two that hit her really hard. I still think she hasn't taken it in. She's still somehow convincing herself that Myra's innocent. I don't know how she stays sane.

Although Myra's mother and her husband Bill were living together, they were barely speaking because he would spend as much time as he could in the pub. He said: 'When she got life, so did we. We shall suffer for ever. Our lives are in tatters. We just want to be left alone to forget the past.' He said that if she were ever released then she could not stay with them.

> I do not want to see her or talk to her again. Myra is on her own. Her mother's health is going down fast. How do you think she feels when she reads these dreadful stories about her daughter? She is a broken woman. Stories about Myra being a beast and evil obviously upset her, because in her heart she loves her.

On the 29 May 1987, Winnie Johnson wrote again to Myra:

> Dear Miss Hindley,
>
> I write yet again, both in hope and despair. On June 12 will come the birthday that Keith is no longer alive to celebrate, four days later will

be the twenty-third anniversary of his disappearance. Both dates for me will add to the agony and trauma I have suffered constantly since my son disappeared and the situation is infinitely worsened by the newspaper reports I keep reading which suggest that Mr Topping will end his search for Keith and Pauline Reade unless any discovery is made at the spot he is now searching.

If that does happen then for me life will be at an end. After your decision to make a full and frank confession and give the police every help you could my spirits soared and I truly believed that after all these years the nightmare would finally end. But it begins to look as if that might not happen because the police cannot pin down on the moors where Keith and Pauline are buried.

It is for that reason that I am writing to you again. From newspaper reports I have read it is obvious that Ian Brady is either still unwilling to help or too mentally ill to help end this horrible mystery so everything depends entirely on you. You have been courageous and honest in opening your heart to Mr Topping and indeed me to a certain extent. I now ask you to please, please search your heart and memory again, to recall those terrible crimes you have tried so hard to forget to see if there is any additional information you could reveal to Mr Topping which would enable him to find the bodies of Keith and Pauline. I know it has been such a long time and I know the memories hurt but please try. It is obvious Mr Topping needs more information, one of the newspapers said he was suffering from 'Moors Madness', things like that hurt very much, I know you are both trying to bring all the pain to an end, and I need you both to keep trying. I am the mother of eight children, and the grandmother of fourteen others. June 12 always brought an empty hopeless feeling with it since Keith disappeared, but even recently myself, my husband and my seven other children hoped that this time we would be able in some way to wish him a happy birthday, because we know where he is, and we just want to bring him home, please try and help again.

Yours Sincerely
Mrs W. Johnson

A seemingly helpful breakthrough was made in early June, when Ian Brady told Topping that he was willing to help in the search for the two missing bodies. Reports in the press claimed Brady had refused to help and, angered by this, he wrote to Topping, who replied immediately and told Brady that if his offer of help was genuine then he would take him up to Saddleworth Moor.

Brady received Topping's reply on 9 June, and one of the staff at Park Lane Hospital phoned the detective the same day to say that Brady wanted to speak to him. Brady wanted to know what form of transport would be used to take him up to the moor – he wanted to go by helicopter as the journey would be over within thirty minutes that way, but Topping said it would also cause unwanted attention from the press. He refused to discuss anything else over the phone and asked to see Brady in person.

A week later, Myra wrote an open letter to Brady, a copy of which was in newspapers as well as on TV and radio. In part, it read:

> If you are withholding vital information, for God's sake help those poor families. [If you don't] the only conclusion is that for your own selfish and morbid gratification and don't ever want this whole ghastly nightmare to end.... What difference can it make now to acknowledge those two crimes? We both know we will never be free.

Benedict Birnberg, Brady's solicitor, released a statement: 'He has not received this letter and he does not wish to receive it. If the letter arrives he will instruct the hospital authorities to send it back unopened. He regards the whole thing as a public relations stunt.'

Myra had no idea that Brady was already talking to Topping and Lesley Ann Downey's mother.

# 10

# Finding Pauline Reade

On 17 June 1987, Myra rang Topping; she wanted to tell him about the letter she had written to Ian Brady and of her letter to Winnie Johnson. Topping took the opportunity to go over again what Myra could remember on the night Pauline Reade was killed and buried. She was able to tell him that the grave was further into the moor than that of Lesley Ann Downey but, as it was dark when Brady buried her, she was unable to say whether or not she could see the road from the location of the grave. As they discussed where she had sat at the side of the body, for the first time – whether she meant to say it or not – she told him that she could clearly see the rocks of Hollin Brown Knoll silhouetted against the night sky.

The detective subsequently spoke to Brady to see if he had anything to add. Brady told him he had lowered his demands and was willing to cooperate with the investigation provided that, instead of being given the means to commit suicide, he be given a 'human

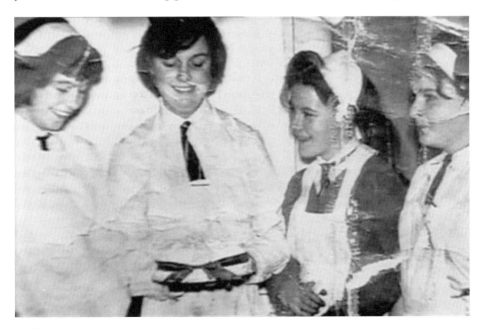

Pauline Reade (third from left).

week'. To Brady, this meant a week of food that he chose himself, a drink of alcohol (preferably Drambuie) and watching the occasional TV programme of his own choosing. He also wanted to be allowed to watch old movies, such as *Gone with the Wind*.

Topping visited Brady two days later and he told him that his request for a 'human week' was not possible. He said he had discussed it with the prison authorities but was told that it was an impossible request. Brady suggested that Topping take him out of the hospital and put him in secure police accommodation in order to be granted his week there, but the detective told him that too was not possible.

Brady then resorted to blackmail and said he would write to the parents of Pauline Reade and Keith Bennett and tell them that the Home Office were stopping him from helping the police by denying his small request. Topping's response was that that the public would view him poorly he refused help because he wasn't allowed to watch a few films or eat some food.

The following day, Brady wrote to Ann West, in reply to a letter he had received from her husband:

Dear Mrs West,

Many thanks for your last letter. The reason I have not replied sooner is that many things that are happening must not reach the press yet. I suppose you've seen or heard that the Home Office, on the strength of my information, are reopening the case. I can't tell you anything else. You'll see or read about it soon.

Sincerely,
Ian Brady

Topping and his team visited Brady again, where they discussed him going up to the moor. Brady told them that he did not want his doctor, Dr Strickland, to accompany him on to the moor, but wanted his Social Worker, Bob Fitzpatrick, and a nurse nominated by him. He was still maintaining that he wouldn't go up to the moor without having had his 'human week' first, but he was making more plans with the detectives should he go up there.

He was determined to know exactly how many police officers would be around him, who would be in his group, how the police would keep the press away and whether or not he would be given a pair of binoculars to use, as he said he would need to view some objects on the moor from a distance.

On the 1 July Topping took time off from digging on Saddleworth Moor to visit Brady again. This time, Brady had drawn up a list of ten points that he wanted to discuss, the last being an extremely odd request; he wanted a full face and profile picture of David Smith's eldest son, as well as his blood group. He refused to explain why he wanted them. It soon became clear to Topping that Brady was trying to suggest that he might be the child's father. He was clearly hoping that his suggestion would get back to Myra and Smith as a way of upsetting them, but there has never been any suggestion that Brady and Maureen had ever slept together.

After four hours of questioning and discussions, Topping received a phone call at 14.45 from officers searching at Hollin Brown Knoll. They told him that they had discovered a slight change in the vegetation where they were searching and after a few minutes' careful work they had uncovered a girl's white stiletto-heeled shoe.

They had discovered Pauline Reade's remains after more than 100 days of searching, just 3ft below the ground and, amazingly, only 100 yards from where Lesley Ann Downey had been buried. It was just 250 yards from the A635.

Topping told Brady that there had been a 'significant development' and that he and his team needed to leave.

Pauline Reade's shoe is found.

Topping told Knupfer back at Hollin Brown Knoll to act as normal, not to excavate any further and to leave as normal at the end of the day so as not to alert the press who were camped out there. He was determined to tell the family of Pauline Reade before they found out in the press.

He drove straight back to Manchester and met up with the rest of his team where they notified the Coroner, Home Office Pathologist for the area, forensics, police photographic and video teams and senior officers. He then took the team back to the site. Dr Geoffrey Garrett, the Home Office Pathologist, recalled:

> I got a call at the hospital that they'd found a body and was advised to make my way up after 6 pm when the scrum of reporters hanging about would have gone away. They were told that nothing significant had happened and the diggers got into their police cars and drove off, secretly leaving just one man behind to guard the site.

When he got up to the grave site Pauline was still buried and lying in a small hollow with just one foot and shoe protruding through the earth. When the earth and peat were cleared away they discovered that Pauline's body had been remarkably well preserved, to the point that Dr Garrett was able to state that her family could quite easily have identified her.

It was clear for all to see that Pauline had had her throat cut, and as the excavation continued Pauline was laying on her left side and facing the main road. According to Dr Garrett:

219

Her head was retracted and her left arm was folded across the front of her body with her hand on her right shoulder. Her right arm lay along her side.

Her thighs were extended and her knees were bent so that her heels were tucked up close to her buttocks. The right shoe, the one that led to the discovery, was in place but the other was resting on her thigh, clearly positioned there by the hand of her murderer before she was covered over with earth.

Pauline was wearing a heavy woollen coat. The skirt and underslip were pulled up above her waist and we could see stockings with suspenders at mid-thigh but no knickers or suspender belt. She had been wearing a suspender belt the night she had vanished.

As the body was moved gingerly on to a plastic sheet to wrap it up and take it to Oldham Mortuary, the right hand, the wrist joint ruined by time, became detached.

When Ian Brady heard that her body had been discovered he issued a statement to the press, through his solicitor, saying that he was prepared to go to the moors and help the police in their search.

The following day, Dr Garrett was joined by Dr Mike Green (who had worked with the original Moors inquiry pathology team of Professor Cyril John Poulson and Dr David Gee) at the mortuary. Dr Garrett commented:

Bits of peat and soil that had stuck to the clothing were brushed away and the coat was carefully cut off with scissors. All the clothes were given to forensic expert Dr Karen Mashiter who did a remarkably good job of reconstructing the items and proving that they had belonged to Pauline.

The removal of the coat revealed a handknitted cardigan that was also cut away, but we left the sleeves in place. They would act like a false

Pauline Reade's remains are taken from Saddleworth Moor.

skin to hold the tissue and bone structure of the arms together. The left hand became detached now and it was clear that although the body was in relatively remarkable shape there had been, as expected, major deterioration.

Under the cardigan were a black blouse and lurex patterned skirt. A brassiere was fastened at the back, and a slip and nylon net petticoat were intact...

Underneath the collar of the cardigan was a small section of gold chain, broken off from the rest of its length. There was a deep cut across the front of the throat and the coat collar, with its lining, had been pushed into the wound. Whatever force had done that had taken with it the rest of the chain, which we found inside.

*Right*: The burial site of Pauline Reade.

*Below*: Aerial view of the Pauline Reade crime scene.

221

*Above*: Aerial view of the Pauline Reade crime scene.

*Below left*: DCS Peter Topping searching Saddleworth Moor.

Below right: DCS Peter Topping at Hollin Brown Knoll.

Topping told the press who were waiting at Hollin Brown Knoll:

> It's been a team effort. You see us up here on a fine day, but I have a small squad of officers and we have endured terrible weather conditions, not just for weeks but for months. Had we unfortunately not found anything up here I would, quite properly, have been asked to justify my actions – and I could have done. There have been a number of reasons why we continued this investigation: the interests of justice, the families and the

222

public. Finding the body brings some peace to the family of the victim. But it is a day when you have got to have mixed feelings. We are pleased and relieved but also realise the dramatic effects on the people concerned.

Pauline Reade's mother, Joan:

> I never thought Myra Hindley or Ian Brady was to do with it all because her sister was a near neighbour – next door but one. She went visiting there. Myra Hindley was talking to me normally and saying she was sorry about Pauline, knowing she'd done that.

Ever since Pauline had been abducted, Joan had suffered with her mental health and spent time in hospital. That evening Topping rang Ian Brady, who gloated that the police had been on top of the body the whole time. Brady also said that he had plans to make things difficult for the former Lancashire Police DCI Joe Mounsey because he had Pauline Reade's body under his nose the whole time and had not found it.

He then told the detective that he was desperate to get up to the moors and show him where Keith Bennett was buried. He said that he now wasn't interested in his 'human week' and just wanted to get up there. He said that he would show the detectives where the grave site was but didn't want to be there when the body was excavated, and he didn't want to discuss the killings. It was highly likely that he simply wanted to see if the police were anywhere near to the site of Keith Bennett's body. If they were, he may have told them. But if they weren't, then he could say what he wanted, and he would keep his 'perfect murder'.

Topping acted quickly in case Brady changed his mind and, already having permission from the Home Office, decided to use the same officers he had when Myra was taken to the moor.

At 03.00 on the 3 July Ian Brady was woken in his cell and twenty minutes later he was taken in a three-car convoy of unmarked police vehicles out of the gates of the hospital. Brady was not as cooperative as Myra had been about wearing clothing to match everyone else. He wanted the press to see him and insisted on wearing his long

Ian Brady on his way to Saddleworth Moor.

223

overcoat and dark sunglasses. The convoy used the M62 motorway which stretches from Merseyside to the Humber as the quickest way to get to Saddleworth Moor.

The convoy stopped at the lay-by near Hoe Grain which Myra said they had used on the night Keith Bennett was murdered; Brady, unhandcuffed, was allowed to lead the way. They walked along Hoe Grain until they reached the junction with Shiny Brook and then Brady pointed to an exposed slope at the top of the bank on the right-hand side and told the officers: 'There's a spade in there.'

Brady was almost silent as he continued to walk, and it appeared that he knew exactly where he was going. As they reached the top of Hoe Grain, Brady turned right into Shiny Brook which was the opposite direction to where Myra had led them. They walked along the streambed until they came to an area known as the sheep pens, where small dry-stone pens had been built years previously.

Brady told the officers that the pens had moved since he was last there and said that they had been a few yards closer to the stream. He said this was where he and Myra used to go for target practice with the guns, using cans as their target.

They then walked through the pens to the junction of Shiny Brook and the next gully, called Near Most Grain. Brady stopped, looked up the steep stream bank and said: 'There's the Eagle's Head', (a rock formation that looked like an eagle's head).

Brady wanted to go up to a rock formation above there to get his bearings, and one of the search party, Sergeant Ron Peel, was told to stick as close as possible to him in case he tried to jump off.

Saddleworth Moor search.

As they walked along, Brady told the officers that he had once had an argument with a shepherd on the right-hand bank; he had threatened to shoot Brady's dog. The officer's hopes raised at this point, as Myra had told them that on the day of the row with the shepherd Brady had unwittingly pointed out to her the location of Keith Bennett's grave. This was when the dog had been sniffing around a dead lamb's carcass.

They carried on walking, but Brady said that the place had changed a lot since he was last there. He said that quarrying had taken place and damaged the area, but records show that no quarrying had taken place in that area.

They then crossed the weir and Brady headed to the top of a steep and dangerous bank. When they got up there, he said he was looking for a large rock, 5ft tall, which he said was similar to those at Stonehenge. The area was searched but no such stone was found, and Brady now appeared lost. They finally stopped when they were looking down over a wide valley and two reservoirs. There was a group of rocks on top of the moor, Grey Stone Rocks, which resembled those Brady had described. The detectives took him to them, and confirmed they were what he was looking for. After that, Brady said he wanted to find a gully with a sandy bottom and described its appearance and location.

Then, out of the blue, he described to the officers how he buried Keith Bennett's body. He said that Myra had been positioned near to the burial site to act as lookout and she had the rifle with her. The search was called off 15.00 as Brady seemed completely lost.

Knupfer later recalled:

> We took him up there and he marched off directly to the spot where Myra Hindley had taken us. The place where she recollected Keith Bennett was buried. It was only when we got down there, which is probably three-quarters of a mile from the road, that he became very confused, and I'm assuming he was genuine. He really couldn't get his bearings other than saying, 'It's round here somewhere'. He also said, 'Who's moved that mountain?'

Ian Brady recalled:

> We stepped onto the moor at dawn. Helicopters and private planes kept circling us and the police seemed determined they would not get any photos. Police kept surrounding me when a low-flying helicopter came at us. Of all hated papers, the *Sun* got a full-length one, sharp and clear! The moors had changed a lot in my eyes over the twenty-odd years that had passed. Many of the changes were real, some imaginary. It was weird seeing the place again, all that space and vastness.

As soon as Brady got back to Park Lane Hospital he released a statement to the press via his solicitor criticising Topping for ending the search too soon and offering to go back again. His said that the landscape had greatly changed but had he been given more time he would have located the grave.

Brady's solicitor later said: 'Mr Topping informed me that he is entirely satisfied that Mr Brady tried his utmost. He gave his all, physically and mentally, in the task.'

225

*Above*: Ian Brady (glasses) talking to DCS Topping.

*Below left*: Ian Brady is shielded from the press helicopter by the team of detectives.

*Below right*: Ian Brady talks as DCS Topping listens on.

Topping, however, later stated:

> The nurse from the hospital who had been with us all day and his social worker, Bob Fitzpatrick, felt he had done everything he could to help us. At the time – and to this day – I was not entirely sure. It had occurred to me that he might have been playing games with us. When he set off purposefully, perhaps he really did know where he was – and perhaps he later decided to play at being lost and confused so he would not have to show me the grave site. Perhaps he did what he had accused Myra Hindley of doing: intended to help but 'bottled out' when he got there. Or perhaps he was laughing up his sleeve all the time, just using the day to check up that we had not got close to the grave. His mind is so devious that it is impossible ever to know exactly what is going on inside it.

However, Myra later said of the moor: 'Ian's attention to detail was such that major landmarks on the horizon, viewed from a particular vantage point on the roads across the moors, provided a perfect grid reference for his trained mind. Ian had spent months planning the murders and plotting each location.' It was more than likely that Brady had simply gone to see that the police were nowhere near where he had buried Keith.

Brady himself later commented:

> It was weird seeing the place again, all that space and vastness. Keith Bennett is buried three miles into the moor from the A635. I put a boulder on his grave as a marker after we buried him. Myra knows this. She was a few feet away. I didn't indulge myself on the day, thinking about the luxury of walking on the moors I had loved so much when I was free. I knew I would be back in my matchbox within hours.

Topping went back to see Brady on the 5 July. Oddly, Brady showed him the photographs that Myra had got her mother to send to him. When asked why he was showing them, Brady replied that it was so he could see how the landscape had changed. Was he telling the truth? Or was he teasing the detective and the location of the grave was in one of those photographs? We'll probably never know.

On the 7 July, as the search was continuing, Police Chief James Anderton went to Saddleworth Moor and told the gathered reporters:

> We regard it as our basic and fundamental duty that the missing children be discovered, identified and properly laid to rest where the families can thereafter pay their respects which has been denied them all these years.
>
> I hoped this search would lead to the final story being told, the book being closed on one of the most horrendous series of crimes involving children ever known, certainly in this country.
>
> I have come here to congratulate my officers on their outstanding success and achievements against all odds and to wish them well in the continuing work.

Topping added: 'We've now got an area to be searched, and we know what we are looking for. We've got to pinpoint the area where we hope to find the grave of Keith Bennett.'

He then went to visit Brady again, and this time was more forward than he had been previously. He told Brady that the changes he was claiming to the terrain simply hadn't happened, and that the police, RAF and shepherds had all said and shown that the changes had not taken place.

Brady told him that it was possible that he had taken a different route to Shiny Brook on the day Keith Bennett was murdered and buried, but then dismissed that idea. He did, however, seem determined to find the body because Myra had helped to find that of Pauline Reade.

He then told Topping that some of the landmarks that he had wanted to find, such as the Eagle's Head and the views of the reservoir, had no significance to the grave site, but he had become confused and wanted to use them to get his bearings. He then showed the detective some slides that he had taken in the 1960s along with some he had taken of Scottish scenery in an area between Loch Long and Loch Lomond, which he said was significant but didn't say why.

Brady was informed that there was no chance of him paying a second visit to Saddleworth Moor and a few days later he wrote to the BBC TV reporter, Peter Gould, telling him in as little detail as possible about five further murders that he had claimed to have committed, which he called 'happenings'. Part of the letter read:

> Yes, it was weird seeing the place again, all that space and vastness. But when we reached the slope where Keith Bennett was, I couldn't find the ravine. We searched from early morning till late afternoon, and I wanted to continue, but a police convoy picked us up. I kept repeating to Mr Topping that I needed a second chance at it, but without any success.
>
> I've also given Mr Topping details of happenings, but he doesn't seem interested in them, i.e. a man on a piece of waste ground near Piccadilly, a woman in a canal, a man in Glasgow, and another on the slopes of Loch Long etc (the latter two were shot at close range). So that's how things stand at the moment.

But then he added:

> There's another on the opposite side of the moor road, one had a rag tied on the wooden post as a marker, but, unknown to me, all the wooden posts had been changed to plastic.

## The man on a piece of waste ground

He told Topping that he had left Myra parked in a car on a road which runs off London Road, directly under the Piccadilly railway complex. On wasteland behind the station he had had an argument with a man and had, in his own words, 'bricked him'. He said that the attack was not premeditated and that something had just come over him.

Only one case seemed to fit this location. In the early 1960s the body of a railway worker was found on waste land near Manchester's Piccadilly Station. His murderer was never caught, but there was no evidence to link Brady to his murder.

## A woman in a canal

Brady told Topping that he murdered a woman near a canal near the Rembrandt pub. He said he had been drinking heavily and had got into an argument with her, he had picked her up and thrown her over the parapet wall into the canal. He heard a splash, and then left. He did not know whether she had drowned.

As far as the police were concerned, there were no unexplained canal deaths at the time. To drag every inch of the miles and miles of canals in Greater Manchester was never even considered an option by the police.

## A man in Glasgow and another on the slopes of Loch Long

Brady told Topping that he saw an old woman whom he thought was a tramp, with matted hair hanging down from a cap or bonnet in the Salt Market area of Glasgow. Her hair reminded him of the fetlocks of a Clydesdale horse which he had seen killed when he was 8 or 9 years old after it had fallen and injured itself. He said that a man was treating the woman badly. He followed the man along a canal for some way and then stabbed him with a sheath knife. He said he was not sure that he had killed him, but that he had used 'full force' so assumed that he had. He cleaned the knife blade by submerging it in Nitric Acid, which he said took all the chrome off the blade, leaving it with a dull, bluish tint. He said the knife was among his possessions which had been taken away by the police after his arrest for the murder of Edward Evans, and that it had been returned to his family after the trial.

Brady said that there had been a 'significant incident' between Loch Long and Loch Lomond, but didn't want to speak about it. There was never any evidence to link Brady to any crimes at these locations.

## Another one on the opposite side of the Moor road

When Brady was taken on to the moors by Topping he said that he wanted to look at some road markers, but it had not been possible because of the press presence. Topping asked him why they were significant, and after a short silence told him that one of the markers indicated where another body was buried – that of an 18-year-old youth. He said the youth was someone he knew. He was not sure on the exact location as he said he was not driving. Topping asked him if Myra had been driving but he said no. He said there was a third party involved, but it was not David Smith. He said it was someone who had done him no harm, and he did not want to get them involved. Topping thought that Myra had been the driver and he was trying to protect her.

This was the first and last mention by Brady of anyone else buried on the Moor. Myra denied all knowledge and there was no evidence to suggest that Brady was being truthful.

On the 8 July, Dr Garrett was able to carry out the rest of the post-mortem on Pauline Reade. Her body had been immersed in a solution to enable her to be laid out straight, and it became very clear to him that: 'there were two parallel knife wounds to the neck, one very severe, three inches below the point of the chin, and a second, less deep, two inches below that. 'In addition there was a swelling on the forehead the diameter of a kitchen mug.' Pauline had been hit hard on the head. Internal examination showed that one of the throat cuts had been delivered with such force that it severed the spinal cord... There was no other sign of injury we could detect and, such was the extent of the body's deterioration, we were not able to investigate whether there had been any sexual assault.'

At the later inquest, the following details were given:

> There are two separate incised wounds running horizontally across the midline, one four inches in length which gapes and one more superficial, two inches in length ... the upper incised wound almost completely divides the stylomastoid muscle and appears to involve the anterior surface of the cervical spine.
>
> The swelling in the centre of the forehead appears to be a haematoma and is consistent with the application of blunt force, either with a fist or an instrument.
>
> Post-mortem deterioration of the perineum and anus precludes any examination of sexual assault... The pushing of the collar of the coat into the wound of the neck appears to have been deliberate rather than accidental during the burial of the body and could well have been carried out in an attempt to reduce the amount of bleeding.

Soon after this, Topping rang Brady to tell him that the investigation had reached a climax over the site of Keith Bennett's gravesite. Brady was told that there was no gully like the one he had described and that they had failed to find the spade that both Myra and Brady had said was buried.

The detective asked Brady to describe his journey back to the car that night and he said that it was very dark, and that both he and Myra had difficulty getting their bearings. He then said that at one point Myra had lost her shoe and they had to go back for it. He then said something significant – he told Topping that they had followed the lights of the cars on the road to guide them back – it was not possible to see the road from the Shiny Brook end of Hoe Grain.

The detective, along with many people involved with the case, was astounded that Brady, Myra and Keith Bennett had managed to walk as far onto the moor as both Brady and Myra had claimed, especially as it was dark and boggy and all three were wearing normal shoes.

Brady then told Topping that when he and Myra came off the moor they had to walk along the road from the Yorkshire side to the car and he had unwrapped the rifle that Myra was carrying in case someone was near the car waiting for them.

James Anderton, the Chief Constable of Greater Manchester Police, again visited the scene on Saddleworth Moor and told the awaiting press:

> I have come here to congratulate my officers on their outstanding success and achievements against all the odds. Mr Topping has done a tremendous job under enormous pressure and at times tremendous hostility. I would hope this operation will lead to the final story being told – the book being closed on one of the most horrendous series of crimes against children ever told.

Topping:

> We've got an area to be searched and we know what we are looking for. We've got to pinpoint the area where we hope to find the grave of Keith Bennett… There have been some changes in the landscape and, of course, it's been a long time since he has been up here. Please don't get at me if something doesn't happen today, tomorrow or the day after.

The truth of the matter was that the area he wanted to search was under water and he needed at least two weeks of warm, dry weather to clear it up.

There was still no sign that Topping and the search team were any closer to finding Keith Bennett's grave, so the following week he took videos made by the search team to show Ian Brady, who watched them reluctantly. He then, for the first time, told the detective that he was ashamed of what he had done and that he had tried to recall the specific details of what had happened on the night but he was thwarted by 'blocks' which came down in his mind. He then went further and said that he was ready to be interviewed formally, although he did not want to talk about how he had killed the children and did not want to discuss what had happened in Scotland.

He then gave Topping more details about the 'happenings'. He said that in the case of the un-named 18-year-old who was buried on the other side of the A635, they had approached Saddleworth Moor from the Holmfirth side and after they had walked on to the moor, not far from where he had gone with Keith Bennett, Brady had shot him with a .38 revolver. He said that he had buried the body with a spade 'which was always in the Mini Traveller'. He said he and the youth had gone about a quarter of a mile into the moor and were shielded from the road by a rise in the land.

Brady refused to name the victim because it could link it to the name of a third person whom he didn't want to involve. He said that this person had done him a favour by murdering someone for him and disposing of the body in the River Ouse.

The conflicting reports on this 'happening' are astounding. He gave different sides of the road as burial areas for the body, and said that the driver wasn't Myra, yet he then said that the car he used was hers.

He then changed details regarding the Glasgow murder, saying that he didn't follow the man along a canal bank. He said instead that he had followed him through several side streets and then into Argyll Street and into a park where he had stabbed him several times. He subsequently said that he had stabbed him underneath railway arches in the

Carlton area of the city after he had witnessed him hitting a woman in the Saltmarket area.

He claimed that he had told the detectives in the original investigation about the 'happening' in Loch Long, but they had looked at Loch Lomond instead. He said that he and Myra had gone to Scotland and that he often got her to pull into a petrol station near the village of Arrochar just so that he could hear a Scottish voice. He said that on this occasion they had stopped the car by the side of the road and he was looking at the landscape through his German binoculars when he caught sight of a hiker, probably in his twenties, with a rucksack and decided to speak to him, but the man surprised him by having an English accent rather than Scottish.

He said that he had a sudden urge to kill and shot the hiker in the back of the head with his revolver 'in such a way that it was a complete surprise, he had no warning'. He said burying him became difficult as he didn't have a spade, but he managed to do it by using the flat metal tin that the hiker was carrying. He took the rucksack back to the car and later threw it into a pine forest as they drove past.

Topping asked for a description of the man that Brady claimed he had killed on wasteland behind Piccadilly Station, and Brady seemed troubled by this. He said the man was between 20 and 30 years of age, wearing baggy trousers and looked like a workman. He couldn't remember what the argument was about, but the man had bumped into Brady, who had been drinking heavily. In a frenzied attack Brady hit him with a brick or lump of concrete, almost battering him to a pulp.

On 3 August, the inquest into Pauline Reade was opened at the Magistrate's Court Building in Oldham. It was simply a matter of satisfying the Coroner about the identity of the body, to enable it for release for burial.

The following day, Topping and Knupfer went to Cookham Wood to talk to Myra about the 'happenings' which Brady had claimed took place. The detectives didn't believe his stories for a second but were duty-bound to investigate them. They also wanted to show Myra the videos that had been shown to Brady of the moor to see if anything jogged her memory, but they found her in a slightly hostile mood. She was annoyed that they hadn't been to see her since their last visit and annoyed at the amount of time it had taken to find Pauline Reade's body. She became even angrier when she discovered that the detectives had looked for the box Brady had said was buried before looking for the body.

She was unable to identify the area where Keith Bennett was buried and when she picked out possible sites on the videos they were over a mile apart. When asked about the picnic she had had with Brady and the Waterhouse children at Grey Stone Rocks, she remembered it but wasn't so sure it had taken place in that location. She also confirmed what she had said previously that, when following Brady and Keith Bennett to the spot where he was murdered, she was carrying only binoculars, and not a rifle as Brady had said. She also said she did not carry a spade.

In relation to the possible 'happenings', she said she did remember one occasion when she and Brady drove to Manchester Piccadilly Station one night after work and she dropped him off outside the Queen's Hotel. He said that he was going to the cinema, and she assumed she was going with him, was told that he was going alone and that she had to pick him up at 23.00 under a railway arch in Store Street.

She was angered by this but drove home and went to visit Maureen, where she had a bath and put her hair in rollers. She then realised that she might be late in picking Ian Brady up, so she put a headscarf over her hair and drove off to meet him. She waited in the agreed place at the agreed time but he didn't turn up. She grew bored so got out and went up the stairs to the station approach to look for him, knowing that he 'had a thing for railway stations'. She couldn't see him so returned to the car, but he still wasn't there. Eventually, at 01.00, he turned up, drunk. She asked him where he had been and he replied that it was none of her business.

She said that she hadn't noticed anything that might suggest that he had been involved in a struggle, and she and the detectives tried to figure out a date of when this had happened. Myra was sure that it was after the death of Pauline Reade and that she had gone to Maureen's flat in Hattersley, which meant that it was after July 1965.

She said Brady annoyed her by going quiet instead of arguing (something he had said of her, too) and that on the way back that morning she sped up and then slammed on her breaks, nearly sending him through the front window. He reacted by punching her in the side of her head, which nearly embedded one of the rollers in her head. He then laughed, and began to talk to her normally, but still would not tell her where he had been.

Of the body buried on the moor, she said that the only person she ever dropped off on the moor was David Smith and that was when they were going for target practice. The only men she had met via Brady were Gilbert Deare and a man in Hull named Douglas Wood.

When she was questioned about the trips to Scotland, she said that they often went to Loch Long, but Brady never left her to return with a rucksack. She said they normally camped in the area and slept in the car, but didn't recall a village named Arrochar.

Pauline Reade's funeral took place on the 7 August at the church of St Francis in Gorton, where she had worshipped as a child (and where Myra Hindley had converted to Roman Catholicism), and was buried at Gorton Cemetery. Her mother, Joan, was allowed out of a psychiatric hospital to attend the service alongside her husband Amos and son Paul. The disappearance of her daughter had had such an effect on Joan that she was in and out of care for the rest of her life. She later recalled:

> I was in hospital and I remember my husband saying that Pauline had been found. I had her shoes brought to me. A terrible feeling. Out of my mind I was, really. It was a dark world.
>
> Two nurses brought me home to the funeral. I remember everything about the funeral, everything. I remember following the coffin and the people putting flowers on, throwing flowers down. I remember putting the dust on Pauline and putting my flowers on.
>
> Well, as years went on, I was saying my prayers about it and it seemed to lift me like a cloud lifting off my shoulders. I began to feel more pleasant about it, although I never forgot her any day. Even now I think about her every day and the way she had to go. That's never to be forgotten.
>
> She's not suffering now. Nobody can hurt her now. I feel her so close to me. But I miss her very much. I still do. She's my little girl.

Patrick Kilbride, Ann West and Winnie Johnson also attended the funeral and Pat Cummings, who should have gone to the dance with Pauline, sent flowers with a card that read: 'Pauline, No words can express how I feel at this moment.'

A few days after the funeral, Topping went to see Myra again, asking for her help to find Keith Bennett's grave. She still did not tell him that she and Brady had taken marker photographs of his grave. Just two years before her confession to Topping she had written in her unpublished autobiography, which Topping had no access to, that: 'Little did I realise then that his graves would be marked by photographs and not headstones.'

*Left and below*: Pauline Reade's funeral.

Years after the investigation had slowed down, Myra wrote another version of her autobiography, in which she admitted to being less than honest with Topping and his team. They had shown her photographs of her and Ian Brady on the rocks at Hollin Brown Knoll, and while she wanted to take credit for finding the missing children's graves, she didn't want to admit the depth of her involvement in their deaths in case it undermined her case for release.

In the autobiography, she wrote: 'I wanted them to know, without saying in so many words, which grave was in which area.' She suggested Topping got the photographs blown up so that the enlargement would reveal the expiry date on the tax disc in her car, which would have shown them that John Kilbride and Pauline Reade had already been killed by that point, and as the picture was clearly not of John Kilbride's grave then: 'it had to be marking the location of Pauline Reade's grave, which, in turn, meant that Keith Bennett's grave was in the Hoe Grain/Shiny Brook area (where similar 'landscapes' were taken).'

Topping went to see Brady on 20 August in order to question him formally about the disappearance of Pauline Reade and Keith Bennett. Brady didn't want to be interviewed formally but, when asked, he did say he still wanted to find the grave of Keith Bennett. The detective talked about the description Brady had given him of the grave and Brady suddenly said that Myra knew 'the location of the grave on that slope'.

Brady was asked about Pauline Reade and how he had disposed of the knife used to cut her throat. He replied that he had, on a number of occasions, offered to show the police where he had thrown the knife and was still willing to do so, but the detectives thought this was simply a ploy for him to get another day out of the secure hospital. Topping did all he could to get Brady to admit on tape that he was responsible for murdering both Pauline Reade and Keith Bennett, but he would only answer questions evasively. They did, however, already have enough evidence to charge him if the case went to court.

When the tape was switched off Brady was happy to continue talking informally and told the officers that he had only ever hit Myra twice – but he couldn't remember when the first time was. The second time, he said, was at the time of Pauline Reade's murder, when he realised that he had dropped to the depths of depravity, but Myra had said something to Pauline Reade before she was killed that made him realise that she had 'dropped even further'. He refused to say what she had said.

Topping then offered to tell Brady Myra's account of the killing of Pauline Reade. He made comments as the account was read out to him:

- The sun was shining until late, so there was no need to flash lights when picking her up (Hindley had said that he was behind her car on his motorbike, and he had flashed his lights when a suitable victim was spotted).
- Myra picked up Pauline Reade by asking the girl to help carry a pile of records to the van, which she said was parked on Cornwall Street. He was at least an hour behind them going up to the moor.
- Myra had not set out to pick up Pauline Reade specifically, and said that it could have been anyone.
- Myra took Pauline Reade up to Hollin Brown Knoll on her own, and that was where they met.

- He agreed that he was introduced to Pauline Reade as Myra's boyfriend and that they told her they were looking for a lost glove.
- He disagreed with Myra's version that she had left him with Pauline while she went to the van. He said all three of them went on to the Knoll. Myra had said that she was in the car when Pauline was killed, and Brady said it was true in 'general terms'.
- Myra was there when the body was buried, and that was when he had hit her. When he was asked a second time if Myra was there when Pauline was killed he said 'yes'.

Topping then moved on to the abduction of Keith Bennett. Brady said:

- Myra was on her own when she picked him up.
- She drove them to the Ardwick area to meet Brady in Bennett Street.
- He couldn't remember the excuse given to Keith, but they went to Saddleworth Moor.
- Myra had a spade and a rifle, wrapped in a plastic mac or a piece of plastic.
- Keith walked with him on to the moor.

Brady was then shown the aerial photographs taken by the RAF of the moor and was asked if the site where Keith was buried was in his 'Tartan Album', which was shown at his original trial. He replied: 'Thank Christ the police didn't get to them', and hinted that Myra had destroyed them between their subsequent arrests (Probably in the file she admitted to destroying at Millwards). He also suggested that Myra would have destroyed the 'left luggage' ticket if she could've got back into her house and the contents of the suitcases. He said that everything photographic, including the negatives, had been destroyed.

Police finally called off the search of the Moor on 24 August, having failed to find Keith Bennett's body. This, however, did not mean that the investigation was over.

The following day, Topping and his team went back to HMP Cookham Wood and spent five hours talking with Myra, but learned nothing new. When asked if the envelope she had burned at Millwards contained negatives of photographs, Myra said she didn't know and had destroyed them quickly because she was in a hurry and very frightened. She said that to the best of her knowledge it contained only plans for bank robberies.

It was at this meeting that Topping first mentioned hypnosis to Myra. He told her that it would not be used to get evidence to prosecute her with, but would be used to try and trigger any small detail of the location of Keith Bennett's grave.

Having heard that the search of Saddleworth Moor had come to an end, Lesley Ann Downey's mother, Ann West, wrote to Myra to see if she could persuade her to tell the police everything. She had to wait nearly two months for a reply:

Dear Mrs West,

Thank you for your letter, and I'm sorry it has taken me so long to reply to it. I think I know how difficult it must have been to write to me, and this reply is going to be even more difficult, because I find it almost impossible to express the way I feel about the indescribable suffering I have caused you, your family and the other families concerned.

It is true what you say in your letter about my never having written to you during all these years to express any sorrow or remorse, but I want you to know that in the early 1970s, after having read something about you in the press, I did ask the authorities in Holloway if I could write to you (rules about correspondence have changed in the last few years) and if I could ask you to visit me, despite your threats to kill me if you ever got the chance. But I was advised against writing, and an adamant refusal was given for a visit to take place.

In retrospect, I know the letter I would have written then would not have been as frank as this one, because you must be aware that it has taken me a very long time – much too long – to come to terms with what Ian Brady and I did all those years ago.

I could not even face the truth myself, let alone tell the truth to anyone else. This is unforgivable, and I do not expect anyone, especially yourself, to understand the reason for my long silence, and many denials. I know almost everyone describes me as cold and calculating – 'evil Myra' – but I ask you to believe that I find this deeply upsetting. I was evil, and I make no excuses whatsoever for my part in any of the past.

The letter from Mrs Johnson last October absolutely devastated me, and made me realise finally that I could no longer remain silent, whatever the cost to my family or myself. In February this year I gave as full and detailed account as I could to Mr Topping of what happened to your daughter.

I now want to say to you, and I implore you to believe me, because it is the truth, that your child was not physically tortured, as it is widely believed. I said at my trial, and I say to you now, that my involvement in the events on that tape-recording were indefensible and that I accepted any derogatory adjective used to describe my conduct. But please believe me – not for my sake, but simply in the hope that it will give you even a little peace of mind, that however monstrous and unforgivable the crime was, your child was not tortured to death.

I want to take this opportunity to say that there was no 'third man' involved in your daughter's case. Ian Brady and I lied at our trial about my former brother-in-law's alleged involvement. If this led you to believe he was implicated, as I recollect was the case, then this liberty over the years may have been a source of distress to you. But he didn't have anything to do with it, and I have done him a worse justice in this respect than he did me by giving false evidence for the Crown about the death of Edward Evans, when in fact he should have been charged and put in the dock with Ian Brady and myself.

But to return to your letter, you say 'I could never blame your mother for what happened. It wouldn't be right. So I don't expect you to blame me for all the heartache I have had over these years.' Of course it wouldn't be right to blame my mother. She, and Mrs Brady, are, in a different sense, two more innocent victims of Ian Brady's and my perpetrations. My own mother, and my family, have endured terrible sufferings through me, and are still serving, like yourself, an unbearable life sentence. This is yet another burden of guilt I carry, and the weight of it is almost more than I can bear.

The same is true of the sufferings and heartaches I have caused you and the other families. How can I possibly blame you for the thing I am responsible for? And how can I blame you for the more than understandable hatred you feel for me? I do understand your hatred, of course I do, but believe me Mrs West, you couldn't hate me more than I hate myself. I have asked God for His forgiveness, but I couldn't ask you for yours, for how can I expect you to forgive me when I cannot forgive myself? I have to live with the past for the rest of my life, with self-inflicted wounds to my mind and heart which I doubt will ever heal.

Having finally and fully acknowledged and confessed these heinous crimes, and realised the dreadful enormity of them, the guilt and remorse I feel is agonising – the wounds have reopened and are raw-edged and festering. But I deserve it all, because irrespective of how I became involved in those monstrous crimes at the age of 20, I was a woman, a young one, but still a woman, and an utter disgrace to womankind, as you yourself have said, as have others, and rightly so.

Mrs West, can I ask you to believe the woman I now am, aged 45, that I am not what I was all those years ago, and to accept that my sincerity is genuine in respect of my deep regret and remorse for all the pain and heartache I have caused you and your family. No words can adequately express what I feel, or what I wish with all my heart you could understand. To say 'I'm truly and deeply and sorry' sounds so futile, but I am truly and deeply sorry, and sorry also for taking all these years to say so.

In the past it seemed an impossible task to write to you when you were quite rightly fighting so hard against my release from prison. There is no need to do that any longer, because I have finally accepted my fate, and know that release from prison is no longer a practical reality. I have written to the Home Office and the Parole Board to say I do not wish to be considered for parole in 1990, and my belief is that I shall remain in prison until I die. So be it. I've brought it all on myself.

Since my confession to Mr Topping in February this year, the police have been able to find Pauline Reade's body, and her family have been able to give her a Christian burial at last. I am deeply sorry that the case is not yet true for Keith Bennett. I pray and hope with all my heart that the police resume the search, and I promise you, as I'm writing to Mrs Johnson to promise her, that I will continue to do everything possible to help them find her son so that she and her family can be relieved of some of their grief.

It is true I wanted to send a message to the Reade family, but I was advised against it, as it was feared it would intensify their grief. But Mass was said here for Pauline and her family and I will write to them when I feel they are able to accept a letter from me.

There is one last thing I would like to say to you. As I wrote above, I do understand your hatred, and I've said that you couldn't hate me more than I hate myself. I know that nothing can change the past, and that you can never forgive or forget the loss of your child, or that any words of mine can bring her back to you. But what I do wish for you, Mrs West, is that eventually your hatred can subside to enable you to gain some measure of peace of mind. I know from my self-hatred that it corrodes the spirit and leads to despair that is unbearable to live with. You've suffered more than enough; please don't add to your suffering by a hatred that I'm not worthy of, and will fester in your heart and mind more than it already has, through my fault.

This has been a very long letter and will have been painful for you to have read, just as it has been painful for me to have written, knowing that it will have reopened your own wounds yet again. I want to say to you from my heart, as God is my witness, that my sorrow and remorse for everything is truly genuine, and I hope that you accept it as the truth.

If you can't bring yourself to believe me – and I have no ulterior motive in writing to you, other than my genuine wish to answer your letter – I will try to understand, and will continue to pray for you, for peace for you, and a healing of your pain and heartache.

Yours Sincerely
Myra Hindley

It was around the 12 October that Myra first petitioned the Home Office to be allowed to be put under hypnosis in an effort to find Keith Bennett's grave, but she was turned down and told: 'The Secretary of State is not sufficiently persuaded of the likely utility of hypnosis in this instance to grant your request.'

Topping and his team went to visit Brady again on the 16 October at his request, claiming that he 'now knew where he had gone wrong'. However, when the detectives got there Brady had nothing new to say and was just critical of DCI Mounsey for not finding Pauline Reade's body during the original investigation.

He then began to suggest that Keith Bennett might actually be buried in a different area of the moor and was warned not to invent things in the hope of getting another visit to the moor.

They discussed a railway sleeper, which Brady said was on the opposite side of the road to where Pauline Reade and Lesley Ann Downey were buried, and said that it was used for target practice and also as 'a marker to other matters'.

Topping was starting to believe that it might be necessary to take Brady back up to Saddleworth Moor, believing that a second visit might help to clear up any confusion in Brady's mind. In subsequent visits, Brady hinted that the police were close to finding the grave and that they only needed to look at how close the original investigation had been in uncovering Pauline Reade's grave. He was asked if that meant that they were close to the grave in the Shiny Brook area, to which he replied that given a shovel he would find it.

Brady had seen Myra's letter to Ann West, which had been published in a national newspaper, and said that she was trying to downplay her role in the murder and that, in fact, the opposite was true. He claimed that after the murder of Pauline Reade, he and Myra went to the cinema and watched *The Lost Patrol*. It was a popular movie and the soundtrack was in the charts. He said that whenever one of them whistled it, the other knew what they were thinking about.

He then stated that when he had followed Myra's ex-fiancé, Ronnie Sinclair, and thought of killing him, Myra had insisted that he remove Sinclair's false teeth first in order to humiliate him. He used this to show that Myra was far more vindictive than he was. He said that although he had killed people, they didn't know that it was about to happen. With Myra, she wanted them to know what was about to happen to them.

He also knew that Topping had applied to the Home Office for permission to take him back up to the moor and said that he needed to get there by the end of the month as he was 'in a race against the snow'.

It was around this time that 16 Wardle Brook Avenue was demolished. Because of its notoriety, the council had found it difficult to get tenants to live there for longer than a few months, especially when the tenants made it public that there were strange noises and smells in the house, along with a strange atmosphere.

Nellie Moulton, Myra's mother, went to watch it being demolished but so did Ann West, and an angry scene soon emerged. Ann West shouted to Hettie: 'You brought a monster into this world!'

On the 8 December, a police team arrived at Brady's hospital at 05.00, only to be told that he no longer wanted to go to the moors. For security reasons, he hadn't been told that he would be going until that morning.

16 Wardle Brook Avenue after the police investigation in the 1960s.

Brady was still in bed and argued with Topping that it was too late in the year to go to the moor as there would be little daylight and the weather would be bad. After talking with his Social Worker, Bob Fitzpatrick, Brady finally agreed to go and they left the hospital at 07.20, finally arriving at the moor at 08.45.

The temperature was barely above freezing and there was a frost on the ground. Brady was not happy! He was taken, in a Land Rover, down the Water Authority's private road near Wessendon Head to the reservoir and the plan was to work back from there to where they had started at Hoe Grain last time.

Brady was stronger than last time and very cooperative. He accepted that the terrain hadn't altered and any changes had simply been in his mind. He concentrated on the Shiny Brook area, and tried to establish whether he had walked on to the moor down Hoe Grain or Near Most Grain. They carried on working until the light began to fail around 16.00. Brady was back in his room in hospital by 17.40.

Ian Brady (shielding his eyes) with DCS Topping in front.

Ian Brady leaning in to DCS Topping.

241

Later that day, Brady wrote to Alan West, step-father of Lesley Ann Downey:

Dear Mr West,

I've just come back from the moors and I wish to get developments down while still fresh in my mind…

I got no warning when my door was opened at five o'clock this morning and I was told that the police were coming to collect me. I had been trying non-stop from July to get back to the moor, yet the Home Office dragged its feet till December and the <u>shortest</u> day of the year. When we got to the moor everything was covered by frost and frozen water. But it was all worth it because within an hour I rectified the big mistake that had been made. And when I saw it I felt a great surge of relief and satisfaction. It greatly reduced the search area to a spot where a sheep pen is and a junction of two streams. I <u>know without any doubt</u> that the gully and the area I was searching <u>is</u> there. We then spent the rest of the day trying to locate the precise spot but I was zigzagging up and down logically in order to make sure I didn't miss anything. Mr Topping gave me plenty of support and allowed me to go wherever I spotted something, or possibilities. But I was racing against time and I had to keep hurrying before the early darkness fell.

On the return journey in the van I asked Mr Topping what he intended to do next. He said the weather was too 'inclement' at the moment and that no search would be organised. I was deflated by this – if it was good enough to take me there it should be good enough for a search. I'd like to see forty or fifty policemen on that slope tackling <u>every</u> gully.

I'm grateful for all the help you gave me to get back there, and it wasn't wasted – I <u>know</u> it's there, and I've no intention of letting go of the matter until I find, or the police find, that gully. And I'll continue to need any help from you.

Sincerely
Ian Brady

Winnie Johnson grew frustrated that her son Keith Bennett's remains still had not been found and wrote a letter to the Home Secretary, Douglas Hurd:

Dear Home Secretary,

I am at my wits end as yet another Christmas and another year approach and there appears to be no end to the nightmare I have lived every day since my son Keith died at the hands of Ian Brady and Myra Hindley more than twenty-three years ago.

It is now just over a year since I was given fresh hope that my son's grave would be found on Saddleworth Moor. But, as has happened so often in the past, my hopes have been shattered. The search for Keith's grave at the Shiny Brook area of the moors was called off and although Mr Topping keeps trying to reassure me he is still doing everything he possibly can, I cannot help feeling that my family and I are doomed to suffer through this dreadfully unjust ordeal for the rest of our lives.

Mr Home Secretary, I am begging you to help. You are the last chance we have of giving Keith a proper Christian burial and finding peace of mind. In the past few years my husband's health has deteriorated and my own health, both physical and mental, is suffering. Must we continue to be 'victims' of the Moors Murderers for the rest of our lives?

I appreciate that considerable resources have been used on the moors in the past year. I have nothing but the highest praise for Mr Topping and his team. They know approximately where Keith was buried. Yet two people – Ian Brady and Myra Hindley – know exactly where he was placed.

I know that between them, my son's murderers have made three short visits to the moors and the two visits by Myra Hindley enabled the police to locate the grave of Pauline Reade at Hollin Brown Knoll. And if it was possible for them to find Pauline why can't my son's grave be found?

It appears that both Brady and Hindley have cooperated with the Manchester Police and they have indicated they will do so again. Surely they are the only two people who can possibly help the police to solve this case once and for all – and end my suffering.

There are a number of people who say this is a waste of time and money and that I should forget it all and be content with some sort of memorial on Saddleworth Moor. I ask any parent in the land to put themselves in my position. On the evening of 12 June, 1964, I waved goodbye to my son as he set off to visit his grandma. I never saw him again.

Now from what the police have told me I know that he lies buried at Shiny Brook. I have walked over that area and wept and known that I can never find peace of mind until my son's body is found and laid to rest with God.

What else can I do except hope and pray that Hindley or Brady may be allowed out of prison again to help the police pinpoint the site of my son's grave? I know they are serving prisoners and there are many problems involved in releasing them. There were protests and cries of outrage when they were released to help police before. Again, I would ask any parent in the land to put themselves in my place. More than anyone else I know the horror of their crimes. I am still suffering because of them. But I fear that without their help, this case will never be solved.

I beg you sir to use your authority to make this last part of the Moors Murders case a priority and make it possible for Brady and Hindley to again be placed in a position to help the police and find my sons grave.

Yours Sincerely
Mrs W. Johnson

A couple of days after his last visit to the Moor, Brady told Topping he wanted to go back again but was told in no uncertain terms that his request was impossible as the Home Office would never sanction it.

Brady then asked if it would be possible for him to meet Myra, in order that they could discuss the location of Keith Bennett's grave, but was again told that it wouldn't be possible. Topping commented:

> I do not know whether he really wanted to see her to further the search for Keith Bennett, or whether it was just for old time's sake. Despite the fact that he was at times very critical of her, and despite the fact she had not hesitated to outline his crimes, I felt they both still had a lingering regard for each other. Neither seemed to want to hurt the other. Although they were both vindictive towards David Smith, they were each careful never to criticise the other.

On the 4 January 1988, a Home Office report concluded, after reading Topping's report on the visit of Ian Brady to Saddleworth Moor, that:

> …the visit was successful in resolving some of the confusion arising from the earlier visit and confirming the routes taken onto and off the Moor on the evening of Keith Bennett's murder. In that sense, therefore, the visit has confirmed that the police have been searching the right part of the Moor. However, the visit has not brought the police any closer to finding the body and, as the area has already been thoroughly searched, Mr Topping does not intend to renew the search as a result of the visit.
>
> The police now seem to believe that the only hope of finding Keith Bennett's body is for Myra Hindley to undergo hypnosis. This may mean a request from the police for the Home Secretary to reconsider his decision once they find that Myra Hindley's request has been refused. Their support for and interest in that request were, however, taken fully into account.

Ten days later, Allan Green, the Director of Public Prosecutions, announced that it would 'not be in the public interest' for Ian Brady and Myra Hindley to stand trial for the murder of Pauline Reade.

# 11

# Myra Hindley – 'til Death

Ian Brady wasn't alone in his criticism of being taken onto the moor in December; in his book *Stalker*, Deputy Chief Constable John Stalker of the Greater Manchester Police was also critical of the search taking place so late in the year. In February 1988 Ian Brady wrote to Ann West about this and about his frustration:

> I know precisely what I'm looking for and so does Hindley. But she simply took the police to the general area re Pauline Reade when in fact she could've taken them to the precise spot. And she didn't bother to tell the police that clumps of grass had been torn up and transplanted on the site to hide it, so the police took weeks to find it, and even then I think it was pure luck – either that or Hindley became impatient with the police bungling around and told them of the transplanted grass.

Behind the scenes, detectives were working hard to get the Home Office and Douglas Hurd, to change their position with regard to Myra being allowed to undergo hypnosis. Dr Una Maguire, the hypnotist that Topping wanted to use, said at the time that:

> Ninety-eight out of every hundred people are receptive to hypnosis and given that Hindley was anxious to help, I feel sure it would have been possible to work with her. It would have taken about an hour altogether, and in that time I could have taken her back mentally to the evening when she and Brady took Keith Bennett up to Saddleworth, and we could have recreated the whole journey across the moor. We could have ascertained exactly where the car was parked, and where they entered the moor.

The inquest into Pauline Reade's death was held on the 12 April and at the end of proceedings the Coroner, Bryan North, recalled Topping to the stand:

> I am well aware that you have conducted your investigation in the face of considerable scepticism and ill-judged comment. You and your team have also had to contend with the harshest of terrains and weather conditions during your long and arduous search. And I am sure you have brought much comfort to the family by your efforts.

Mr North told the jury:

> It is possible, although I think it unlikely, that her death could have
> occurred in another place other than the place of discovery. I think that
> unlikely particularly in view of the evidence of Dr Garrett in relation to the
> wounds and bleeding. It is not a place where a young girl would go alone
> to carry out an act of harm against herself.

He said that because of this, there was only one verdict for them to return: unlawful
killing.

Mr North said he had sought the views of the Director of Public Prosecutions about
any future court action. In a letter dated 17 March 1988, he was told: 'I confirm that the
director has decided not to institute criminal proceedings against anyone in respect of the
death of Pauline Reade.'

Following the inquest, Topping told the gathered press that he hoped the Home
Secretary would reconsider his decision regarding Myra Hindley undergoing hypnosis.

> Hypnosis is a controversial issue and I understand the problems, but we
> are talking about a very small session with a trained practitioner. I feel
> there is everything to be gained and nothing to lose and I believe it is
> something that should be reconsidered by Mr Hurd for the sake of Keith's
> family. It may be that another piece of insignificant information could
> come from Myra Hindley under hypnosis and could help us to recover the
> body of Keith Bennett.

The following day Topping took Winnie Johnson and one of her sons back to Saddleworth
Moor and as close as they could get to Shiny Brook. From there they started to walk and
the areas searched by police were pointed out to Mrs Johnson. When they reached the
approximate area where they believed Keith was buried, Mrs Johnson was allowed to sit
by herself for a while and as they left, she told Topping that she was satisfied everything
had been done to find him.

Back at police headquarters, Topping talked with her about how Keith had been taken
on to the moor, and how he had been killed. He explained that Keith's death had not been
as horrendous as Pauline Reade's.

Topping explained that there was nothing more the police could do and they both
agreed that hypnotising Myra would be the only chance of getting the information they
needed – even if all it did was to confirm that they had been searching in the right
place and that the body was no longer there. Topping said of the refusal to authorise the
hypnosis of Hindley:

> it is cruel and unnecessary of the Home Secretary to turn down what
> is almost certainly Mrs Johnson's last hope of finding her son's body.
> Douglas Hurd has not given me a reason for refusing to allow hypnosis,
> and the reasons he has given Mrs Johnson are not, in my view, defensible.
> The factors that worry the Home Office do not apply in this case: Myra

Hindley is not a witness; there are no criminal proceedings to be taken and therefore no legal difficulties: and her prison doctor did not raise any objections, so there are no medical arguments…

In my opinion the real reason was fear that it would be successful, and thereby give credibility to a practice the Home Office did not support.

On 25 July, after being transferred to HMP Gartree, Brady wrote a letter to Lesley Ann Downey's mother, telling her he was certain he could find Keith Bennett's grave:

As for my two visits to the moors, the first took me completely by surprise. I did not ask to go, nor was I given any warning. I said that I would only take half an hour and that I had no wish to wait around. But, after twenty-three years inside, the moor looked all different to me and destroyed my concentration. The second visit again took place without any warning, <u>six months</u> later and when the police <u>knew</u> in <u>advance</u> that I did <u>not</u> wish to go back up there in December as those are the shortest daylight hours of the year, and the moor was under ice at 5 degrees below zero. I argued with the police for <u>two hours</u>, but I was told that if I didn't go then, I wouldn't get another chance. So, I had no choice but to go up.

I <u>know</u> I can pinpoint KB to a distance of <u>twenty paces</u>. The police have <u>bungled</u> it twice. Again, why should I fight the police or Home Office reluctance to give me the opportunity to close the case?

DCS Peter Topping and Winnie Johnson.

I <u>want</u> it closed, that's why I fight. The whole situation is a farce, what with this red-herring about Hindley and hypnosis etc. It's all just an excuse, a diversion – a <u>cheap</u> PR gimmick to avoid doing the obvious.

Brady again wrote to Lesley Ann Downey's mother:

> When I discovered that MH had been deliberately misleading the police by 'distancing' herself from the sites by not giving the precise locations which she knows and knew, I felt deep anger, in view of the efforts I had made in the worst conditions.
>
> She, as I predicted to the police, still wishes to impress the Parole Board by appearing to help the police while at the same time suggesting her innocence by pretending not to know the precise locations.

Mr Michael Forsyth, the Minister of State, met with Keith Bennett's mother and members of her family. He explained that hypnosis could only take place with Myra Hindley's consent, that hypnosis was unlikely to produce positive results and that the media attention that granting the application would attract would put further strain on the family. Having considered these factors Mrs Johnson still asked that the application be granted. The Minister therefore approved Myra Hindley's application on the basis that everything possible should be done to help the family in their quest to find Keith Bennett's body.

He then wrote to Mrs Johnson:

> Dear Mrs Johnson,
>
> Thank you for calling me today to discuss Myra Hindley's application for hypnosis. Having read all the previous correspondence on the subject I thought that it would be useful to meet and discuss all of the issues. I hope that you found our meeting helpful.
>
> As I explained, hypnosis can only take place with Myra Hindley's consent. We believe that she is currently willing to be hypnotised but should she change her mind the Prison Service cannot by law force her to undergo the process, nor would it wish to do so. Similarly we understand that she is not prepared to take the 'truth drug' and again the Prison Service cannot by law forcefully administer the drug.
>
> It remains unlikely that if hypnosis goes ahead it will provide useful information. In practice it would be for the Greater Manchester Police to decide whether the information gained, if any, was such as to justify a new search. Even if a search is to be undertaken it is unlikely to produce positive results.
>
> I remain concerned that the considerable media attention that granting this request is going to attract will put further strain on you and your family. However, I think that you deserve every assistance in your long-standing quest to find Keith's body and give him a Christian burial. I am therefore prepared to grant this request.

We will now proceed by making arrangements with Myra Hindley about the use of the material obtained from the hypnosis, and also establish certain safeguards to protect against inappropriate media reporting of the hypnosis session. She will also have to be examined by the Prison Medical Officer and a visiting psychiatrist to ensure that she is not suffering from disturbances of her mental state and therefore is fit to undergo hypnosis. We will start making arrangements immediately but it is likely to take a few weeks.

Although it would appear highly unlikely that allowing Myra Hindley to be hypnotised will lead to the discovery of your son's body, I am prepared to grant this request to ensure that all possible avenues have been explored.

On 7 February, Julia Morgan (Home Office) also wrote a five-page report to Ann Widdicombe (Minister of State for Prisons) regarding the current stance on hypnosis for Hindley and is recreated in part, here:

In January 1995, after meeting Mrs Johnson, (mother of the victim, Keith Bennett), Mr Forsyth agreed to Hindley's request that she should be hypnotised in the hope of locating the burial place of Keith Bennett. The Minister did so solely in response to the wishes of Keith Bennett's family, and on the understanding that costs would be met by Myra Hindley. It is now clear that Myra Hindley cannot meet the cost. There is no end in sight to the delay that has already arisen, and the funding issue has come to undermine the neutrality of the Home Office's position. This submission has been prepared in discussion with legal advisers…

Although lie detector tests have been allowed for some prisoners, the use of hypnosis is, as far as we are aware, without precedent particularly in the respect that it will be funded by public money. Hypnosis presents a series of technical difficulties for the three psychologists who have been advising us and handling difficulties for the Prison Service. Given that hypnosis has never been used before these could not have been foreseen at the outset, nor can we be totally confident that all of the problems have yet been identified.

Agreement to the hypnosis of Myra Hindley rested on the understanding that it was a privilege, granted to the prisoner at her request, but for the benefit of the victim's family. It was also understood that the costs would fall to the prisoner. As the arrangements progressed it became clear that the costs could be considerable (perhaps in the region of £11,000) and that Myra Hindley did not have sufficient funds to meet them. She has recently confirmed this position.

When it first became clear that the prisoner could not meet the emerging costs it was decided that the Prison Service should meet the costs in keeping with your predecessor's wishes to respond to the needs of Keith Bennett's family. Myra Hindley is aware of this.

We received legal advice that by funding the psychologists the Service would assume responsibilities as their employer and potential liability in the event of litigation should Myra Hindley suffer injury as a result of hypnosis. Funding would also impair the neutrality of the Prison Service. To avoid this, legal advisers suggested the money be made available to Myra Hindley thus transferring employer responsibilities to her. You expressed concern about this suggestion and said that if the psychologists were not prepared to waive their fees then the police or prison service must be persuaded to pay. The police have refused to do so.

If public money were to be used the only way of protecting the Home Office/Prison Service would be through letters of agreement with Hindley and the psychologists.

A team of three psychologists are required for the hypnosis which could take up to twelve sessions. Each of them has indicated their intention to seek remuneration for their services which ranges from £200 to £400 per session. Advice and direction offered by them to date has been without charge.

The Home Office Circular 66/1988 concerning the use of hypnosis by the police in the investigation of crimes notes that there may be a danger, in some cases that hypnosis may cause long term harm to the mental health of the subject either because of some latent psychological condition or by causing the subject to relive a traumatic experience. The collective view of all three psychologists is that there is unlikely to be any lasting damage to Myra Hindley. She may be subject to depression if the sessions reveal little that is of use in the search for Keith Bennett's body but she is unlikely to become psychotic. This view is echoed by the directorate of healthcare who identify no contraindications in this case.

These views notwithstanding the legal advisers suggest, and this seems entirely sensible, that we cannot be totally confident that all of the risks can be identified in advance. It must be the case, therefore, that Hindley will be made fully aware of the risks as they are known before she embarks upon the sessions. It will also be explained to Myra Hindley that given the uniqueness of the hypnosis situation an accurate assessment of all of the risks cannot be predicted. She will be given the opportunity of her own medical advice of she so wishes although she will have to meet the costs for this.

Although her physical condition is improving and she is now ambulant, Myra Hindley still requires close medical attention. There is no indication that she is physically fit for hypnosis nor is it possible to say when she will be fit. Recent discussions with the staff of Durham suggest she may raise objection to the arrangements for recording the hypnosis, thus prolonging the period of preparation.

Home Office Circular 66/88, which is concerned with the use of hypnosis by the police in the investigation of crime, concluded that the use of hypnosis in police investigations was 'a fallible and limited instrument for obtaining reliable evidence', but it does not imply that hypnosis is never of value.

XXXXX, in a letter to the Home Office dated 4 February 1995, point out that the weight of informed opinion in the scientific community might advise that hypnosis is valueless since its use presupposes that the technique can evoke recovery of lost memories, a view which attracts little support. He suggests that the way forward could be to set up a panel of experts to decide when hypnosis would be useful in particular cases.

In this case hypnosis may not reveal any information that would be of use in locating Keith Bennett's body. If information should be forthcoming, it would not necessarily result in a renewed search of the moor. This is a matter for the police to determine. This was explained to the family of Keith Bennett at the outset, and our views on it have not changed. However hypnosis represents a final opportunity for the family to find Keith Bennett's body and was agreed to on that basis.

Contracts with the psychologists and Myra Hindley will need to record an undertaking on their part not to divulge information gathered through the process of hypnosis to anyone without approval. It will also need to make clear that neither the Home Office nor the Prison Service can protect Hindley, solicitors or hypnotist from media interest and pressures.

Contracts with the psychologists will also make clear that it is impossible for the Home Office or Prison Service to indemnify them against legal action by Myra Hindley should she suffer as a result of hypnosis. She herself will have to sign an undertaking to the effect that she undergoes hypnosis willingly though any adverse effects of the process cannot be assessed and that the Home Office/Prison Service cannot accept responsibility.

If hypnosis takes place, a precedent will be set which may become difficult to argue against. This will become more difficult if the cost is met by the Prison Service rather than by Myra Hindley. In effect the Prison Service is funding the continuation of a criminal investigation.

The position has changed since Mr Forsyth took the initial decision to grant Myra Hindley's request. The complexity of the hypnosis process (which we are told requires three psychologists and numerous sessions) has become clearer. This has resulted in a significant increase in costs, which cannot be met by the prisoner. The use of public money undermines the Prison Service's position of neutrality and places us in the position of employers of the experts. Myra Hindley shows no eagerness to proceed and is preoccupied by her medical condition and parole-related matters. Only the early view that the chance of the exercise leading to the location of the burial place remains small prevails. In the circumstances, hypnosis is unlikely to proceed in the near future yet neither side can easily withdraw from the agreement. In view of the position we have considered possible courses of action of which there are at least three.

First, to maintain the current position and, should the hypnosis proceed, to take every care that the letters of agreement reached with Hindley, the psychologists and the solicitors give the Home Office and the Prison Service as much protection as possible against any subsequent litigation.

A second option is to return to the original decision and to argue that the hypnosis can only proceed if funds are made available by Myra Hindley. If funds were made available by Myra Hindley's supporters they might seek to influence arrangements such that the Prison Service would lose the control conferred by its current faciliatory role. However Myra Hindley is already aware that the Prison Service, seeking to support the victim's family, has considered taking responsibility for payment for the hypnosis. This arrangement is not known to Mrs Johnson.

A third option might be for you to reconsider Mr Forsyth's decision and reach the conclusion that approval for hypnosis should be withdrawn on the grounds that twelve months had elapsed and Hindley had not presented herself for hypnosis; that the only way in which hypnosis could proceed would be if public money was spent, and this would undermine the neutral position of the Prison Service/Home Office and was seen to be committing public money to an exercise no informed person believed would achieve its objective. Such a decision would be criticised by some as reneging on an agreement given by your predecessor to the victim's family, albeit that the agreement was on the basis that public funds would not be used. It would also have the effect of destroying any hope Mrs Johnson has of recovering her son's body; hopes which were raised by the original agreement. On these grounds the option is not recommended.

Winnie Johnson wrote to Hindley on 15 August:

Dear Myra,

It is now more than eighteen months since you agreed to be hypnotised in an attempt to identify the place where my son Keith is buried. I have not troubled you in the intervening period because your health has not been good and I understand your need to be completely fit and in control before commencing hypnosis. Nevertheless, I was elated when you first agreed and, naturally, have invested a great deal of hope that the process might just bring with it the information I have so longed for.

I have heard recently from the Home Secretary that your health is now much improved and that you will soon be well enough to participate. I write to you to urge you to initiate the process as soon as you are able. I understand, of course, that there can be no guarantee that hypnosis will help to find Keith. However, even if not successful I, and the British public, will know that you have done your best. In return, you will have the peace of mind of knowing you have done all in your power to give Keith back to me.

I am not getting any younger, Myra, and each year that passes eats at my soul. I want only to pick up the threads of the life I unwittingly let go of when I crossed Keith over the road to visit his gran, all that time ago. Your fulfilment of your promise to be hypnotised might just enable me to do that.

Yours Sincerely
Winnie Johnson

Myra had grown tired of the letters from Winnie Johnson and asked her solicitors to tell her to stop writing to her.

On 3 February 1997, Home Secretary Michael Howard confirmed her whole life tariff. He took into consideration the fact that when the decision was made that she should serve a minimum of twenty-five years, it was not known that she would later confess to her part in a further two murders. He told her:

> The Secretary of State does not accept that a <u>minimum</u> tariff period of twenty-five years as recommended by Lord Lane is adequate to reflect the gravity of these offences. Having regard to all the circumstances of your case the Secretary of State has concluded that a whole life tariff is necessary to satisfy the requirements of retribution and deterrence in your case.

In October 1997 Hindley was moved from HMP Durham to HMP Highpoint, near Newmarket, Suffolk, for accumulated visits from Patricia Cairns. This was, at first, a temporary transfer for one month but was soon made permanent. As a convicted prisoner, Hindley was entitled to accumulated visits and to apply to be temporarily transferred to take her visits at another establishment suitable for her age, security classification and gender.

In 1998 Detective Superintendent Tony Brett was put in charge of the case, and he assembled a team of specialist officers. DC Dave Warren mapped the moor and carried out an audit of all the searches for bodies; DC Gail Jazmik studied Brady's photographs; DC Andy Meekes read every word that had been written on the case; DS Fiona Robertshaw gathered intelligence; DC Phil Steele checked that nothing was missed. The main purpose was to make sure Hindley was never released and if they found Keith Bennett along the way then that was a bonus.

DSI Tony Brett was told by government lawyers that he could not charge Hindley with anything relating to the murders of Pauline Reade and Keith Bennett and they would be ruled an 'abuse of process' because fifteen years earlier, after she had confessed, the families of Keith Bennett and Pauline Reade had sought a new trial. The Director of Public Prosecutions had put a stop to it on the grounds that, as there was no prospect of release, a lengthy court case would be a waste of taxpayers' money.

On 30 March 1999, the Supreme Court heard Hindley's further appeal against her whole life tariff and in a unanimous judgement drafted by Lord Steyn, the appeal was dismissed. At the end of his speech, he said:

> The Secretary of State was therefore entitled to take into account that the two murders of which she had been convicted in 1965 were the culmination

of a series of five murders committed by her and Brady. They abducted, terrified, tortured and killed their victims before burying their bodies on Saddleworth Moor.

Hindley was a woman of competent understanding. The argument that she was not the 'actual killer' must be put in perspective. Her role in the murders was pivotal. Without her active participation, the five children would probably still be alive today. The pitiless and depraved ordeal of the victims and the torment of their families, place these crimes in terms of comparative wickedness in an exceptional category. If it be right, as I have held it to be, that lifelong incarceration for the purposes of punishment is competent where the crime or crimes are sufficiently heinous, it is difficult to argue that this case is not in that category. In my view, the decision of the Secretary of State to maintain a whole life tariff in the case of Hindley, is lawful.

In August, Myra released a statement to the *Independent* in which she once again told a reporter her version of her involvement in the murders:

I was under duress and abuse before the offences, after and during them, and all the time I was with him. He used to threaten me and rape me and whip me and cane me. I would always be covered in bruises and bite marks. He threatened to kill my family. He dominated me completely. He raped me anally, urinated inside me and, while doing so, bit me on the cheekbone, just below my right eye, until my face began to bleed. I tried to fight him off strangling me and biting me, but the more I did, the more the pressure increased.

Somehow, on 25 October, two-and-a-half months after Lord Longford passed away, the *Sun* newspaper managed to get hold of a copy of Myra's list of twelve people that she wanted at her funeral. They were her mother, Sharon and Bill Scott, Nina Wilde, Andrew McCooey, Trisha Forrester (believed to be Pat Cairns), David and Bridget Astor, Solicitor Carolyn Taylor, QC Edward Fitzgerald, Rev. Michael Teader and his deputy Sister Carmel.

By November, Keith Bennett's brother, Alan, had visited Myra a handful of times and managed to get Myra to describe the area to him where she said Keith was buried. Planned meetings with detectives in attendance had been postponed twice and were never rescheduled due to her deteriorating health. Father Michael Teader was present at the meeting and drew a map as Myra described it. He recalled:

Alan Bennett approached Myra differently to everyone else. He was willing to speak to her, to work with her soberly, in order to see if Keith could be found. She did her best. We had photos of the moors to sift through – I think they were sent via a solicitor – which we looked at together. I asked her various questions, hoping to draw memories out of her, such as where she had sat, what she could see and hear, that sort of thing. Anything, really, to jog her memory. And from what she told me I drew a map, the one that was published everywhere, Myra's map. But if you look at the handwriting you'll see that it's mine, not hers. I drew it to her instructions because she wasn't able to do so herself. There was no question of Myra returning to the moor again – she needed a walking frame to get about [due to a diagnosis of osteoporosis], so it would have been physically impossible. She did what she could.

At 18.00 on 11 November it was noted that Hindley was having trouble breathing and was moved to the Health Care Centre. She was no better the following day and it was believed she had a chest infection. She was taken to West Suffolk Hospital at 20.15 that evening and it was expected that she might need to spend a few days on the ward to recover. However, on 14 November her condition worsened to such an extent that the hospital staff informed those at HMP Highpoint that Myra was not expected to live much longer.

At 16.58 on 15 November 2002 Myra Hindley passed away, aged 60. She had asked for the last rites to be given by her friend, the Rev. Peter Timms, but she passed away before he arrived. The Home Office Pathologist, Dr Michael Heath, who later carried out the post mortem examination at West Suffolk Hospital in Bury St Edmonds, said she died of bronchial pneumonia due to heart disease. She suffered from high blood pressure and poor blood supply to the heart, resulting in blocked coronary arteries. Her last words were cries for her mother, who was herself too frail to visit her daughter and was living in a nursing home in Manchester.

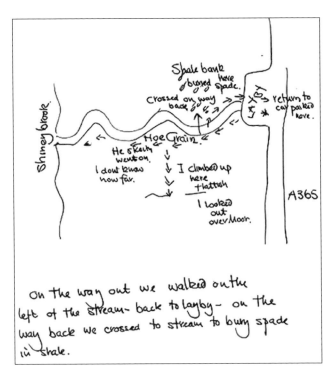

Map described by Myra Hindley.

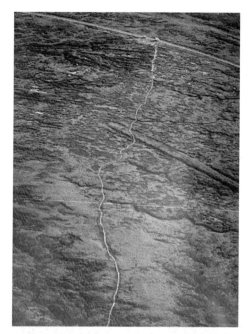

*Left*: Police search the area described by Myra.

*Below*: Aerial view of the area described by Myra.

Hatred for Hindley and her crimes was such that a couple of days later a spokesperson for the hospital in which she died said: 'The room has been cleared of everything that was used during her care and has been redecorated.' Prison staff had been instructed to incinerate every article in that room, from the bed linen to Hindley's clothing.

She was cremated at the City of Cambridge Crematorium shortly after 19.30 on 21 November 2002. Twelve people turned up, including a former lover Nina Wilde, but no family attended. The only sign of any protest was a poster left at the crematorium's gates which read 'Burn in hell'.

The inquest into her death was held on 23 February 2003, where it was revealed that Hindley was on a daily cocktail of drugs for a long list of ailments: osteoporosis, angina, insomnia, hypertension, raised cholesterol, depression, menopausal symptoms, headaches, back pain, asthma, bronchitis, arthritis and irritable bowels.

At the close of the hearing, Greater Suffolk coroner Peter Dean asked all those present in court to stand for a minute's silence in tribute to Hindley's victims.

Her ashes were scattered at Stalybridge Country Park, at the foot of Saddleworth Moor, by her former partner, Patricia Cairns.

Following her death, police launched Operation Maida, and again searched Saddleworth Moor for the body of Keith Bennett. It was a far lower-key search than previously; the officers read through the statements of Brady and Hindley and also studied the photographs taken by them. They consulted images of the area taken by a US satellite used to look for evidence of soil movement, but found nothing of any significance.

*Right*: Myra's coffin.

*Below*: Myra's coffin is carried into the church.

I, MYRA HINDLEY, of HMP Highpoint, being of sound mind, declare this document to be my LIVING WILL.

If, for any reason, I become severely incapacitated or am left in a persistent vegetative state, it is my wish that no attempt whatsoever be made to resuscitate me or keep me alive by artificial feeding or treatment.

It is also my wish that no organs or limbs or other parts of my body be removed under any circumstances or for any purpose after my death.

It is also my wish to be cremated, and for the cremation service to be conducted by the Rev. Michael Teader and for my ashes to be disposed of at his discretion. Furthermore, I would like Albinoni's Adagio to be played during my cremation, and would like Masses to be offered for the repose of my soul.

Signature. M. Hindley

Dated Wednesday 12th January 2000.

*Left*: Myra's will.

*Below*: Stalybridge Country Park, where Myra's ashes were scattered.

# 12

# Ian Brady – 'til Death

On 19 October 1999, Brady was seen by Consultant Forensic Psychiatrist Dr Madden at Ashworth Hospital. In his subsequent report he states that Brady complained to him about being forcefully moved to another ward; he was given no warning of the move, was manhandled by guards who had entered his room and forced him face-first onto his bed, stripped him, carried out a full body search, and then forcefully dressed him in a change of clothes. At this point Brady was informed that a van was coming for him and he was being transferred to Lawrence Ward.

Brady was then raised off the bed, held in head and wristlocks, walked down the corridor and into the van. The same procedure was carried out in reverse when he reached Lawrence Ward; Brady told Dr Madden: 'It took a very long time. I was trying to do it myself, trying to lie down on the bed but I was completely unable to move because I was restrained.'

Brady was held face down on the bed with his head facing the wall until Mr Kendrick, Head of Security at the hospital, arrived. When Brady asked why he had been moved, he was told: 'We don't know anything. We were told about the move an hour ago, we knew nothing until then.' Due to this move, Brady immediately went on hunger strike.

He was visited later by his new Responsible Medical Officer, Dr Collins, who had also found out about the move an hour before it happened, but had not been told the reason. Brady was placed on continual observations by two staff members and spent six days with only a bed in his room.

Dr Madden reported:

> Mr Brady appeared shaken by his experiences but, in terms of psychiatric symptomatology, his mental state was similar to that observed on our last meeting, as described in my previous report. He was angry and distressed by the move and his treatment. He was never threatening and spoke politely throughout. He said that he was determined to continue with his legal actions, and wondered if his treatment had been an attempt to deter him, on the part of the hospital.
>
> I asked Mr Brady about his refusal of food, and he said that he was taking drinks sweetened with low-calorie sweeteners i.e. of no nutritional value.
>
> While he gave no specific conditions under which he would end his hunger strike, he made it clear that his motivation was the unjust treatment which he had received. He made reference to previous hunger strikes, which he saw as his only way of protesting against injustice.

Dr Madden found:

> Despite a recent stressful experience there has been no significant deterioration in Mr Brady's mental health and I see no reason to change the recommendations in my previous report, that he is medically fit to attend a hearing outside the hospital, and that such attendance would be unlikely to have any significant effects upon his mental disorder. Of course, it would be necessary to revise this opinion if his hunger strike continues, and if his physical or mental health deteriorates as a result of starvation.

Since 1998 Ian Brady had been visited by Jackie Powell, a Mental Health Advocate (an independent specialist who represents psychiatric patients). Brady said that he understood the effects that his murders had had on the families of his victims and was remorseful, but 'If you ask me to say "sorry", that is a word I cannot use because it is meaningless.'

In 2002, she told how Brady could be manipulative, obnoxious and arrogant and that he felt he had to be in control of every situation.

> He can control a conversation and will not allow others to get inside his head. This is part of the behaviour they categorise as schizophrenic, but to him it was a battle of wills he was not prepared to lose. He is adamant he is not mentally ill.
>
> At the court hearing [2000], the psychiatrist at Ashworth, and the final judgement, listed fifty-seven personality disorders, including his tendency to be legalistic – using lawyers too much.

Jackie Powell said that Brady sometimes spoke to him about Myra:

> He was very angry with Myra Hindley. He felt betrayed because they had always agreed to do everything together. She wanted parole, but he never did. He would say 'What is the girl playing at?' whenever he heard she was trying to win her freedom.
>
> He always called Myra 'The Girl' and said she was the only woman he'd ever cared for, apart from his mother. Hindley later accused him of raping her and keeping her prisoner, but he denies that 100 per cent. He was bitter when she died from a chest infection in 2002. He said she'd got what she wanted and said he wished he had cancer so he could die.

In September 2002 Brady's mother, Peggy, was taken ill and admitted in to Manchester Royal Infirmary. She asked to see her son one last time before she passed away and the Home Secretary, David Blunkett, sanctioned the visit under armed guard on the 25 September. He stayed with her for around an hour.

On 1 July 2009, Greater Manchester Police officially gave up their hunt for the body of Keith Bennett, saying that 'only a major scientific breakthrough or fresh evidence would see the hunt for his body restart'. Detectives were also reported as saying they would never again give Ian Brady the attention or thrill of leading a search on the moors.

Detective Chief Superintendent Steve Heywood, head of Greater Manchester Police's serious crime division, told the press:

> As a force, there is nothing we would have liked more than to draw a close to this dark chapter, and we are very disappointed that we have not located Keith's remains, but we will never close this case and remain open to any new lines of inquiry which may come about as a result of significant scientific advances or credible or actionable information.

Still officially on hunger strike and being fed through a nasal tube (although often seen eating biscuits), on 13 September 2009 Brady began a campaign to be transferred to a Scottish prison; in Scotland he could not be force-fed via a tube, so he would be allowed to die.

While his case was being considered, a privately funded search for Keith Bennett's grave began on 27 March 2010. Winnie Johnson, now 76, said she hoped to find her son and bury him before she and Brady died. Donations from members of the public allowed the search to be conducted by volunteers from a Welsh search and rescue team, but his body was not found.

On 5 May 2012 David Smith passed away. He had moved to Ireland with his wife but suffered from cancer in his later years. His funeral was held at Oughterard Church and he was buried at Kilcummin Cemetery. In July the same year, Brady suffered a seizure and had to spend several nights in hospital. Jackie Powell told the *Mirror* newspaper:

> At first, they thought it was hiccups. Quickly, they grew more severe. Suddenly, he collapsed and went into a full seizure. He lost consciousness for several minutes. Help was called and several doctors and nurses rushed in. His heart stopped. He was dead. That should have been that. He had told the hospital years earlier he did not wish ever to be resuscitated. He put it in writing. They knew that, but still used a defibrillator.
>
> I had to see him in an interview room with an observation window. He was in extreme pain. He told me he had fractured his T6 and T10 vertebrae. Doctors told him the fractures had been caused by the violence of

Police search Saddleworth Moor.

the seizure. He does not recall the seizure and was furious that he had been resuscitated. This is the one thing he has always said he does not want.

Much of his behaviour stems from his legal battles with Ashworth Hospital. He is adamant that he is not mentally ill. He says he committed the murders at a time when, if he had been distracted by something else, they might not have happened. He talks about understanding the effects the killings had on the families of his victims.

This episode resulted in a delay in the mental health tribunal which was considering his request to move to a Scottish prison. The tribunal had received information concerning Brady's medical condition following his admission to hospital and it also received submissions on Brady's behalf from his QC Mr Hugh Southey, and from Miss Eleanor Gray QC on behalf of Ashworth Hospital.

The tribunal accepted that Brady's medical condition was such as to preclude his attendance at, and participation in, the hearing in public; however, because his participation in the hearing had been a significant factor in the decision to grant a hearing in public, it was considered improper to continue in his absence.

It was also claimed that month that Brady may have given details of the location of Keith Bennett's remains to Jackie Powell. Shortly before Winnie Johnson passed away on 18 August 2012, Brady allegedly wrote a letter to her, with strict instructions that it was not to be opened until after he was dead. Jackie Powell claimed that she had received a sealed envelope from Brady, thought to contain this letter.

Martin Bottomley, Head of Investigative Review of Greater Manchester Police's Major and Cold Case Crime Unit, recalled: 'As soon as we were made aware of the existence of this alleged letter, we made exhaustive attempts to obtain it to establish whether or not its contents would assist us in finding Keith's body.'

Police searched Jackie Powell's home near Llanelli and took away bundles of documents following a search that lasted ten hours. She was also detained on suspicion of preventing the burial of a body without lawful exercise. Brady's room at Ashworth Hospital was also searched.

At Jackie Powell's home they discovered an envelope with the words 'to be opened in the event of my death' written on the front. It was believed to be in Brady's handwriting, but there was no letter inside. Martin Bottomley:

> That in itself does not prove or disprove the letter's existence – it might have been destroyed, it might be hidden elsewhere, it may be in someone else's possession, or it may simply never have existed in the first place and this has been yet more mind games by Brady.

As far as Ashworth Hospital was concerned, Jackie Powell wasn't vetted and was classed simply as a 'visitor'. She was originally paid legal aid but that funding stopped shortly before her claims that Brady had given her a letter saying where Keith Bennett was buried and she continued to represent Brady for free. Her position became further clouded when she also claimed to be a co-executor of Brady's will and it was in this role that she said she was given the envelope to deliver to Winnie Johnson following Brady's death.

262

Martin Coyle, Deputy Chief Executive of Action4Advocacy, said it was puzzling that she had both roles as there could have been a conflict of interest. Ordinarily as a Mental Health Advocate, she would owe Brady a duty of confidentiality but this did not apply if there was serious risk to someone else or a risk of breaking the law. As a co-executor of his will, however, she had an 'obligation' to report any wrongdoing. She was not a solicitor so was not bound by client confidentiality.

Jackie Powell herself told Channel Four's *Cutting Edge*:

> I received a letter and a sealed envelope which said on the front 'to be opened in the event of my death'. He says he doesn't wish to take his secrets to the grave and within the sealed envelope is a letter to Winnie Johnson. Within that is the means of her possibly being able to rest.

Winnie Johnson passed away in a hospice following a long illness. John Ainley, a senior partner at Oldham-based solicitors North Ainley Halliwell said:

> She will be sadly missed and was much loved by her family and friends. She has died without knowing Keith's whereabouts and without the opportunity to finally put him at rest in a decent grave. It is a truly heart-breaking situation that this opportunity has now been irrevocably lost. Winnie's health deteriorated in the last few days. She died not knowing of the letter's possible existence but with the steadfast conviction Ian Brady can resolve the situation.

Keith's brother, Alan Bennett, issued a family statement saying:

> Winnie fought tirelessly for decades to find Keith and give him a Christian burial. Although this was not possible during her lifetime, we, her family, intend to continue this fight now for her and for Keith. We hope that the authorities and the public will support us in this.

Following his mother's funeral, Alan Bennett later released another statement:

> As far as I am concerned, until Keith is found then he is still in the possession of Brady and Hindley. Our fear as a family is that now my mother is no longer with us, this may be seen by the police and the media as some sort of closure to the case. This must not be allowed to happen, both out of respect for Keith and my mother's memory and for those of us who loved them both.

On 28 June 2013 Brady (now going by the name Ian Stewart-Brady) was in front of the cameras again. The media were able to see him via a TV relay as he gave evidence at his Mental Health Tribunal at Ashworth. He wanted to be sent back to a prison where he could complete his hunger strike without intervention.

He refused to answer questions directly about whether or not he would kill himself if he was sent back to prison but told one of his correspondents: 'I have had enough. My objective is to die and release myself from this once and for all.'

He considered himself to be intelligently superior and no longer wanted to be mixing with those who were mentally ill. He disputed that he had any mental disorder and that he had ever been suffering from schizophrenia. He said that the symptoms he exhibited in 1985 were faked so he would be moved to a hospital because the situation in HMP Gartree was no longer tolerable and that he understood that Ashworth 'wasn't a political dustbin. It wasn't a place where they forced anti-psychotic medication on you to embalm you into a zombie.' He continued that it had also offered him educational opportunities.

However, two doctors who had treated him spoke of incidents in which he clearly showed evidence of continuing hallucinations, talking to himself and of paranoia. They told of an event that had happened in late 2012, where he had been on a reducing dose of morphine following his seizure in July 2012 which made him increasingly irritable.

For some time prior to the seizure he had been making comments about a female member of staff. One morning, Brady went to collect his medication from the dispensary, but upon seeing this member of staff in there he walked out and sat far away, where he said in abusive terms that he would not have his medication 'when that filth is on the ward'. He told one of the doctors, 'you have deliberately given that scum the med keys to try to wind me up'. Brady was extremely angry and repeatedly abusive, before storming off to his room and slamming the door closed.

A short while later Brady asked to use the telephone, but was still extremely angry. He went back over to the doctor and 'leaned over, pointing his pen approximately five or six inches away from my face, stating "you can stop trying to soft soap me, you daft cunt. You and her [referring to the nurse he had abused] should keep out of my way".' The doctor lent back in his chair and Brady thrust his pen towards him; if the doctor had not leant back, it would have made contact with him.

Brady went to make his phone call from the telephone booth; the staff knew that if he was allowed to do that it was likely to have a calming effect.

Out of sight, another patient was reading a magazine; when Brady finished his phone call he walked over to this man and said: 'You're a fat fucking slug, you fat bastard, sat there.' The patient asked what Brady was talking about and he responded by putting his pen between his knuckles making a fist around it and said: 'Do you want to do something about it?'

Members of staff rushed in and told Brady to go back to his room. He continued to be abusive and on his way back to his room he claimed that a patient had been throwing cereal around and smearing honey on the chairs to annoy him. Brady later spoke to another doctor and said that the patient reading the magazine had provoked him because he was deliberately slamming doors shut and was making 'pig noises' which were specifically directed at Brady, so he went to tell him to stop.

That evening Brady was overheard in a lengthy, prolonged conversation, but there was no one else in his room and he was talking to his television in the corner.

At the tribunal Brady was asked about this and he denied being threatening:

> It doesn't matter whether it's a patient or a member of staff attention seeking. As I'm the sole high profile patient they've got, they only have to mention my name and that's it. Everybody jumps on the wagon train. And Collins especially eagerly grasps any negative information he can

use against me by collusive patients or staff'. He denied that he had been aggressive to any of the staff and called it 'a classic set up.'

The doctor at the tribunal concluded that Brady's conversation with the television was Brady responding to an auditory hallucination. Summing up, it was announced that:

> The tribunal accepted that the evidence did establish that Mr Brady had been suffering from schizophrenia at the time of his admission to hospital. Furthermore, the Tribunal accepted that it had been present for a substantial period but had fluctuated in its severity. At times the symptoms had abated but particularly, at times of stress and upset, they had become more pronounced. Clearly his condition had deteriorated after his transfer from HMP Wormwood Scrubs but with his transfer to hospital the symptoms had reduced. It was a serious illness which had been present for years with varying degrees of severity. The Tribunal accepted that it was severe and chronic. Its nature and degree were such as to make his detention in hospital for treatment appropriate. The Tribunal regarded Dr Grounds' assessment of its duration … as being the minimum period and that in fact, the history established that the condition continued over a longer period.

The tribunal then announced their verdict:

> The tribunal has concluded that Mr Ian Stewart-Brady continues to suffer from a mental disorder which is of a nature and degree which makes it appropriate for him to continue to receive medical treatment and that it is necessary for his health and safety and for the protection of other persons that he should receive such treatment in hospital and that appropriate medical treatment is available for him.

On 2 November 2013 John Dilworth, head of the CPS North West Complex Case Unit, announced that there were to be no charges brought against Jackie Powell:

> We have completed our review of the evidence concerning an alleged failure by Jackie Powell to disclose information about the location of Keith Bennett's remains. This allegation centred on a letter, supposedly written by Ian Brady, which may have led police to where Keith Bennett was buried.
> The only offence that might have been committed by Ms Powell was preventing a lawful and decent burial. It is possible to prosecute a person for preventing a lawful burial through a failure to act, but there must be sufficient evidence to prove that the suspect either prevented the burial or intended to do so when they chose not to act.
> After careful consideration, we have decided that Ms Powell should not be charged, as it cannot be established that she knew what the contents of the letter referred to, that the letter in question existed or what information it might have contained. The only evidence of the

letter's existence was in comments given by Ms Powell to an interviewer and she stated only that she believed it may contain information about Keith Bennett.

Even if it could be proved that this letter existed, there is no evidence to suggest that Ms Powell ever knew the nature of its contents and there is insufficient evidence to prove that she genuinely believed it contained the information in question.

As such, it could not be established in court that Ms Powell either prevented Keith Bennett's burial or intended to do so.

We understand that this is still a very sensitive matter for the relatives of Keith Bennett. We have written to Keith Bennett's brother to explain our decision and have offered a meeting to discuss this matter.

In 2014 Brady suffered a fall and broke two bones, including his hip. He was taken out of the secure hospital and treated at Aintree University Hospital six miles away.

He died on 15 May 2017 at 18.03 at Ashworth Psychiatric Hospital; although he had been receiving palliative care from cancer nurses, he passed away from heart disease. His lawyer, Robin Makin, was with him less than two hours before he died: 'I got a call that he wanted to see me – he was obviously well aware that his death was imminent.' They discussed Brady's legal affairs and funeral arrangements but there was no mention of Keith Bennett.

Makin said 'I would be very surprised if he really had information that was useful. He did go to the moors a long time ago and I suspect that if there had been information for him that he could have provided, he would have provided it then.'

He called the search for Keith a 'frenzy' but said he had no information that could assist but hoped the body would be found.

The inquest into Brady's death was opened at Southport Town Hall with Christopher Sumner as Coroner. It was found that Brady had pulled out his feeding tube and insisted that he didn't want to be resuscitated if he suffered a cardiac arrest. He had 'retained capacity throughout'.

Mr Sumner told the hearing:

> I would like an assurance before I [release the body] that first of all the person who asked to take over responsibility for that funeral has a funeral director willing to deal with the funeral and that he has a crematorium willing and able to cremate Mr Stewart-Brady's body.
>
> Emotions are high, they are bound to be, in the Manchester area. I also wanted to have assurance that when Mr Stewart-Brady is cremated his ashes will not be scattered on Saddleworth Moor. I think that's a right and proper moral judgment to make.
>
> I think it would be offensive if Mr Stewart-Brady's ashes were scattered on Saddleworth Moor.

It emerged that just hours before Brady passed away, the police had tried unsuccessfully to gain access to his papers so they could carry out any possible future search of the moors.

In his ruling, Chancellor of the High Court, Sir Geoffrey Vos, wrote:

> I decline to permit the playing of the fifth movement of the Symphony Fantastique at the cremation as Mr Makin requested.
>
> As the composer's programme notes describe, the theme and subject of the piece means legitimate offence would be caused to the families of the deceased's victims once it became known it had been played.
>
> It was not suggested by Mr Makin that the deceased had requested any other music to be played or any other ceremony to be performed, and in those circumstances, I propose to direct that there be no music and no ceremony.
>
> I have no difficulty in understanding how legitimate offence would be caused to the families of the deceased's victims once it became known that this movement had been played at his cremation. I decline to permit it.

The piece of music that Brady had wished for was written by Berlioz and is about a satanic dream. The artist sees himself in the midst of a ghastly crowd of sorcerers and monsters assembled for his funeral. The air is filled with strange groans, bursts of laughter, shouts and echoes. Suddenly, the artist's beloved appears as a witch, her theme distorted into spiteful parody.

Pathologist Dr Brian Rodgers, who carried out a post-mortem, said Brady weighed 9st 8lb at the time of his death with no sign of 'emaciation'. He found that Brady's body was in 'fairly good condition'. His lungs were very severely diseased, however, and 'essentially stuck to the chest wall'.

Former Detective Chief Superintendent Peter Topping, whose reinvestigation of the case in the 1980s found the body of Pauline Reade, recalled:

> The fact that Brady's passing has come quite frankly is a good thing because he was never going to give any more information. It ends a chapter, a very important chapter. Brady is gone, no longer a drain on the state, which I think is a good thing. He is no longer able to do his manipulation and use people. For that, there is a form of closure but, as far as the case is concerned, I will never get closure and my team that worked on it in the 1960s – and others who worked on it after that – you can only get closure after they have found Keith Bennett's body.
>
> Brady tormented the families of the victims. Having committed these horrific murders of the children of those families he then cruelly tormented the families, first of all denying his guilt when he was arrested by a team of detectives in the '60s. He resisted helping them to locate the bodies of those children.
>
> I took both of them to Saddleworth Moor on two occasions. There was a very detailed search by a team of detectives and we recovered the body of Pauline Reade and that had a tremendous effect on the health of Pauline's mother Joan, who had been really suffering with her health, not knowing what had happened to her daughter. That was a tremendous

thing and I think that poor lady and her family, they did benefit from that discovery, the confessions – and the recovery of Pauline's body.

We got a lot of information from Hindley and Brady – mainly Hindley, about the possible location of Keith Bennett's body, but despite the very dedicated work that was done, by the skilled team of detectives, we were not successful in finding his body.

The information we had at the time was searched to exhaustion, the case will always remain open and any information that comes into the hands of the police will be fully investigated by them, to see if there is any hope of recovering Keith's body. The man was always a cruel and manipulative person, he always looked to his own ends.

He said, if you give me the means to kill myself I will give you information. No sane person, never mind a police officer, would give a person the means to kill himself, he knew that, that is why he was making this taunt. That was the sort of man that Brady was.

Had he really wanted to kill himself, as anybody will tell you – who have known people take their own lives – they will find a means of doing it, they don't ask for the means, but this was Brady trying to manipulate the police and trying to manipulate the authorities. Brady was very demanding; he wouldn't allow anybody with me when I was with him and he wouldn't allow me to take notes.

The head of Greater Manchester Police's cold case review unit, Martin Bottomley, said that his force would never give up the search for the remains of Keith Bennett.

While we are not actively searching Saddleworth Moor, Greater Manchester Police will never close this case. Brady's death does not change that … I do not want to comment on Brady at all. The thoughts of everyone within Greater Manchester Police are with the families who lost loved ones in the most painful and traumatic way. It is especially saddening for the family of Keith Bennett that his killers did not reveal to police the whereabouts of Keith's burial site. A week hardly goes by when we do not receive some information which purports to lead us to Keith, but ultimately only two people knew where Keith is. I want to stress that our aim, as it always has been, is to find where Keith is buried and give closure to his surviving family members so they can give Keith the proper burial they so desperately want.

Former Detective Inspector Geoff Knupfer, who was second in command to DCS Topping, said that he believed now more than ever that Keith Bennett's body would remain unfound.

You're talking about a remote, peat bog in the middle of the Pennines. The chances of it being found, even at the time, were small. I'm sure that we searched the area faultlessly. There have been several searches by police and by others, and I'm as satisfied as I can be that the body is gone, unfortunately.

I'm equally satisfied, incidentally, that Brady – until the time of his death – was suffering from severe mental issues and didn't know where the body was. I know there was a myth that he knew where it was and was hanging on to this – I don't think for one second he knew where it was.

Shortly before he died, Brady gave Dr Alan Keightley (former head of religious studies at King Edward VI College, Stourbridge and confidant to Brady for 25 years) various items from his cell. One of the items was 200 handwritten pages which Brady asked him to delete any repetitions, type up and then send on to his solicitor in London.

Brady decided that he wanted to let the readers of the paperwork know about things that had happened in the past, now that both he and Hindley were dead. He clearly indicated another murder had taken place:

> With Myra dead and me on the brink … certain long withheld information can be safely revealed for the first time, particularly in regard to our final year of freedom together…
>
> When Myra personally wished to experience the capacity of the .38 Smith and Wesson snub nose, she had the opportunity to cancel a liability we had up in Yorkshire. Fortunately the evening was bright and fine for a lengthy stretching of the legs over rough terrain. As we reached the chosen appointed spot Myra affected some trouble with her shoe. Halting, ostensibly to wait for her, I gave the landscape a 360-degrees with the binoculars. For the all clear I then casually distanced myself from the target by several paces while maintaining a particular song that was in the current hit parade as the trigger.
>
> Luckily the single shot went straight through and high, obviating any need for messy ballistic retrieval. The brown peat naturally absorbed all surface traces. The usual depersonalisation and disposal procedures were completed smoothly and without incident at the pre-prepared nearby site. Frequent post-incident scans indicated a clear run, and back at the car we relaxed with a whisky, listening to the radio tuned to Radio Caroline and discussing remaining logistics to sanitise the car interior before nightfall.

He also claimed that he was fully aware of everything he had ever done and played the system to fake being mentally ill:

> Statistically, psychotic symptoms are considered more valid grounds for transfer to a mental hospital. And the linchpin of psychosis consists of delusional, hallucinatory experience and history. In Gartree prison I therefore began to manufacture and exhibit symptoms, reinforcing them with a devised false history that, hitherto, I had supposedly managed to conceal for a fear of ridicule.

I had embarked on a subtle number of other psychotic symptoms – distraction, preoccupation, withdrawal, etc., avoiding explanation or engagement of any description. Simultaneously, whenever I had to be seen to be eating, I later regurgitated so that my weight continued to fall dramatically, and I was moved to the hospital wing of the prison. Whenever a prison warder thought I was unaware that I was being watched, I would either move my lips as though speaking to an invisible presence or answering imaginary 'voices', or sometimes actually speak the words aloud, simulating agitation and anger.

Occasionally I would focus my attention on the radio (switched off) or radiator while having these supposedly unseen conversations. At night I would pace my cell talking aloud to myself and gesticulating at an imaginary person. I had also stopped going to bed, remaining in a chair huddled over the radiator and mumbling whenever I heard prison warders stealthily approaching to observe me through the spyhole. My letters to people outside also had to show degrees of irrationality and paranoia, of course – which was the most demeaning and hardest part of all. It is one thing to perform secretly behind prison walls, but quite another to sacrifice one's expectation and self-esteem in the eyes of relatives and friends.

Fortunately, without acting out of character in the role I was playing, I could periodically return to being my normal self and obtain some relief from the constant stress of performing by having conversations with intelligent individuals. I had to sustain enactment of all these symptoms, and more, for well over a year, maintaining the consistency of pattern and theme.

One night, after regurgitating food, I slipped on the wet floor and fractured my hand, the bones being brittle as my weight had fallen to under eight stone. But I maintained the appearance of irrationality by not reporting the broken bone, knowing that someone would eventually notice how swollen my hand had become.

When asked to explain how it happened, I returned to my psychotic role, stating I had punched the wall in rage, knowing they would attribute the rage to the delusional characters I was arguing with. This was only one example of how I had to keep innovating to sustain the image of a well-rounded psychotic in florid mode, feigning forgetfulness selectively and, paradoxically, therefore having to retain a good memory.

Because on top of all this I was having to field interviews with doctors, specialists and Home Office officials, and stay in character when talking to other prisoners, some of whom could be informers or provocateurs sent to test me by the authorities.

Suffice it to say that, if ever called upon to prove the success of my marathon performance, I could now give a detailed account of every day, action and conversation I had during that period of simulated 'psychotic breakdown', even though it took place over twenty years ago.

I possess almost total recall of every significant event in my life.

However, on 15 June 2017 a letter from Dr Noir Thomas, Brady's responsible clinician, to the Senior Coroner that Brady (whose NHS alias was Ian Steel) stated that:

Mr Brady was admitted to Ashworth Hospital on 29 November 1985 from HMP Gartree. Prior to this, he had spent twenty years isolated within maximum security prisons, including HMP Durham, Parkhurst and Wormwood Scrubs.

The nature of his index offence is well known. In 1966, he was convicted of three counts of murder, the victims being Edward Evans aged 17, Lesley Ann Downey aged 10 and John Kilbride aged 12. During the investigation of these murders, the police also enquired about the disappearance of Keith Bennett aged 12 and Pauline Reade aged 16, for which he later accepted responsibility.

**Mental Disorder(s):**

Mr Brady suffered from paranoid schizophrenia, marked by perceptual disturbances, delusional ideation, disorganised thought and speech. There are accounts of disturbed and bizarre behaviour relating to psychosis, to include assaults against peers.

This diagnosis came to the fore in 1985 alongside recognition that he suffered from a severe underlying personality disorder of prominent narcissistic and antisocial sub-types. He was also thought to suffer from a number of deviant sexual disorders, to include (sexual) sadism and paedophilia.

Mr Brady had been offered antipsychotic medication over the years, though medication was administered against his will on a very small number of occasions during his early admission. He since declined to accept antipsychotic medication. He also refused to engage with either psychological assessment or therapy throughout.

His thirty-two-year detention at Ashworth Hospital was largely marked by hostility, opposition to his care and treatment, allegations of brutality, serial complaints and insistence of interference by the Home Office. He was also subject to intense, often hostile media interest.

In 1999, he commenced what he termed 'hunger strike' in protest against a ward move to which he objected. He was subsequently fed by nasogastric tube (NG), though this was largely under his control. His NG feed was often coupled with an acceptance of diet and fluids from select staff.

Mr Brady was of the view that his acceptance of diet from certain staff was covert, though this was always accurately recorded by staff on intake charts. All food given to Mr Brady was sourced internally, via the hospital catering and/or canteen department.

Over the years, clinical teams regularly sought to bring an end to his reported 'hunger strike', recognising that he was regularly accepting diet and fluids, alongside or substituted for his NG feed. However, any attempt at negotiating a discontinuation would be met with hostility such that Mr Brady would then commence absolute fluid and food refusal, necessitating the use of the NG feed.

Over the last two years, brief periods were sustained, lasting maximally eight weeks, whereby Mr Brady tolerated the absence of his NG tube, accepting diet and fluids regularly. However, each episode ended with Mr Brady recommencing absolute food and fluid refusal for a period in excess of forty-eight hours, such that an NG had to be passed again. He would then invariably accept fluids once the NG tube was re-sited. Mr Brady continually refused to be weighed but was not considered to be of low body mass index warranting concern. Where possible his dietary index and use of NG feed was advised and supervised by dieticians.

Mr Brady serially pursued remittance to prison with the verbalised intent that he might commit suicide. His detention was upheld at each Mental Health Tribunal, to include a public hearing in 2013.

In recent years, there was ongoing evidence of intractable narcissism, with marked grandiosity, a lack of empathy, demanding and entitled behaviour. There was also ongoing evidence of paranoia and persecution, though no florid evidence of psychosis. There had been no incidents of violence, but he maintained a verbally abusive, derogatory and confrontational stance against the hospital.

**Physical health conditions:**

A summary of Mr Brady's physical health conditions is as follows:

- Bullous emphysema (also known as chronic obstructive pulmonary disease, or COPD) with recurrent chest infections and type II respiratory failure. The natural history of such a disorder is that of an irreversible and progressive deterioration in lung function, and it is thought secondary to cigarette smoking. Mr Brady smoked heavily until Ashworth Hospital became a non-smoking environment in 2008;
- Cataract (left cataract removed 08.10.11, right removed 07.12.13)
- Collapse and isolated seizure, June 2012, leading to fractured thoracic vertebra;
- Ankylosing spondylitis (a chronic spinal inflammatory condition);
- Benign prostatic hypertrophy. He had an in-dwelling urinary catheter for a number of years and, associated with it, recurrent urinary tract infections. He declined surgery;
- Haemangioma lower lip. He declined surgery.

Mr Brady's physical health was monitored internally by the (Primary Care) Health Centre at Ashworth Hospital, further supported by visiting physicians.

As was policy, his NG tube was due to be re-sited (every twelve weeks) and staff were prepared to do so on 10 May 2017. He was asleep when initially approached. He was then frustrated that the procedure had not been undertaken and was reported to have removed the tube himself later on 10 May 2017.

It was not unusual for Mr Brady to remove his NG tube himself in frustration. The tube was not subsequently re-sited in view of his ailing physical state and the associated risks of the procedure, in line with the views of Dr J Raj.

Mr Brady's physical health deteriorated further on 12 May 2017, with minimal fluid and dietary intake, coupled with increasing breathlessness and agitation. Advice was sought from the on-call palliative care service, who advocated increasing use of benzodiazepines and opiates.

He was at the time observed by nursing staff on level 3 (constant) observations, day and night.

Due to an increasing reluctance to accept oral medication, he was commenced on a subcutaneous syringe driver on 13 May 2017.

On 14 May 2017, Mr Brady was reviewed by Dr K Marley (Consultant in Palliative Care) who noted that his presentation was rather more settled, in terms of agitation, though recognised that he was nearing the end of his life.

He was assessed again on 15 May 2017 (1230 hrs) by Dr J Raj and colleagues from the palliative care team, who noted further deterioration and the observation that Mr Brady was in the final hours/days of his life. He was unresponsive at times, laboured in his breathing, and agitated.

He declined chaplaincy. He asked for his solicitor to be notified and requested that his locked briefcases be removed from his room. These were sealed by security staff and locked in the Director of Security's office.

He was administered 2.5mg diamorphine and 2.5mg midazolam subcutaneously in addition to his syringe driver to settle his presentation. A further 2.5mg diamorphine and 2.5mg midazolam were given twenty minutes later with positive effect.

His physical health deteriorated further over the course of the afternoon, with laboured breathing. His death was considered imminent.

I attended Newman Ward, having had a conversation with Dr C Bell (Speciality Doctor) at 1750hrs who observed that Mr Brady was increasingly laboured in his breathing, termed Cheyne-Stokes breathing, commonly seen preceding death.

On my arrival on the ward, I was advised that staff believed that Mr Brady had died; he was unresponsive with no evident signs of life.

Following examination, I certified his death at 1802hrs on 15 May 2017.

Operation Chrome was subsequently initiated.

Three police officers arrived on Newman Ward at 1925hrs.

He then listed the 'regular' and 'as required' medication prescribed to Brady. His summary read:

> Mr Brady was detained at Ashworth Hospital in excess of thirty-two years, on account of his severe mental disorder(s) and risk. He was resistant and oppositional throughout, refusing medication and therapy, and regularly challenging the grounds for his detention. He was pending a further Mental Health Tribunal scheduled for late July of this year, which he was seeking to be heard in public.
>
> His care and treatment in recent years remained largely unchanged, in line with the manifestations of his mental disorders which were considered resistant to treatment. In recent years, his deteriorating physical health has been the source of concern and significant specialist input. Even at the end stages of his lung condition, it was felt that he was best placed within a high secure hospital setting and not returned to prison.
>
> His death (15.05.17) was expected, given the progressive deterioration in his physical health, and directly related to his obstructive pulmonary disease. This I understand is supported by the initial post mortem findings.
>
> This care and treatment of Mr Brady at the end of life was supported throughout by external specialists, whose services were invaluable in allowing us to ensure that all aspects of his care were managed accordingly.

Brady was cremated without ceremony on 25 October 2017 in Southport. His body was collected from the Royal Liverpool Hospital's mortuary by a council official and a pathologist who had attended Brady's post-mortem at around 21.00. The van was then escorted by an unmarked police car to Southport Crematorium. Brady's body did not enter any public area and it was placed in a standby cremator, where the cremation began at 22.00. There were no flowers, no music and the only people in attendance were Brady's solicitor Robin Makin, the two police officers who escorted the mortuary van, council officials and two crematorium workers.

At 00.45 Brady's ashes were handed to council officials and the biodegradable urn, made of Himalayan rock salt, was taken in the unmarked police car to Liverpool Marina. The weighted urn was designed to sink to the bottom of the sea immediately before dissolving over the space of a few hours.

While the Crematorium was undergoing a deep clean by professionals, the urn was taken aboard a boat from the North West Police Underwater Search and Marine Unit accompanied by the council official and a police sergeant. His ashes were dispatched at sea at 02.30. In a statement, Tameside and Oldham councils said:

> We are pleased that this matter is now concluded and we are grateful for the support and professionalism shown … to ensure Ian Stewart-Brady's body and remains were disposed of expediently at sea in a manner compatible with the public interest and those of the victim's relatives.

# Epilogue

It soon became clear that Brady had given two locked briefcases to his solicitor, Robin Makin, shortly before he died. Alan Bennett's lawyer, John Ainley, recalled:

> I was aware of the briefcases, which have not been provided to the police, as I understand it. Certainly Alan Bennett would be very interested in these being opened and the contents being seen, because there may be information in there. It may not be relevant to anyone else but with all the knowledge Alan has, it may lead to the spot where Keith is buried. So we would ask Mr Makin to provide those either to the police or to Alan Bennett.
>
> In fact, we would like all his papers because they may give Alan, with his knowledge of the case, some information which may lead him to finding where Keith is buried.

Terry Kilbride, brother of murdered John Kilbride, said: 'There must be something in those briefcases for him to go to those lengths to hide them away. It's all the hope we have for finding Keith.' And Terry West, brother of Lesley Ann Downey, added: 'I would like to know what's in those briefcases. Fingers crossed there might be something that would finally help us to find Keith's body.'

On 29 October 2018 Pauline Reade's body was exhumed and reburied after Greater Manchester Police discovered they had kept some of her remains at the University of Leeds following an audit. Her family said that these included a jaw bone and some hair. Nine months after that discovery, the police handed back to Pauline's relatives her shoes and some jewellery.

This chain was given to the family of Pauline Reade and they were told that it was the one that was pushed into her neck wound. None of her surviving family recognise it. Could it have been given to her by Brady or Hindley?

One of Pauline's best friends, Pat Garvey, who attended her reburial, recalled:

> I couldn't believe who had done it – we knew her, we grew up with Myra Hindley. My mum used to mind David Smith. David lived in the same street as Pauline. We used to play with Maureen. She lived in the street next to me. I couldn't take it in that Myra could do such a thing.

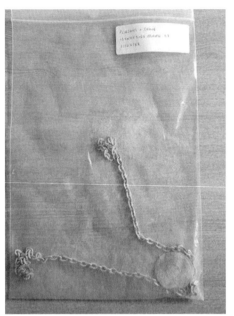 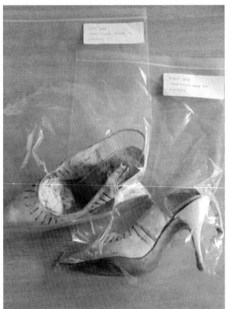

*Above left*: Pauline Reade's locket.

*Above right*: Pauline Reade's shoes.

*Below*: Necklace.

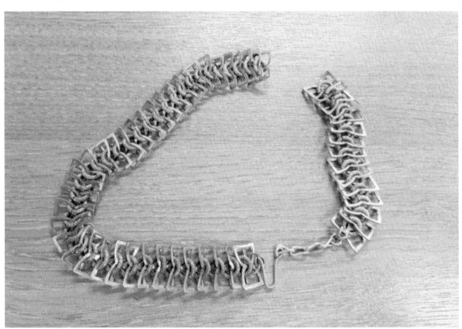

She was my best friend. We had been friends since we were little, tiny little girls. She was really timid, shy. I still miss her. She was twelve months older than me. I come to her grave regularly, it upsets me every time.

By February 2020, the locked briefcases being looked after by Brady's solicitor still hadn't been opened. Robin Makin had refused all pleas from family and the police to open them and reveal if they contained anything that could be of use in finding Keith Bennett.

Following Brady's death, Greater Manchester Police applied for a court order to examine the contents, but were denied on the grounds that there was no longer any prospect of an investigation leading to a prosecution. Keith Bennett's brother Alan said:

I am sure you will understand that there is a desperate need to look for anything that may help in the recovery of Keith's body and there may be something in those cases.

We cannot be sure [but] we need to know for sure – one way or another. During my correspondence with Brady many years ago he stated that he had left instructions in his will for me alone. He did not give any further detail but it was at a time when I was searching on the moor and asking him about routes taken, areas of the moor, landmarks.

The refusal by Makin to help any further is a great cause of distress considering that my brother's body still remains on the moor while all the other victims have been returned to their loved ones for a proper burial. There seems to be no compassion or thought for Keith or his family.

The solicitor was criticised by the High Court in October 2017 for being 'secretive about how he was intending to dispose of the deceased's body'. A judge had ruled that he should not be trusted with Brady's ashes.

The Home Secretary at the time, Sajid Javid, said: 'I have instructed my officials to contact Greater Manchester Police urgently to establish the details around this case and determine whether there are any legal gaps that the government should consider.'

The Home Secretary even wrote to Labour MP Yvette Cooper, who chaired the Commons Home Affairs committee, promising to get to the bottom of the matter.

He added: 'I appreciate that Alan Bennett and his family will be suffering continued distress, and that such auctions will not swiftly resolve matters. I promise to provide further clarity on this matter based on the outcomes.'

To this day, the suitcases remain unopened in the care of Brady's solicitor Robin Makin.

# Statement from
# Greater Manchester Police

Martin Bottomley, Head of Greater Manchester Police's Cold Case Review Unit, said:

Since Keith was first reported missing in June 1964, Greater Manchester Police has been committed to finding him and providing desperately deserved answers for his family. In 1965 we made extensive and concerted efforts in searches of Saddleworth Moor – which led to the discovery of the bodies of two children, Lesley Ann and John, who were both murdered by Brady and Hindley. Further searches of the Moors in 1986 and 1987 uncovered the remains of Pauline.

Between 1988 and 2003, a number of searches by volunteers, geologists, family and friends of Winnie and Alan were conducted, but to no avail. In 2003 a team of GMP detectives began another operation to locate Keith. Seeking Brady's cooperation, they visited him at Ashworth Hospital but he was not forthcoming. Specialist police search teams – using cadaver dogs – with the assistance of geologists – conducted extensive digs and analysis of groundwater samples for isotope analysis between 2005 and 2008.

In 2009, GMP formally announced that these searches had been unsuccessful and that physical searches would only recommence in the event of a major scientific breakthrough or fresh evidence coming to light. We made it clear, however, that this case will never be closed, we would continue to support Keith's family and take appropriate action should intelligence or evidence lead us to believe we would be able to locate Keith's body. That remains the case to this day.

In July 2012, a lawyer representing Channel 4 News informed us that an associate representing Brady had told one of their journalists that they had received letters from Brady via his solicitor.

We were told that one of these letters contained a further letter, addressed to Keith's mother, Winnie Johnson, and Brady's associate believed that this letter contained some information to indicate where Keith's body was buried.

Acting on this information, GMP officers arrested the associate, searched their premises and at the same time searched Brady's belongings at Ashworth Hospital – including two briefcases. Neither of these letters were found.

It is likely more documents have accumulated over the years but no further examination of the briefcases, or of Brady's papers, has been allowed in the seven years since GMP were granted access under authority of a warrant in 2012.

The day after Brady died in May 2017, a detective applied for a further warrant to allow access to examine Brady's papers. This application was denied by a District Judge. In the following days, advice was sought from the Coroner with responsibility for conducting the inquest into Brady's death, but we were informed that there is no legislation available to allow access to Brady's papers in these circumstances.

Officers then approached Brady's solicitor, seeking his permission – as executor of Brady's will – to examine Brady's papers. After initially agreeing to this course of action, at a pre-arranged meeting at Ashworth Hospital in June 2017 for the purpose of examining the papers in the solicitor's presence, Brady's lawyer suddenly withdrew his cooperation. We were not allowed to examine any of Brady's papers. In September 2017, further contact with Brady's lawyer failed to resolve this. Two further requests by officers to Brady's solicitor have gone unanswered.

I must emphasise that Greater Manchester Police remain committed to providing Keith's family with the support and answers they deserve. As with so many crimes of this nature, we rely on advances in forensic science, new witness testimony, fresh evidence and most importantly the cooperation of our community.

We have steadfastly pursued all these options over the last fifty-five years and will continue to do so. However, I fear that without a significant breakthrough, Keith's family may remain taunted and haunted by Brady from beyond the grave, as was his clear mission in life.

Two questions remain … What is in these briefcases? And where is Keith Bennett?

# Bibliography

Garrett, Geoffrey and Nott, Andrew *Cause of Death* Robinson 2001

Goodman, Jonathan *The Moors Murders* David & Charles 1973

Harrison, Fred *Brady & Hindley* Harper Collins 1987

Keightley, Dr Alan, *Ian Brady: The Untold Story of the Moors Murders* Robson 2017

Lee, Carol Ann *One of Your Own* Mainstream Publishing 2010

Marchbanks, David *The Moor Murderers* Leslie Frewin 1966

Potter, John Deane *The Monsters of The Moors* Elek Books Ltd 1966

Rhattigan, Tommy *1963 A Slice of Bread and Jam* Mirror Books 2017

Ritchie, Jean *Inside the Mind of a Murderess* Angus & Robertson 1988

Smith, David with Lee, Carol Ann *Evil Relations* Mainstream Publishing 2011

Staff, Duncan *The Lost Boy* Transworld Publishers 2007

Topping, Peter *Topping* Angus & Robertson Publishers 1989

Various Authors *Moving Targets – Women, Murder and Representation* University of California Press 1994

West, Ann *For the Love of Lesley* Warner Books 1989

West, Terry *If Only* Wild Wolf Publishing 2018

Wilson, Robert *Devil's Disciples* Express Newspapers 1986

Wilson, Robert *Return to Hell* Javelin Books 1988

The main files accessed for research at the National Archives were:

ASSI 84/425–430, DPP 25366, HO 287/4035, HO 287/4361, HO 336/12–15, HO 336/19–22, HO 336/24–28, HO 336/31–35, HO 336/44, HO 336/48–50, HO 336/54, HO 336/58, HO 336/79, HO 336/86, HO 336/93–95, HO 336/97–98, HO 336/102, HO 336/104, HO 336/108, HO 336/110–111, HO 336/115, HO 336/120, HO 336/126–129, HO 336/131–132, HO 336/139, HO 336/141, HO 336/145, HO 336/148, HO 336/156, HO 336/174, HO 336/176, HO 336/179, HO 336/622, HO 336/895–896, HO 336/901, HO 336/910–11, HO 336/913, HO 336/926, HO 336/928, HO 336/931, HO 336/933, HO 336/938, HO 336/940, HO 336/942–43, HO 336/946–948, HO 336/1014–1015, HO 336/1034, J 267/446–447.